The **Garden** Book

The
Garden
Book

With a foreword by

S TEFAN B UCZACKI

First published in Great Britain in 1996 by
Hamlyn, a division of the Octopus Publishing Group Limited
2–4 Heron Quays, London E14 4JP

Copyright © 1996, 1999, 2001 Octopus Publishing Group Limited
Paperback edition published 1999

ISBN 0 600 60414 4

A CIP catalogue record for this book
is available from the British Library

Executive Editor: Julian Brown
Art Editor: Paul Tilby
Editors: Sasha Judelson, Mary Lambert, Emily Wright
Production Controller: Clare Smedley
Consultant: Richard Bird
Picture Researchers: Sally Claxton, Jenny Faithfull
Indexer: Hilary Bird

Designed by The Bridgewater Book Company Limited
Produced by Toppan
Printed and bound in China

Some material in this book has already appeared in other Octopus
Publishing Group publications.

The authors and publisher will be grateful for any information
which will assist them in keeping future editions up to date.

Jacket Acknowledgements

John Glover front cover top centre left/
Janis Ridley front cover bottom left.

Octopus Publishing Group Limited front cover
bottom centre left,/Guy Ryecart front cover centre.

S&O Mathews front cover top left

CONTENTS

FOREWORD

In performing this very agreeable task, I am reminded of the Introduction to a very old gardening book that I possess in which the author felt obliged to justify his new creation for no other reason than that "there are very many gardening books in the world already." If this was true when it was written in 1873, surely it must be more than ever true today. For yes, the output of gardening titles seems to increase year by year, but there can be no denying that the purpose of a great majority is to keep photographers, rather than gardeners, in employment. How refreshing, therefore, to find a new book that genuinely has something useful and practical to say; and says it in a manner that will be immediately comprehensible to the beginner but will serve as an invaluable reminder to the more experienced.

I'm delighted to see the emphasis that is laid on planning and designing your garden before you go too far with your planting. And the numerous excellent sample plans on which you can base your own scheme are not, as so often in garden design books, merely flights of fancy for someone with limitless resources and time. They can stand on their own as guidelines for small backyards but, for a large area, two or more could be combined to create a larger whole. And yet, unlike so many gardening books that lay stress on the value of design, the mistake is never made here of allowing it to slide into becoming a do-it-yourself manual. It remains throughout a book written by a gardener for a gardener.

There are countless practical touches to reveal that the text comes from someone who genuinely has done each particular task. And this evidence of practicality comes, too, in the lists of recommended plants; it is both reassuring and rewarding to discover that I could almost have drawn them up myself, so closely do they reflect my own views, based on much trial and error.

I can think of no other single-volume book that covers so much ground, so succinctly and usefully, and I commend it warmly.

STEFAN BUCZACKI

DESIGNING YOUR GARDEN

LEFT: all the pleasures of
a fine, mature garden begin
with a well thought-out,
carefully planned design.

GARDEN PLANNING

The essence of good garden design lies in creating an area that is visually pleasing but one that also fits in with your needs and that you are able to maintain in good condition.

ASSESSING THE SITE

THE MOST important thing in deciding how to make a new garden or how to improve an existing one is to know about your area, for the character of a garden is influenced by climatic conditions, soil, aspect, views (or lack of them), the buildings around you and so on. The combination may seem so unpromising as to be difficult, but no site is incapable of being improved by thoughtful design and carefully chosen plants.

Whether your backyard is brand new or an old, established plot, the same principles apply to planning and designing your garden. First, assess what you have got, then decide what kind of garden you want and whether you can achieve it. Assess your yard's potential, its strengths and weaknesses, and then decide how to take advantage of all that is good about it and play down the bad points. But, remember: nothing happens overnight, and you will not wake up the next morning to find the perfect garden!

LEFT: use the yard's natural features, such as mature trees to frame the flower beds.
RIGHT: to fill damp areas, choose moisture-loving plants such as "yellow loosestrife."

See also: Design guidelines pages 18–23

Climate and microclimate

CLIMATE IS all-important because it dictates the kinds of plants you can grow, which will influence your design. If you have moved to a new area it is easy to discover average temperatures and rainfall, but you must always allow for extremes.

Regional climate is influenced by fundamental geographical factors like latitude, altitude, proximity of large land masses and the sea and the influence of major ocean currents. Some neighborhoods also have their own local weather patterns such as seasonal winds.

Then there are microclimates, natural and artificial. For example, some cities are nearly frost-free because of the artificial heat exuded. Consequently many tender plants can be kept outside while in colder country areas they have to be protected or over-wintered in frost-free places.

Though it is necessary to learn about your local climate, it is equally important to set about creating your own special microclimate. You cannot do much about the weather but you can do a great deal to minimize its effects, perhaps by putting up a protective windbreak against icy winds; this will allow you to grow a wider range of delicate and more interesting plants. In cold areas, frost and snow will do no harm provided you grow hardy plants suited to your area.

Soil types

THE BETTER the quality of the soil in your garden, the better your plants will grow. If your soil is poor and infertile you will have to improve it. But first, since soils vary hugely in texture, structure and quality,

begin by working out what type of soil you have in the garden.

Most gardeners need only know whether their soil is clay-like or sandy, since this influences your choice of plants. Clay retains moisture, is difficult to work and sticky when wet, and sets very hard with surface cracks in a dry summer. It needs regular breaking up over winter with a soil conditioner although it is often very fertile in its own right. Sandy soil is easy to work and dries out quickly, but needs plenty of well-rotted manure or compost to improve moisture retention. Alluvial silt in a flood plain is an exception to the sandy rule; it is easy to work,

ABOVE: in cold areas, tender plants will have to be kept in a well-protected, frost-free place.

RIGHT: the giant-leaved gunnera grows well in moist soil and flourishes by a garden pool.

fertile and, though free-draining, excellent at retaining moisture.

Acidity and alkalinity

YOU MUST also know the character of your soil. Is it acidic or alkaline? If it is alkaline you will not be able to grow lime-haters such as rhododendrons or camellias. In very acid soils limestone plants such as philadelphus, clematis and dianthus will not thrive. You can easily buy cheap pH testing kits, which you should apply to different parts of the garden since conditions will vary. To confirm your readings do a little reconnaissance, talk to people, ask local gardeners for their advice and opinions, and look around the neighborhood to see what plants are growing well in other people's gardens. If you want to increase soil alkalinity add lime, but think carefully before you do this as it is long-lasting. It is not so easy to increase the acidity. The best way is to create raised beds, or special enclosures, filled with acid soil for heathers (ericaceous plants).

See also: Elements of design pages 24–27; Hardiness zones pages 108–109

Sun, shade and shelter

THE QUALITY of light will have a major influence on your garden design. Shade is usually more of a problem in urban areas than rural, as next-door buildings and neighboring walls and fences tend to cast shadows for at least part of the day. If only a corner of your backyard receives sun then it makes sense to reserve this area for an outdoor bench, patio, or greenhouse. Do not waste the sun you do have.

Shelter is something else to consider. For the best possible results, plants need a sheltered place. Ideally, your garden should provide an enclosed haven in which they can thrive. Wind can be a major problem since it dehydrates the soil and stunts plant growth. If your site is badly exposed the first thing you should do is build some kind of windbreak. Although it may seem like a good idea to build a solid wall, this does more harm than good because the wind will eddy over the top of the wall and swirl down, creating a whirlwind effect in your

ABOVE: use hedges and walls to make a sunny, wind-free haven.
BELOW: trees and hedges give dappled shade.

garden. A filtering windbreak like an open-work fence or hedge is the best idea.

Frost protection is as important as wind protection. Frost in winter is seldom a problem given that there are in excess of 60,000 hardy plants to choose from. Even the coldest areas can be planted up to suit most tastes. Frost at the wrong time of year, on the other hand, will kill plant growth. In valleys or ground hollows you may well get what is known as a "frost pocket." This is when the cold, frosty air sinks at the lowest part of the landscape and collects beneath walls and closely-planted hedges. Frost will also collect under a closely-planted hedge or solid wall. If you thin or remove trees or walls, you will let the cold air flow through rather than trapping it.

Dimensions

IN ORDER to get the most out of your space, you will have to familiarize yourself with its dimensions. Size matters, but only in so far as it might limit the number of different

See also: The look of your garden pages 28–32

areas you can create and the size and number of plants and features within them. If the yard is small, there are several ways of putting what space is available to more efficient use: vertical surfaces, for instance, offer scope for climbers, wall plants and hanging baskets. Raised beds and terraces extend the growing areas, and containers make maximum use of paved areas. Although most gardeners find themselves with limited space rather than too much, too much space can be a problem. In this case, strategic planting, with the emphasis on trees and shrubs underplanted with ground cover, will help make the garden seem smaller.

Shape

THIS INFLUENCES design considerably. Few plots are symmetrical, but that really does not matter. An L-shape or a triangle can even offer more design potential than a rectangle. Perhaps the most difficult shape of all is a square, particularly when it is too small to subdivide as in many yards in front.

A design for an awkward shape needs to be carefully thought out. A long thin area, for example, can be divided into contrasting sections with barriers across its width, but by leaving a narrow view running through from one end to the other you create an additional sight line. Furthermore, by placing an ornamental feature like a statue or seat at the far end, you gain the full benefit from the site's length while the screens minimize the disadvantages of its shape.

LEFT: a small square area, often found in urban yards, is one of the most difficult to design. Here a circular, shell-edged bed gives variety of shape, and a profusion of plants such as violas and lilies adds color.

Topography

THINK TWICE before leveling slopes in your garden because, surprisingly, a level site offers less exciting design potential than one with interesting, gradual changes. Slopes and changes of level all offer the opportunity for building terraced levels, retaining walls or stepped growing beds, or introducing something such as a water or rock feature.

Division

HEDGES, WALLS and fences make ideal screens and can introduce different moods and styles as you walk through the garden. They are also invaluable for screening off unattractive areas like the compost pile and garbage storage areas, but do not just build screens and forget about them: they ought to be attractive, architectural features.

Atmosphere

THE MOOD of your garden is an important consideration. Even when you are working on a bare site, the potential of the space needs to be assessed and compared with the "feel" you want to achieve. Walk around the area, take measurements, and observe natural features. The emphasis is on making use of your natural resources, and converting the apparently insignificant areas into eye-catching attractions.

LEFT: this design skilfully breaks up a long narrow area while retaining and even emphasizing a sense of distance.

See also: Drawing up your plan pages 16–17

What you want from your garden

HAVING ASSESSED your backyard's advantages and disadvantages, next examine your own particular needs. What do you want from the garden as a space and as a reflection of your lifestyle? Do you want a place in which to rest and relax, enjoy a barbecue, grow vegetables, play games, or build up a specialist collection of plants? In a large yard the problem does not exist—the only concern is how much space to assign to each area, and how to divide the one from the other. But with a smaller yard you will have to limit yourself to one or two areas. The less space there is to play with, the more ingenious the design must be.

Linking house and garden

FROM INDOORS, the view through the windows into the garden is at least as important as the view from any vantage point outside. Your garden design must therefore include views that look tempting from inside, from the rooms where you spend most time. If you are lucky enough to look out over open rural views or a fine cityscape, make sure the garden design blends with the background. A rustic garden-style design is much more suitable for a rural area than a modern design, in the same way as a modern design will look better in an urban area.

Looking back to the house from the garden, the house should be an integral part of the design rather than stand out. A conservatory or sun room can be designed to open on to a patio so that in summer, when the doors are open, the garden feels as though it is extending into the house and vice versa. Climbers and wall plants help soften the harsh outline of a building and act as a link between the house and garden.

Inherited features

IN SOME WAYS, it is best to begin with a bare site. Then you can do more or less what you like with it, providing there are no overwhelming restrictions.

Far more difficult is reworking an established garden. But before you demolish it, do wait one full season. It really is

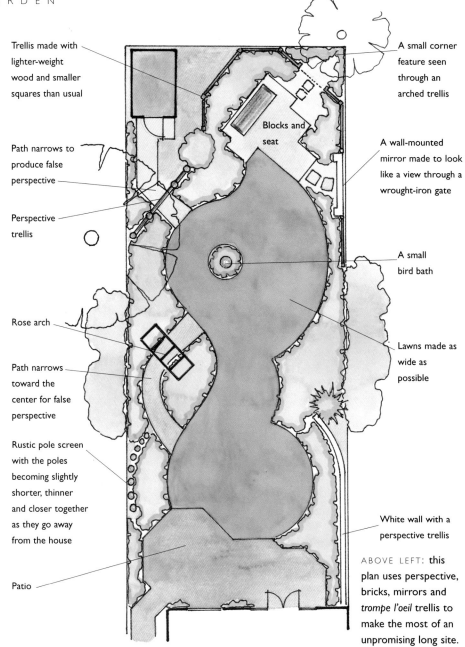

Trellis made with lighter-weight wood and smaller squares than usual

Path narrows to produce false perspective

Perspective trellis

Rose arch

Path narrows toward the center for false perspective

Rustic pole screen with the poles becoming slightly shorter, thinner and closer together as they go away from the house

Patio

Blocks and seat

A small corner feature seen through an arched trellis

A wall-mounted mirror made to look like a view through a wrought-iron gate

A small bird bath

Lawns made as wide as possible

White wall with a perspective trellis

ABOVE LEFT: this plan uses perspective, bricks, mirrors and *trompe l'oeil* trellis to make the most of an unpromising long site.

essential. Even the apparently most hideous layout is likely to have some feature worth preserving, though it may not be immediately obvious.

Note the presence of any existing spring bulbs, shrubs for winter color, colorful fall seedheads, boggy, waterlogged areas, particularly dry hot summer beds. Then decide which of these features you would like to keep.

Obvious features like large trees or natural water courses can cause problems. How will they look when incorporated into a new design? It is impossible to suggest general solutions, but consider the following: is the tree or natural feature particularly fine, rare or special in any other way? Could you

reshape your design to work around the feature? Since maturity is lacking in a new garden, and since the established look is going to be the aim, is it possible to keep the feature for the medium term until the garden has mellowed and matured, and then think about replacing it with your ideal specimen tree or sculpture?

Hard landscaping and architectural and ornamental features present less of a problem than natural features because in most cases they can be dismantled and relocated. The advantage of reusing such existing materials —stone walls and troughs, blocks, millstones, and so on—is that they will be weathered and worn, as compared to the rather sterile appearance of new materials.

See also: Garden plans pages 33–50
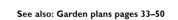

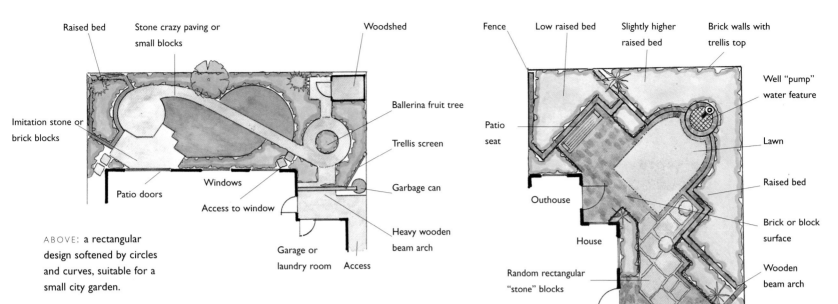

Raised bed — Stone crazy paving or small blocks — Woodshed

Imitation stone or brick blocks

Ballerina fruit tree

Trellis screen

Patio doors — Windows — Garbage can

Access to window

Heavy wooden beam arch

Garage or laundry room — Access

ABOVE: a rectangular design softened by circles and curves, suitable for a small city garden.

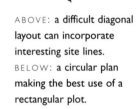

Fence — Low raised bed — Slightly higher raised bed — Brick walls with trellis top

Well "pump" water feature

Patio seat

Lawn

Outhouse

Raised bed

House

Brick or block surface

Random rectangular "stone" blocks

Wooden beam arch

ABOVE: a difficult diagonal layout can incorporate interesting site lines.
BELOW: a circular plan making the best use of a rectangular plot.

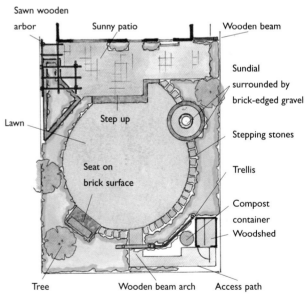

Sawn wooden arbor — Sunny patio — Wooden beam

Sundial surrounded by brick-edged gravel

Lawn — Step up

Stepping stones

Seat on brick surface

Trellis

Compost container

Woodshed

Tree — Wooden beam arch — Access path

Time and money

TIME AND money are two major factors to take into consideration when designing your garden. Only plan a garden that you can afford to make (and, incidentally, that you can comfortably afford to maintain) in a realistic timescale.

The joy of gardening is that it suits every pocket. Landscaping a small area with choice materials and lavish, mature plants is expensive; by contrast, using inexpensive materials, propagating as many plants as possible, and being prepared to wait is the best way to develop a fine garden on a tight budget.

Interim measures have their uses: beds can be filled with annuals until you can afford more expensive shrubs; an arrangement of attractive pots can provide the focal point until a statue or sculpture has been added.

Starting the design

ONCE YOU know all about your site, exactly what you want from your garden, what inherited features are worth preserving and how much time you want to spend on maintenance, you can begin the design. But to generate any useful ideas, first stand in the garden—or on the patch of wasteland that is to become your garden—and think in terms of shapes and colors. As ideas begin to form, you can then explore practicalities and solve problems. At this planning stage, allow your imagination to wander and take plenty of time to consider all the options.

Marking out your garden

THE PRACTICAL business of designing—preparing drawings to scale, organizing plant lists, and so on—appears to be far more daunting than it really needs to be. Accuracy is important but it is not that difficult to achieve; if you are methodical and careful, the site can be carefully measured and a true plan drawn.

If you find it difficult to visualize designs from lines on a piece of paper, there is really no reason why you should not use the backyard itself as your drawing board. The site, if not already clean, will have to be cleared of any trash or unwanted objects before you begin. Then, using sticks and lengths of string (preferably strong and very visible twine) as markers, mark out where everything should go. Keep making adjustments to these markers until you have the layout you want. A length of hose is very useful for marking out areas with curving border fronts.

Complicated details may need a more striking outline, which can be done with whitewash brushed over the ground. It is also worth visualizing height where this is a vital factor. A stepladder set up to the height of a mature hedge will give you a good idea of the ultimate effect. If this looks too tall, obscuring a fine view and casting too much shade, select a different hedging plant. Put a chair in a proposed seating area and try it out. Is this the best place, or will it be ruined by an unpleasant view?

When you have a clearer idea of the arrangement of your site it will be easier to

transfer the details on to paper; this will be essential for reference once the heavy work has begun. Before you draw up the plan, leave the markers in place for a week or so to ensure that the idea really is going to be practical. Then, when you are finally happy with the main elements of the design, draw up the plan.

See also: Surfaces pages 52–53

DRAWING UP YOUR PLAN

When you have decided on your garden layout, you should draw up a scale plan incorporating the main garden features. This may need to be reviewed several times as you dig, plant and build your garden.

LEFT: groups of containers of different shapes—stone troughs, old wash basins, terracotta pots—will add variety to the design.
BELOW: a curving path introduces a pleasing element of informality into a rectangular area.

WHEN YOU have marked out your site, transfer your ideas on to the scale plan. Start by allocating the areas of lawn, hard surface, and border and, when the overall shaping is more or less complete, start to draw in the principal garden features.

It is likely that you will redraw your plan a few times because, even when you set out to dig and plant, weed and build, you may well find that the design alters as you go along. A good garden is a blend of skilful advance planning and on-the-spot alterations over the years to allow the garden to "grow" its own character.

Although a plan is necessary, it should never be rigidly adhered to, otherwise the garden will be "stiff" and out of harmony with its surroundings. Remember that a garden consists of living things that are constantly altering their size and shape; nothing is static, nothing grows in ruler-straight lines, and compromise and adjustment are needed all the time.

Measuring the garden

FOR AN ACCURATE, working scale drawing, measure your garden in detail. Enter these measurements on a couple of preliminary sketch plans first, before using them to produce the scale drawing. The preliminary sketches must bear some resemblance to your backyard, although they do not have to be to scale, and if your site is very detailed and there is a great deal to record, you may well find it easier to make a large number of sketches. A separate sketch of just the house, for example, will give you plenty of room to record doors, windows and drainpipes, all of which must be taken into account if you are going to do a really thorough design job.

See also: Garden planning pages 10–15

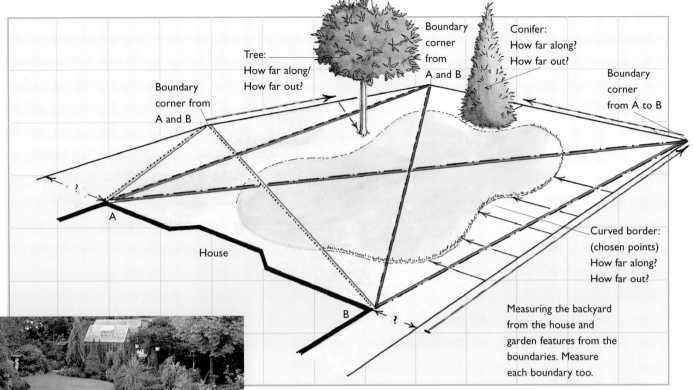

Tree:
How far along/
How far out?

Boundary
corner
from
A and B

Conifer:
How far along?
How far out?

Boundary
corner from
A and B

Boundary
corner
from A to B

? A

House

B ?

Curved border:
(chosen points)
How far along?
How far out?

Measuring the backyard
from the house and
garden features from the
boundaries. Measure
each boundary too.

ABOVE: a sample plan
showing how boundary
corners can be plotted
from A and B, the corners
of the house.
LEFT: a path draws the eye
and leads the visitor to
discover hidden areas of
the garden.

Making a scale plan

THE MOST useful scale to work to is ¼ or
⅛in to 1ft, depending on how big your
backyard is and the size of the paper you
are using. Work out the plan on squared
or graph paper.

First draw the house. Next, plot the
various boundary corners, using a pair of
compasses for accuracy. Take the
measurement between one house corner and
one boundary corner, scale this down and set
your compasses (that is to say, the length
between the compass point and pencil point)
to this length.

On paper, place the point of the compass
on the house corner and, pointing roughly
in the direction of the boundary corner,
draw a broad arc. Repeat the process, this
time using the measurement between the
second house corner and the same boundary
corner. Where the two arcs meet is the apex
of your boundary. Repeat this exercise until
you have reproduced every corner then join
them to produce the boundary. Check your
drawing by measuring the distance from one
boundary corner to the other and scaling it
down—it should be the same as the
equivalent distance on paper.

With the basic framework down on
paper, you can now add other objects.

Starting with the house, carefully
measure and record the length of the walls,
the position of doors and downstairs
windows, along with other house-related
features such as drains; drain covers must be
measured to their center and sketched at the
appropriate angle. Next, measure and record
the length of each different boundary.

Very few yards are actually square, and it
is quite possible that some of your
boundaries are not straight and change
direction more than once. Rather than
trying to record all the corners in relation to
each other, it is much easier to plot them in
relation to two fixed points, such as the
corners of the house. This places every
change of direction and corner at the point
of a triangle. Garden features and plants can

then be plotted off their nearest boundary.

Measure how far along and how far out
at right-angles the object is to the boundary
and enter the measurement on to the sketch
plan. For an object such as a woodshed or
greenhouse, measure two adjacent corners to
get the position and angle of the building
and then the overall dimensions to complete
it. To plot curves off a straight line, use a
series of "how-far-along," "how-far-out"
measurements. Finally, it is also a good idea
to record the size of tree canopies and the
diameter or width of shrubs.

Having marked the position of existing
features, mark the orientation and record the
amount and time of shade cast by the house,
by plants and those outside the boundary,
including neighboring trees.

See also: The look of your garden pages 28–32

DESIGN GUIDELINES

Inevitably, personal taste is bound to govern your final design, but there are basic design principles that affect every scheme. These design guidelines will also help the less confident gardener to become more ambitious and to translate ideas successfully into reality.

ABOVE: a formal design, suitable for a city garden, utilizing crisp white trelliswork and neat brick surface edged by lines of terracotta pots.

RIGHT: constrasting geometric shapes are featured in this design where a circular patio is linked to the main garden by a serrated path.

First steps

TO START with, since the garden will be viewed mostly from the house, go into the house and make all your major design decisions from the appropriate windows. Secondly, do not forget that the house is part of the garden; a garden design completely at odds with the style of your house will not look right.

It is a very good idea to go out and look at examples of different types of garden for inspiration before you start to make your own plans. At least then you will begin to realize that almost anything is possible!

Formality and informality

GARDENS ARE sometimes classified as being either formal or informal, which you might interpret as being regular and geometric or irregular and freehand. Formal gardens are mostly symmetrical, with a central path or lawn and identical features on each side, whereas informal gardens tend to be pictorial rather than patterned and scarcely ever repeat the same idea. They are more likely to consist of flowing curves than straight lines or geometric shapes.

One way of designing your garden is to make the area near the house formal and gradually make the layout less formal the further away from the house you go. This formula works very well since it ties the house into the garden in a gentle and subtle way. But there is nothing to stop you having a completely formal or informal garden, or a bit of both. Why not create a series of "rooms" using alternate formal and informal designs? You will end up with a garden full of variety and surprises which will tempt any visitor to wander further to find out what is around the next corner. Many gardens have an underlying formality that is often masked by a mass of informal planting. This can produce the most delightful results: a sort of controlled chaos.

Before deciding which is visually satisfying, formality or informality, or indeed a mixture of the two, think about what suits you best. Formal gardens tend to rely on tidiness and precision for impact, which means constant weeding and trimming, while informal gardens can be left to grow and are easier to maintain. A formal scheme is not a good idea if you have small children.

Deciding on the basic layout

THE STARTING point to any new design is deciding on a basic layout. Try to resist the temptation to line everything up in a series of parallel lines and instead explore creating more exciting shapes making use of diagonals and curves.

Most gardens have either a rectangular layout, a diagonal layout or a circular layout. A rectangular approach consists of symmetrical features and a lot of straight lines and predictable curves, perhaps more suited to a small city garden than a larger country one. The built-in angle of a diagonal layout will offset features to produce a less predictable, more relaxed and interesting effect. A curved layout is good for large, rambling gardens.

BELOW: this garden shows how a serpentine path shields the patio from public gaze.

GARDEN LAYOUTS

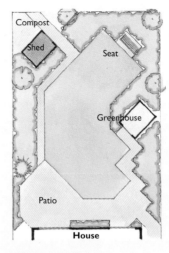

Rectangular layout

This formal, symmetrical design works well for city gardens. Most of the lines will be straight and parallel or boldly curved rather than irregular.

Diagonal layout

A diagonal layout tends to have a semi-formal feel to it. Although it is mostly made up of straight lines, the off-set angle makes it look more interesting.

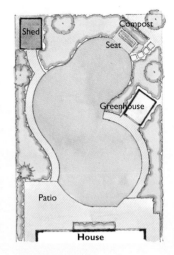

Circular layout

For an informal look, use a curve layout. This creates irregular spaces, borders of different widtl and hidden areas using both straight lines and arcs.

ALLOCATING SPACE

Curving the lawn toward the patio increases the border space. This tends to close in the patio, making it the center of attention.

To open out the patio space, make the lawn circular. This creates more of a balance between hard surface and grass.

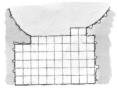

For a less formal approach, stagger the edge of the hard surface into the grass. This is a good way of integrating grass and blocks without dividing up the garden.

Shape and pattern

THE USE of different shapes and patterns is perhaps the single most important element in designing a garden. In a really good garden, the shape and pattern of every component, from the broad outline of a path or lawn to the details such as the contrasting shapes of miniature shrubs in a particular stone trough, will have been thoroughly thought out.

Shapes introduce movement, balance and punctuation to a garden design. Movement can come from the repeated use of upright shapes like arches, which takes the eye away into the distance. The effect will work either in a formal symmetrical context or in a more informal zigzag fashion. Balance will help

the garden to look restful to the eye: a dramatic upright shape can be countered by an adjoining low mound, and the two can be held together by some horizontal shapes.

Some patterns, like squares and circles within squares, are static and restful because they are self-contained shapes that do not lead anywhere, whereas diagonals and curves are active and full of movement since they lead from one place to another. A static design is appropriate for a formal, regularly shaped garden, while an active design is better for an informal garden. Make sure all the lines of your pattern lead the eye toward some focal point, be it a specimen tree or a statue. This will create the "pace" of the garden and link it up into a coherent and satisfying whole.

Apart from these structural uses of shape, a garden is kept alive and interesting through its detail, by the constant interplay between neighboring plants.

Horizontal and vertical surfaces

USE VERTICAL structures—walls, fences, screens, gateways, arbors, and garden buildings—and horizontal structures—drives, paths, patios, and steps—sensitively, as certain shapes and materials relate to one another while others do not. For a successful garden design you should use the vertical and horizontal together in a pleasing and harmonious way, to create a unified whole. Try to achieve a balance between both planes: for example an arch will complement a straight pathway, and so will a low wall built around a patio.

Contours

NOT EVERYONE is blessed with an easy, level site for a garden, and those who are often long for a more varied terrain. But, whatever your preference, there is no doubt that level ground makes gardening easier and that changes of level pose a set of problems, both in planting and with access.

Steep slopes can be used for streams or waterfalls but to maximize on planting space you can terrace the slope using either retaining walls or sloped sod. Groups of Mediterranean-type plants like lavender and santolina will thrive on sunny slopes, where drainage will be quick and efficient. These are also the exact conditions for a scree garden (*see Glossary*), which will be more interesting to look at than a single planting. Cold, shady slopes make good woodland gardens, but will equally make an ideal site for a terraced alpine garden because they are naturally well drained, fully exposed to light, but without the drying heat found on a sunny slope.

What you decide on also depends on the relationship of the slope to the house. A garden that slopes up from the house is far more dominant than one that slopes away. Sites that slope away from the house are less

LEFT: a square garden softened by curved hedges which bracket a focal point, the terracotta pot.

See also: Drawing up your plan pages 16–17

LEFT: a basic design principle is that the pattern of the garden should lead the eye toward a focal point, as demonstrated here.

BELOW: the narrow shape of this patio is enhanced by the siting of pots and variations in the pattern of flagstones and brickwork.

PLANNING ON PAPER

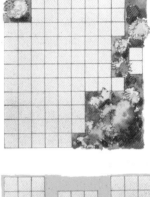

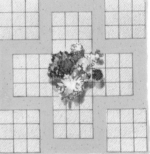

Before committing yourself to any one design, try out several schemes on paper first. Here, four simple designs create very different effects. The most basic design (top left) shows how simple it is to break up the regularity of the square while retaining a feeling of space. A more complicated version of this (top right) consists of the same stones removed but in a more intricate pattern. The most formal design (bottom right), has grass and hard surface arranged in a static, symmetrical pattern. This makes the space seem smaller, but detracts from the garden's squareness. The most active design (bottom left) has a diagonal line across the square. This simple division helps to create two complementary areas.

imposing and throw into the distance. If the view is good, and it can be relied upon to remain so, then make the most of it, but if you want to keep the focus within the garden, try using a formal arrangement of large pots or upright conifer trees. These may not mask a poor view but they will give details of some substance to attract the eye.

Irregular changes of level within a garden can make it more interesting and offer the chance to create surprise views and features. The move from one level to another does not necessarily have to be negotiated in one go; a flight of steps can be split up and intermediate levels inserted in between. If the garden contains large mounds or depressions, consider enlarging them to create a major feature, such as a pond or rockery.

See also: L-shaped garden page 40; Split-level garden page 41

Manipulating scale

IF YOUR backyard is small or an awkward
shape, you can disguise the fact by using
various design devices. Most people want to
increase the apparent size; others to make a
broad site with little depth appear longer than
it is; or to make a long and narrow garden
seem less tunnel-like; or the aim may simply
be to make a small yard seem less confined.

Making a small site appear less cramped
is often most successful when you avoid any
single, unified design, which tends only to
emphasize the size of the site. If you break
the space down into even smaller portions,
your eye will quickly move from one part to
another and focus on the details of the
planting and hard landscaping rather than
the larger picture. If you give these spaces
different characters, you will increase a
feeling of diversity within your small site.
Try to create a garden where paths wind in
among the plants in such a way as never to
reveal the full extent of the site.

Long thin backyards can also be treated
in this way, so that it is never possible to see
down the full length of the long axis. It also
helps if you try to arrest the eye with some
major feature in the foreground or middle
distance, such as a circular lawn or a striking
("specimen") tree, or place horizontal
features like low walls, wide steps, blocks, or
hedges across the axis. In a less symmetrical
garden, place features down the sides—
perhaps a painted seat or the striking trunks
of a multi-stemmed tree—so your eye will
swerve and pause.

RIGHT: the same space can be
made to feel completely different by
arranging the elements in different
ways. Here, a pond and blocks are
arranged in four different ways: the
simple approach (*bottom left*) is
most spacious, while the L-shaped
approach (*top left*) makes the area
seem bigger. The diagonal approach
(*top right*) is the most interesting,
while cutting across the front of the
house creates an intimate enclosure
(*bottom right*).

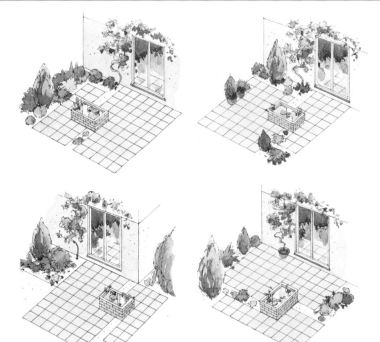

ABOVE: an arbor, flower-
filled containers and pretty
patio furniture can give
great charm to a confined
garden space.

RIGHT: creating different
sections and levels can
make a garden seem bigger
than it is.

REDESIGNING A GARDEN

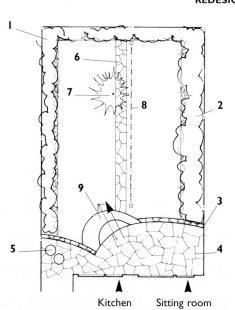

Kitchen   Sitting room

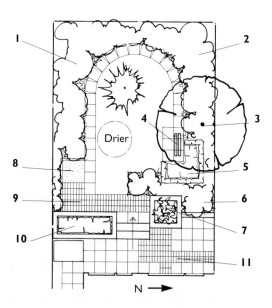

Drier

N →

BELOW: a long, thin garden can be broken up by planting in a random way that seems natural and by avoiding any straight paths or hedges.

Before redesign

Several features spoil this garden and the whole layout adds up to a poor use of the site. The badly laid crazy paving patio (4) clashes with the shape of the house. Retaining walls made from broken cement (3) are unsafe as are the steps (9). The central path (6) divides the rectangular garden into unrelated sections, as do the shrub beds (1, 2) around the lawn and the laundry line (8). Other existing features are a specimen tree (7), and an open corner for garbage cans (5). The aim of the landscape designer is to provide a family garden, with safe, attractive steps and hard surfaces.

After redesign

The patio has been reshaped to provide room for sitting and eating outdoors. It has been resurfaced with neat precast blocks and bricks (9, 11) to provide contrast. The path now sweeps around the garden, ending at a seat (4) under a specimen tree (3) which provides, with the seat, a focal point. The lawns and borders now create strong, flowing curves rather than straight lines. Raised beds are provided for annuals (7) and shrubs and trailers (10). There is a bed for salads or herbs (5), a mixed shrub and herbaceous border (1, 2) and one for roses (6). A play area with sandbox is provided for the children (8).

There are many ways of increasing the sense of depth in a garden. Vistas can be emphasized and "lengthened" by stressing the distant perspective. Eye-catching features can be used to draw the eye away into the distance, but there is no need to rely solely on the contents of your garden to do this. Make use of the landscape outside: let the outside world become the focus of your garden vista. If you are fortunate enough to have a garden with an extensive view, make the most of it. Use trees and shrubs to frame a glimpse of the scene beyond the garden.

Creating false perspective is another useful trick. By placing large plants in the foreground and small ones of the same shape in the distance, they all appear to be the same size although they recede into the distance. It is possible to do the same with foliage by planting thin, airy foliage close by and denser foliage further away. Lawn-mower stripes in a lawn can be used to give direction to a view or to pull your eye in a particular direction, lengthening or shortening the perspective.

Arches, arbors, trellis and fences all have a strong linear impact which can be a tremendous help when you are trying to make sight lines. Trellis can also be used for trompe l'oeil effects, giving the impression of three dimensions where only two exist. There are many ways of achieving these effects. Even mirrors have been used in garden doorways to double the length of a vista. Water too will reflect the garden away and so give the impression of space.

See also: Patio garden page 34; Surfaces pages 52–53

RIGHT: plants can spread most attractively over paving stones.
BELOW: paving is the practical low-maintenance choice in the garden.

ELEMENTS OF DESIGN

Any garden is made up of a mixture of three basic elements: paving, lawn, and planting. Paving is a low-maintenance choice, good if you do not have a lot of time to spend actually gardening. Grass and planting are labor-intensive: grass needs mowing, and planting needs regular watering and weeding. Pick a combination of elements that suits your needs and how much time you have to spend in the garden.

See also: Laying paving pages 62–63; Decking pages 64–67

RIGHT: the luscious blooms of the "Gloire de Dijon" climbing rose need the support of strong trellis to be seen at their best.

Patios

PATIOS TEND to look better laid in symmetrical, formal designs while wooden decking is an ideal alternative for curved, flowing layouts. Decking has a much more relaxed, informal feel to it than paving. It is a material associated with outdoor living and leisure and, being relatively soft, it is a better material than blocks if you have children.

Wood blends in with plants much more than blocks. The texture of blocks contrasts well with that of living material; the one is hard and solid, the other light and full of movement. The two work well together in any garden. There is nothing more attractive than the straight edge of a patio softened by a profusion of trailing plants.

The straight edge of a hard surface can also be used in conjunction with curved flower beds and lawns within one design. The overall effect will be one of contrast: straight and curved lines, and squares and circles.

Paths should be used sensitively and for a reason. A path leading nowhere will not integrate with the rest of the garden. Use curved paths in an informal design and straight ones in a formal scheme. Rather than using a path to split the garden into two equal sections, consider running it along the shadier side of the garden instead.

Lawns

THE IDEAL lawn is both ornamental and practical, and there is a great deal of scope to create an individual and interesting design based on grass. Make sure the shape of the lawn harmonizes with flower beds, pools and other features, but you should avoid complex shapes that not only look fussy but are difficult to mow.

Most lawns are a fairly standard shape: either rectangular or square. A gently curved lawn is a much better proposition as it gives the gardener greater freedom to design with. A lawn flowing through your garden in this way will link up all the separate parts to make a whole.

Grass is the ideal surface for children since it is so soft, but children and adults with sporting tastes can inflict serious damage to lawns. A sandbox is a good idea. In a very small backyard, however, it may be better to discount grass altogether and opt for a mixture of blocks and borders.

Adding the details

ONCE YOU have decided on the framework of your garden, add the decorative details such as arches and arbors, patio furniture, statues and other outdoor ornaments. Resist the temptation to have too many things, otherwise your garden will look fussy and cluttered. Whatever ornaments you are using, they should be placed so as to appear the inevitable outcome of the garden design, rather than just an afterthought.

Introducing plants

GARDENS CAN be made wholly with plants or with artefacts such as walls, paths, patios, steps, pools, statues, and other ornaments added, but the best gardens usually result from a happy blending of everything. The structures will be there all the time, will not change with the seasons, and will give the garden form and character at all times, whereas the plants will be constantly changing in size and appearance, and the annual and bedding kinds will actually be renewed every year, or even two or three times a year. Many beautiful gardens are made by creating a firm design with the architectural components and then clothing this with a rich covering of plants.

Borders and flower beds can be any shape: formal and straight, gently curving, backed by a wall, fence or hedge, or standing in the middle of a lawn as an island bed.

ABOVE: fences play an important part in gardens, marking boundaries and sections as well as providing background support for shrubs, particularly roses.

See also: Patios pages 68–71; Ways with roses pages 168–173; Lawns pages 212–215

Patio ornaments

GENERALLY SPEAKING, decorating your garden is a matter of personal taste and your choice of ornament will create a garden unique to you. Whatever you decide on, it should look good in its own right and be appropriate to the setting, either standing out as a focal point or merging with the surroundings. Choose it carefully: one well-positioned statue will look far better than several pieces dotted around at random.

There are many different ornaments to consider, including statuary and other sculptures, urns and containers, and sundials and bird feeders. Topiary, the art of carving hedges into a variety of shapes, can also be seen as a type of garden decoration but it is a specialized skill.

Most sculpture benefits from a backdrop such as a hedge or wall, perhaps set against a niche for more of an impact. Some look better raised above the ground on plinths or

LEFT: unusual statuary looks effective when raised above the ground.
RIGHT: warm in both texture and appearance, decking is a popular alternative to blocks.

BELOW: patio furniture can be part of the garden design, like this curved stone bench.

See also: Arches and arbors pages 102–103

at the top of a flight of steps. Urns and the more decorative containers also tend to look their best when raised above ground level, standing on some kind of pedestal.

Placing sculpture

CHOOSING THE location for a sculpture is extremely important if the work is to look effective. The best approach is to decide where you want an object and then set about finding a piece that will suit the location. However, more often something irresistible is acquired which must be accommodated in an appropriate setting. Some pieces will dictate a likely location: a Bacchus will look most effective reeling out of the bushes, while a formal statue is ideally placed in a niche or in a more commanding position such as on a pedestal or balustrade.

Be careful always to choose garden sculpture that is in keeping with the architecture of the house and general surroundings, and with the overall atmosphere you are trying to achieve in the garden. For example, a small statue of a pig or a cat, say, which is definitely rustic and informal in character, will look out of place against the formal outline of a grand, dignified house. Such a building calls for a more formal treatment and demands a grand, impressive statue that is more in keeping with its style.

The most dramatic results can be obtained by positioning a sculpture at the end of a vista. Alternatively, it can be placed at the sharp bend of a path, or at the junction of two paths, so that the piece can

be seen from both directions. Sited centrally at the back of an area, it can act as a focal point, but set asymmetrically to offset the curve of a flower bed, the object will create a more relaxed and informal effect. For greater formality, doorways and stairs can be flanked by sculpture. Sculpture can also be used as a counterpoint to a particularly bold plant, or it can be used to distract the eye from an unsightly feature such as a garbage can or a compost pile.

For the most dramatic impact, place a

sculpture in front of a clear-cut background so that it stands out: a smooth hedge or a wall is ideal, as long as it is higher than the statue itself. For the opposite effect, sculpture can be hidden away and used as a means of surprise.

Patio furniture

FURNITURE IS an ideal way to liven up an expanse of hard surface and, as well as being decorative, it is, of course, functional. Patio seats can also be used as focal points, at the end of a garden, for example, or under an arch. They are best sited in a sunny part of the garden that receives some shade during the day.

There is a wide selection of patio furniture to choose from to suit your particular needs. A simple natural wooden seat will look informal, while an ornate wooden seat painted dark green or white will look much more formal. Wrought-iron furniture is one of the smartest types and, on the whole, it will create more of an impact since it does not blend into the garden surroundings in the way that wood does. More temporary patio furniture includes picnic-type plastic tables and chairs and, less durable, canvas deckchairs.

LEFT: this wooden seat is not only a place to rest and enjoy the garden but also serves as a focal point.

See also: Containers pages 174–179

THE LOOK OF YOUR GARDEN

Whether you have a city or a rural garden, it is important to plan ahead to achieve the right look and design.

City gardens

URBAN BACKYARDS have much to offer and provide an exciting, if challenging, opportunity to produce many interesting and original garden designs. A little forward planning and careful thought can go a long way toward overcoming any immediate problems such as lack of direct sunlight, shadows cast from neighboring buildings, poor soil or pollution.

Generally speaking, you will find that city gardens are easier and cheaper to maintain than most rural gardens simply because they are usually smaller. Urban sites also tend to be more sheltered than rural ones and may even be frost-free so you can grow a wide range of tender plants without taking protective measures.

Formality
Formal rather than informal designs tend to be more popular for city gardens because it is easier to incorporate surrounding shared walls into a methodical, precise concept. When choosing your design, remember that the garden will be seen as much from the upper floors of the house as the lower ones, and formal designs tend to look better from above than informal ones.

Size
Size is seen as one of the most common limitations of city gardens, but there are plenty of design options that you can use to help deceive the eye. Small yardss can be made to seem bigger by the use of different levels linked by steps. As for floor treatment, diagonal or circular paving is space enhancing. Creating separate sections within the overall framework of the garden is another way of disguising the limited size of the area. A series of hidden areas that are linked by a winding path can help create the illusion of space.

TOP: small, enclosed city gardens protect plants and are often frost-free.
ABOVE: a gargoyle fountain and striped pots make this patio area unique.

Lack of light
Lack of light is another constraint often encountered in town gardens. For those gardens surrounded by walls, it is possible to paint one or all of the walls white to reflect any light the garden receives.

Choosing plants
Shade cast by surrounding buildings is a common complaint in town gardens, and the only option here is to select shade-tolerant plants. There are many exciting ones to choose from, however, and a careful mixture of foliage and flowering plants will bring much color and interest. Wall plants and climbers play a vital role because they increase the surface area of the garden vertically rather than horizontally. As an added attraction, a plant-clad wall or fence will provide a degree of privacy. Containers and hanging baskets can be used to make up for poor soil in the rest of the garden.

This approach of choosing plants that positively relish the prevailing situation and making the most of the available light, water and space epitomizes city gardening.

See also: Decking pages 64–67; Patios pages 68–71

ABOVE: Oriental poppies,
a rustic garden favorite.
RIGHT: a framing arch.

Rustic gardens

THERE IS AN archetypal image of the ideal rustic garden; from a sleepy road, a gate in a low wall shows a broad flagged path leading to the door of an old house. The path is cascaded with flowers, flowers burgeon from cracks in the paving and roses are prolific. The important point is that it is lovely to look at and that it works by giving the impression of being absolutely right in its context. In the country, fitting a garden into its scene is particularly important.

A natural aspect

The best word to sum up the rustic garden is unsophisticated. It is a style in which a random variety of plants is grown, not particularly for the subtleties of careful plant association but simply as favorites, because they are loved for their own sake or are useful in some way. The garden in which they grow will have a small-scale, purely functional framework, without any grand vistas or extravagant hard landscaping.

Flowers, fruit, and vegetables

In a rustic garden the trees should be fruit trees wherever possible, or at least blossom trees of some kind. Apples, pears, plums, and cherries will all help to create the right atmosphere, as will nut trees such as hazel or almond. If there is space for a large tree, a walnut might do. Try to avoid large upright conifers. Evergreens such as holly or yew will look more appropriate and they can be clipped into shapes which add a touch of fun and formality to the garden if required.

Colorful plants, or perhaps herbs, in simple pots by the door will look right. Make the most of vegetables and fruit bushes, letting them be part of the garden design. Do not be afraid of using rows of vegetables, herbs, bedding plants, or flowers for cutting, especially alongside a path. There is no need to grow only old-fashioned flowers because it is how the flowers are used and grouped that creates the rustic style, not what type they are. Choose as many scented plants as can be fitted into the space available, especially the many varieties of climbing rose and honeysuckle.

The overall effect should be well-tended "disorder," a comfortable mix in which all the plants are allowed to run together. There will be plenty of weeding, but also a great opportunity to grow all your favorite plants in rich profusion.

See also: Rock gardens pages 100–101; Arches and arbors pages 102–103

Low-maintenance gardens

THE LABOR-FREE garden does not exist, but there are ways in which such chores as weeding and tidying can be kept to a minimum. Clearly, what you get out of a garden is in proportion to what you put in, and it will never be possible to expect a plantsman's paradise to thrive on neglect. Those who want beauty without effort are being unrealistic, but there is no need to become a slave. Any means of reducing the more troublesome tasks to a minimum is worth pursuing.

Design options

Much work can be saved by thoughtful design. Instead of grass and borders, have blocks and a few raised growing beds. Blocks are easier to maintain than lawn and, in a small garden, flagstones can look better than grass.

Gravel is a novel alternative to blocks in a low-maintenance garden. It is softer than blocks and flows around curves, and a selection of plants enjoying free-draining conditions will thrive in it. But, most important, gravel laid over soil will suppress weeds and keep the need to weed to a

BELOW LEFT: one important advantage of a paved surface is that it is much less hard work to look after than grass.
LEFT: bulbs are excellent in containers because they need little maintenance as well as giving good long-flowering value.
BELOW: spectacular patio plant, *Festuca ovina* "Glauca."

minimum. Furthermore, it also insulates the soil against moisture loss, so you will not have to water your plants as much as those growing in an open border.

Easy plants

Choice of plants, and their arrangement, exert an enormous influence on the amount of time needed for maintenance. The aim in a carefree garden is to make the plants themselves do as much of the work as possible. Plant shrubs that need little pruning rather than those like hybrid tea roses which require more attention.

Among herbaceous varieties, those that self-seed freely without becoming invasive are ideal in a low-maintenance garden. Ground-cover plants are perfect for filling the spaces between shrubs and give excellent weed control, provided the ground in which they are planted is completely free of perennial weeds in the first place.

See also: Shrubs for year-round interest pages 132–135; Colorful perennials pages 142–145

Patio and container gardens

NEVER LET IT be said that container gardens are second best to gardens in the soil. They may be labor-intensive but, as a reward, they can be as rich and extravagant as your pocket and patience will allow.

Containers solve many problems for would-be gardeners. They are the answer for a paved city courtyard and a roof patio ten floors high, and an excellent solution for people who cannot bend easily to dig. They are an ideal finishing touch: a collection of window-boxes can complete a house front. Whatever the purpose, the choice of containers is enormous.

Upkeep

With container gardening, you should bear in mind certain ground rules. You need to consider the work involved in occasional changes of soil, potting up and repotting; most important of all, you need to consider watering. Do the containers have adequate drainage? Is there a water supply nearby? Will you be able to use liquid feeds? What will happen if you are away or on holiday?

LEFT: container gardens offer plenty of scope but regular watering has to be considered.

BELOW: a peaceful setting for a game of checkers—a brickwork patio with blue table and cane chairs.

RIGHT: an enclosed patio can provide shelter for tender plants such as palms, and its generally linear form can be graced with the foliage of potted bays, camellias, bamboos, etc., providing greenery all the year around.

The question of water

Watering is by far the greatest chore of container gardening and it needs to be done generously and regularly. Rain is never adequate on its own and can fool you into thinking the containers are wetter than they really are. Automatic irrigation is well worth considering for a large container garden.

Planning

It is important to decide whether to plant for a year-round display or to let the containers remain empty during the winter. Remember that many plants which would be hardy enough in the ground may succumb to the cold when their roots are raised up in a container open to frosts. Frozen, waterlogged soil can also burst containers as it expands. Conversely, containers in sun can get very hot in summer and your choice of plants needs to be governed by this fact: it is all too easy to bake the roots of plants.

With these practical points in mind, you are free to choose from the range of container gardening styles. Formal courtyards can be graced with potted bays, cypress, camellias or bamboos. In addition, some especially beautiful pots may look best not planted but used as an architectural contrast. Large cement planters can be filled with trees and shrubs, almost as if they were in the ground. Stone troughs can be planted as miniature gardens of alpines or screes, but they can equally be filled with a single carpeting plant as a piece of living sculpture.

In a rustic garden style, tubs, pots, and even baskets of all shapes and sizes can be clustered to form splashes of color, by doorways or lining steps. Window-boxes and hanging baskets blend in well with this style and provide an opportunity for bold or restful incidental planting in prime locations.

See also: Rock gardens pages 100–101; Containers pages 174–179

ABOVE: Vinca, also known as periwinkle, enjoys sunny and light-shady conditions, provides good ground cover in borders and is attractive when planted in containers.

LEFT: select shade-loving plants such as primulas, lily-of-the-valley, and cranesbill geraniums for shady areas.

Shady gardens

A SHADY BACKYARD is not as disastrous as many people think it may be and, in any case, very few backyards have no sun at all; most have at least a gleam for part of the day. However, sunless spots can be brought to life by plants, for there are many that will grow in shady conditions.

Shade-tolerant plants

Select shrubs that brighten rather than subdue the atmosphere. Choose evergreens with glossy, highly reflective leaves. Camellias, hollies, aucubas, and many others have this attribute, whereas yews and other conifers have dull foliage.

Similarly, variegated leaves have a lightening effect: *Elaeagnus pungens*, *Fatsia japonica*, hollies, and *Euonymus fortunei* are shade tolerant and have forms whose leaves are striped with gold or edged with white.

Shade-loving plants can be brought right up to the house—hellebores and bergenia for winter and early-spring interest; primulas

and lily-of-the-valley (*Convallaria*) can follow; while the summer is a mass of cranesbill (true geraniums), hostas, and a host of others.

Making the most of sunshine

THERE ARE three particularly useful ways to minimize the presence of shade in gardens. They are garden design, tree selection and tree thinning.

Wherever possible, design your garden around the availability of sun. The orientation of paths and vistas may not be able to follow the obvious lines from doors and windows because those ways may not lead to the sun. If the sunniest spot is where the garbage cans normally stand, change it to a seating area instead. Rather than solid boundaries, use trellis or open-work fences which will let in as much light as possible while still acting as shelters. If you do have walls, it helps if you paint these white, so they reflect as much light as possible.

Since evergreens create permanent shade, they frequently make it impossible to grow plants beneath them. Deciduous trees let in winter light, but the choice of species makes an enormous difference. Those that come into leaf late create better lighting conditions beneath their canopies. Acacia, for example, does not begin to sprout until late spring and even then its foliage is frail and lacy, letting in a fair amount of daylight until it is fully developed in mid-summer. Large-leaved trees such as catalpa also open late but when they do they produce a dense canopy of foliage.

Many trees lend themselves to artistic pruning, which is another means of reducing the effect of dappled shade. With practice it is possible to remove whole branches cleanly instead of crudely cutting off their ends, producing a shapely, balanced tree with a smaller, more open arrangement of limbs. Note that this can be tough, even dangerous work, and you may prefer to employ a professional tree specialist or a very experienced gardener.

See also: Garden trees pages 127–129; Hedges pages 130–131

GARDEN PLANS

Planning your garden is wonderful fun. It's the time to really design what you want before the hard work begins in earnest. For some people, this is probably the most exciting time of all in the process of creating a new garden.

This is the time when you can sit down, pencil in hand, and put your ideas down on paper. It's the time to let your imagination run riot.

But careful, constructive planning isn't all about creative instincts. It also requires a cool head. There are raw materials to be considered, lifestyles to be taken into account, practicalities to be weighed up, budgets to be calculated. Above all, there are decisions to be made.

Do you have a small yard to work in or something rather grander? Do you want a formal feel to your garden, or would you prefer something less geometrical, less orderly? Do you plan to spend a lot of time gardening or would you like a low-maintenance option? Is your backyard square, rectangular, or L-shaped, which gives you maximum opportunity for springing surprises? Does your garden take place on just the one level or are there two, or more, different levels to be exploited? Are you content with stone and cement, or do you hanker after something more adventurous? These are all questions that you need to ask yourself.

What follows over the next few pages is a number of different approaches to drawing up a garden plan. Take a look at these and see which of these gardens approximates most closely to the raw materials you have to play with, and which type of garden comes nearest to your chosen style.

Look upon these plans not as blueprints to be copied but as sources of inspiration. See what takes your fancy and let your imagination do the rest.

PATIO GARDEN

Using high-quality paving stones and walling, and a mixture of exciting plants, is always an excellent basis for a garden. This garden is surrounded by an open-weave fence planted with climbing plants. The centerpiece is a raised stone platform, paved on the top with a few plants growing in pockets of soil. Because of careful planting, there is no need for any other ornamentation or complex layout. All the plants have been chosen for their form, color, and texture and are placed effectively around and among the paving stones. Colors in the garden are kept to subtle hues, such as pale yellow, green, gray, and silver, and the flowers are limited to a few delicate colors of white, pink and yellow.

❶ RAISED BEDS

Raised growing beds bring plants closer to eye-level on the patio, making it much easier to appreciate the smaller, more delicate plants, as well as making the fragrance of scented plants more noticeable.

❷ STONE PLATFORM

The central area in this garden is a raised stone platform with a paved top, where plants can be grown in little pockets of soil.

❸ TRELLIS

Trellis with climbing plants such as clematis is another way of maximizing the range of planting within a small garden.

LOW-MAINTENANCE GARDEN

*T*his garden has a simple, low-maintenance design which is exciting and interesting to look at. The uniform paving is complemented by the curved edge of the pond and raised beds. Different types of stone (bricks and cobblestones) have also been used in a stone tapestry-like effect on the ground. There is a tree seat and attractive furniture, both of which add interest.

❶ RAISED POND

A small raised pond may be home to *Nymphaea* (waterlilies), and it will reflect the surrounding foliage.

❷ SHADY SEAT

The white cast-iron seat around a fast-growing *Ailanthus altissima* tree makes an attractive place to sit in the shade in hot temperatures.

❸ CENTRAL PAVING PATTERN

The imaginative mix of bricks, cobblestones and paving blocks in the central ground area creates a kind of decorative masonry rug.

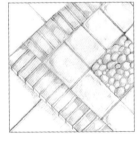

❹ FLOWERING PLANTS IN POTS

A broad range of plants with different growing requirements can be grown in containers and then positioned in sun or shade.

WOODLAND GARDEN

This garden contains many classic features: a lawn, a mass of lovely shrub roses, a mixed shrubbery and a large, open, shaded area filled with herbaceous plants. The great strength of this garden is the way in which these elements have been combined. Leading from the house is a patio paved with plain, rectangular-shaped cement blocks; this space is large without being uncomfortable. Two shallow steps lead down from the patio to the lawn so that the descent is barely perceptible and attention is focused mainly on the plants themselves. The foliage is placed around the lawn area in an informal way so as to mask its edge.

❶ PATIO FURNITURE

On the lawn of a woodland garden, furniture should be lightweight and portable for informal alfresco meals.

❷ PLANTED URN

An urn planted with the tall ornamental grass *Miscanthus* marks a change in level from terrace to lawn.

❸ POTTED FLOWERING PLANTS

Pelargoniums in pots provide bright splashes of red in summer and can be taken indoors in winter to avoid frost.

❹ PAVED PATIO

A spacious patio made of paving blocks, located near the house, provides a dry area for sitting in the sun.

SHRUB GARDEN

Consisting mainly of shrubs, this planting is a low-maintenance solution for a busy family. With a blaze of color, this garden is planted with shrubs that thrive in poor soil conditions. The emphasis is on rhododendrons, azaleas, and other acid-tolerant plants. The chosen plants, all grouped around the lawn, provide color and interest all the year around. The shrubs are interplanted with low-growing perennials and annuals for summer performance. The raised cultivation beds are arranged in an informal, asymmetrical layout to disguise the squareness of the plot.

❶

AZALEAS AND RHODODENDRONS

These shrubs thrive in acid conditions, need little maintenance and produce a dazzling display of blooms.

❷

RAISED BEDS AT DIFFERENT LEVELS

Raised cultivation beds bring variety to a flat, square garden and also make planting and weeding a lot easier.

❹

FOLIAGE SHRUBS

A mixture of evergreen and deciduous shrubs will provide foliage interest and color in all seasons.

❸

CAMELLIAS BY THE LAWN

Camellias, with their showy pink blooms in early spring and glossy foliage all year around, are shown to advantage beside the lawn.

SEMI-FORMAL SQUARE GARDEN

Although based on a formal layout of straight lines, the profusion of plants spilling freely over the cultivation beds softens the look of this garden. The design consists of a square grid of paving and a series of raised beds, with patio seats marking two diagonals and a bench placed opposite the doorway. Containers are placed at random to create an informal feel. There is also a frosted-glass window, which not only protects the garden from wind but also masks the unattractive view outside.

1 PATIO SEAT AND TABLE

A patio seat and table opposite the doorway of the house make this garden into an extra open-air room.

2 CONTAINERS OF SEASONAL PLANTS

The generous use of urns, troughs and other containers provides versatile seasonal color.

3 PROTECTIVE GLASS WINDOW

Instead of a fence, this garden has a frosted glass window to provide shelter without shade on the patio and to screen an unattractive view.

4 TRELLIS WITH CLIMBING PLANTS

A grapevine (*Vitis vinifera*) on a trellis attached to the house wall smothers the brickwork in attractive foliage.

INFORMAL RECTANGULAR GARDEN

The inclusion of an arresting object within a small garden is an excellent way of detracting the eye from adjacent buildings and into the garden itself. The focal point in this garden is an ornate wrought-iron seat, which leads the eye down the garden. The rather austere rectangular lawn is surrounded by a mass of pretty, shrubby little plants, which together help to soften the overall look of the garden.

❶ FLOWERING SHRUBS

Large shrubs in a small garden must have a long flowering season to justify their space.

❷ FOCAL POINT

A pretty, ornate wrought-iron seat, positioned invitingly at the end of a narrow garden, will draw the eye toward it and will beckon visitors to sit on it.

❸ STEPS BOUNDED BY RAISED BEDS

The plain, angular line of stone steps can be softened by building raised flower beds on either side.

❹ SEMI-CIRCULAR RAISED BED

Siting a semi-circular raised bed under the window links the garden to the house in a curved shape and lifts the flowers nearer to eye-level for people sitting on the patio.

L-SHAPED GARDEN

L-shaped gardens offer the ideal opportunity for surprise elements: this one has a hidden dining patio which cannot be seen from the house. It is also built on different levels, the changes in height being linked by similar paving. The high fence acts as a windbreak and a background for plants; it also provides a sense of privacy.

❶ SEATING AREA

In an L-shaped garden the seating area can be out of sight of the house, creating a delightful surprise effect.

❷ PAINTED SHADOWS

A clever way of achieving an effect of sunlight, even on the dullest days, is to paint a shadow on a fence or on a patio floor.

❸ SMALL ORNAMENTAL TREES

Flowering cherry and flowering crab apple are the most spectacular of the small ornamental trees.

❹ MASSED BULBS

A bright springtime splash of color can be provided by massing bulbs such as tulips and daffodils. They are effective in beds or containers.

❺ UNPLANTED ORNAMENTAL VASE

Fine ornamental vases can be left unplanted—one is used here on a brick flanking wall to provide an eye-catching feature.

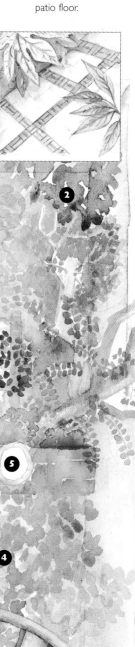

SPLIT-LEVEL GARDEN

*I*n this design, the garden exists on two different levels. Both upper and lower levels are asymmetrical and are joined by some steps, the shape of which echoes the curved retaining wall of an elevated bed. Harsh details that otherwise jar on the eye, such as the imposing end wall, have been softened by a coating of a light color wash and an arched trelliswork with hanging baskets, filled with a mass of colorful trailing plants.

❷ ARCHED TRELLIS

A tracery of unusual white arched trelliswork softens the dominating effect of the wall and accommodates shade-tolerant climbing plants.

❶ HANGING BASKETS

Trailing plants such as fuchsias in hanging baskets are used to minimize the impact of this garden's high brick wall.

❸ RAISED BEDS

Beds planted with shrubs such as *Pieris*, *Potentilla* and *Viburnum* are raised nearer the light on brick retaining walls.

❹ SERPENTINE BRICK STAIRS

A curved flight of brick steps links the upper and lower levels of the garden asymmetrically, following the curved retaining wall of the raised beds.

❺ WATER BASIN

A brick pillar supports a water basin and is surrounded by long-flowering annuals, *Begonia semperflorens* and lobelia.

GRAVEL GARDEN

In this design, the hard, clear lines of paving have been softened by an area of light gravel, which also works as an effective foil for the carefully chosen background plants. The color and texture of the gravel also contrast well with the purple-leaved shrub which dominates the terrace. The height of the plants is accentuated by the smallness of the miniature alpines growing near eye-level in a water barrel.

❶
LAWN AND GRAVEL

Interesting texture contrasts are provided by a small lawn area surrounded by gravel, the broken surface of the gravel setting off the smooth finish of the lawn. The gravel has to be prevented from straying onto the lawn by a hard edging of stone or timber boards.

❷
LEAN-TO CONSERVATORY

Linking house and garden, a lean-to conservatory provides the right degree of shelter and warmth for an extended range of more tender plants.

❸
SUNKEN CONTAINER

A sunken area breaks up a stretch of gravel and is a perfect setting for a pot of zonal pelargoniums.

❹
PAVED TERRACE

Bright new bricks can be chosen for the paved terrace for a look of graphic precision or old, worn bricks for a more mellow, rustic appeal.

JAPANESE-STYLE GARDEN

Timber, brick, gravel and water have been combined to make this Japanese-style garden. The overall design consists of a series of regular geometric shapes in varying colors and textures. Water is used in three ways to produce different textures: there is still water, rippling water and spouting water. Plants are kept to a minimum.

① IVIES CLIMBING FENCE

The highly decorative variegated ivies grow easily and will soon spread over a monotonous stretch of fencing.

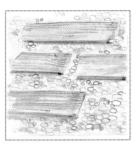

② WOOD SET IN GRAVEL

The interplay of materials, rather than plants, is emphasized in this garden plan. Wooden slats set in a base of gravel contrast with the brickwork and fencing in a series of geometrical shapes.

④ OLD WATER-PUMP

A novel touch—water is fed into the canal by means of an old cast-iron water pump, an idea that works well in the stylized setting of this garden.

③ WOODEN BRIDGE

Simple bridges that can easily be incorporated into a modest-sized garden cross the L-shaped canal, giving access and contributing to the theme of repeated angles.

FORMAL POOL GARDEN

A single pool in a garden tends to dominate. This design shows the advantage of using two smaller areas. Placed between the two ponds is a range of bedding plants that thrive in a shady, moist environment. With formal pools it is important not to have too many overhanging plants that obscure the edges of the pool. Container plants, trees, aquatic plants, and shrubs provide a diversity of foliage, which makes the garden seem larger than it really is.

❶ MINIATURE ORNAMENTAL TREE

Planting a miniature ornamental tree in a container has the advantage that it can easily be moved, giving the best effect at different seasons.

❷ STATUE

A statue serves as a striking focal point in this garden. Statues must be carefully chosen, of appropriate size for their setting. This diminutive statue looks most effective among the irises beside a pool.

❸ SQUARE POOLS

Twin square pools give a strongly geometric aspect to this garden and an island bed of plants has been located between them. The hard edges of the pools have not been obscured by too many overhanging plants—a basic rule when designing formal pools.

❹ CONTAINER OF SEASONAL PLANTS

White petunias and *Helichrysum petiolatum* fill a planting tub to bring seasonal color and variety to a formal garden.

SEMI-FORMAL POOL GARDEN

The focal point of this garden is two curved pools which are separated by a marsh area and a brick pathway. The brick path curves in stark contrast to the horizontal coping stones, while the herringbone paving adds texture and interest. Privacy is created by the brick wall topped with trellis. A corner shed has been stained dark brown so that it is less noticeable. The planting is simple and informal and the background highlights the effectiveness of the vibrant colorful flowers. This garden is refreshingly uncomplicated, while remaining both colorful and spacious, given its small area.

❶ WEATHERED BRICK

The brick walkway between the two pools follows a serpentine curve. The weathered bricks have been laid in a herringbone pattern to charming effect, with straight stone blocks as coping.

❹ SHALLOW STEPS

The shallow steps in the curving brick path encourage the visitor to pause and admire the surrounding display of plants. Even slight changes of level can be highly effective.

❷ BRICK WALL WITH ARCHED TRELLIS

The privacy of this small garden has been achieved by the ingenious use of trelliswork. Arched panels of trellis surmount a whitewashed brick wall, like ramparts on a castle.

❸ FOLIAGE

Most of the trees and shrubs in this design are planted in beds at the foot of the walls. Different foliage shapes are an important ingredient of the scheme—from giant, strap-leaved, red *Phormium tenax* to the rounded, golden-hued *Elaeagnus*, together with buddleias and hydrangeas.

FORMAL ROOF GARDEN

*T*his enterprising roof garden is perhaps best undertaken by an expert, since major alterations on the already established building are necessary if heavy objects such as raised flower beds or ponds are to be supported. The plot is a basic square incorporating two smaller squares placed at opposite corners. One of these squares contains a pond, in the center of which stands a white bird sculpture. An arbor covered with climbers, and a table and chairs, occupy the other corner. There is a raised bed by the side of the pool, which repeats the style of the peripheral raised beds.

❶ SLATTED WOODEN FENCE

A wooden fence with widely spaced slats encloses one side of the roof garden, blending well in color and texture with the mature brickwork of the chimney.

❷ FOUNTAIN

A striking centerpiece sculpture or ornamental pedestal combined with a fountain adds movement and drama to the roof garden.

❸ SQUARE RAISED BED

Large-leaved hostas, elegant irises and long-flowering broom provide a series of contrasts in the square raised beds by the pool, the style of which echoes the raised beds on three sides of the garden.

❹ ARBOR

An arbor of wood sited in a corner makes an attractive seating area. When covered with climbing and trailing plants such as clematis or wistaria it will be shaded with foliage.

INFORMAL ROOF GARDEN

*T*his small roof garden has a patterned floor of black and white paving so, rather than compete with this, the plants are located around the edges. This is especially useful if the roof cannot support much weight. The containers placed around the seating area are lightweight to avoid placing undue weight on the roof. Planted urns are placed at random and window-boxes have been set into the parapet. The roof is at tree-level and surrounded by branches and leaves, so little added ornamentation or planting is needed; also, the striking geometric pattern relieves this roof garden from appearing too dull.

❶ BIRD FEEDER

A roof garden is an obvious center of attention for bird life. The bird feeder here is well sited to attract birds from nearby treetops and is designed to blend naturally with the scheme.

❷ WALL TROUGHS

Flower color is displayed in lightweight containers and window boxes set into the parapet of the roof garden, with red and yellow wallflowers for spring and hardy annuals such as petunias for summer.

❸ CORNER URNS

Substantial urns placed at the corners of the parapet bring a touch of classic style. The urns can be planted with hardy *Potentilla fruticosa*, as well as with summer display plants like begonias.

CONTAINER GARDEN

Every space in this tiny garden is filled with a mass of colorful, fragrant flowers and foliage. An atmosphere of scent and beauty pervades, particularly in summer when everything is at its best. A curved wooden bench (apparent only when you are in the garden) allows you to sit among all the flowers. A trellised wall is covered with climbers; and diverse pots, planters, and high-standing jardinières all enhance the visual effect. The white background shows up the plants to great advantage, and also makes the area seem a lot larger and brighter than it really is.

CURVED BENCH

The curved bench in this tiny garden, hidden in a profusion of fragrant flowers and foliage, makes it possible to linger there in peace and contemplation.

BRIGHT FLOWERS IN POTS

All kinds of pots, planters, and high-standing jardinières to raise plants to different levels can be filled with petunias, pelargoniums, chrysanthemums, and tobacco plants, to provide a mass of color and fill the air with fragrance.

TRELLIS

Trellised walls support a wealth of climbing plants, smothering the garden with flowers—clematis, jasmine, honeysuckle, *Hydrangea petiolaris*, along with climbers like Virginia creeper and *Hedera* "Goldheart" for foliage color and variety.

QUICK TIPS
FOR YOUR IDEAL GARDEN

Practicalities

WORK OUT how much you can afford to spend on your new garden.

• *There is no point thinking up a grand scheme if you can't afford to carry it out.*

Work out how much spare time you have to spend in your garden to maintain it.

• *If you lead a fast-paced life, you may well not have a lot of time to garden, in which case, work out a low-maintenance plan for your new garden.*

Ask yourself what you want out of your new garden. Are you a passionate plant collector? Do you have small children? Do you want to grow vegetables as well as flowers? Assess your backyard and consider what is possible and what is not possible to achieve.

• *If, for example, you have a shady backyard, it's no use having a new design that incorporates large areas of flowerbeds, filled with sun-loving plants. Similarly, if you live in an area of chalky soil, there are certain plants which will not thrive there.*

Ideas

NOW YOU have done all the practical work, start thinking in more detail. Do you want grass or paving? How much border space do you want? More to the point, how much time do you have to keep your borders looking good?

• *On the whole, paving is easier to maintain than grass, which needs regular mowing. However, borders also need a certain amount of work to look good.*

Once you have roughly divided your backyard into areas of paving, grass and borders, or a combination of any two, make a list of features you want.

• *Go out into your backyard and just look around you. Scribble down any ideas that may come to you. Then go inside and imagine what your new garden will look like from both downstairs and upstairs windows.*

If your backyard is a difficult shape, such as short and wide or long and thin, try and work out how to disguise this.

• *Your garden will appear longer than it really is if you have a diagonal layout that leads the eye from a front corner to a back corner. If you want to make your garden seem shorter, divide it into separate "compartments" linked by a winding path.*

Don't be discouraged by sloping ground; in fact a contoured garden is usually more interesting than a flat one.

• *Make the most of slopes by having a rockery or waterfall, or even by making a series of terraces and raised beds.*

Putting pen to paper

FIRST MEASURE your backyard and transfer your measurements to a sketch.

• *Measure all the major distances in your backyard. It makes it much easier if you take a fixed point, such as the corner of your house, and measure everything you can from there.*

Now make a scale plan so you have a realistic plan of the yard as it is.

• *The most useful scale to work to is ¼ or ⅛ in to 1ft, depending on how big your garden is and the size of paper. Work on squared or graph paper.*

Once you have a scale plan, you can draw up your ideas.

• *Mark everything about your new design on your plan so you can carry the scheme out with accuracy and confidence.*

Carrying out your plans

ONCE YOU have decided on your new design and drawn it on your plan, you may need to get professional help with any major soil works or hard landscaping.

• *Don't try to do everything yourself if you do not have the expertise to do so. In the long run, it is much more time- and cost-effective to get professional help.*

CONSTRUCTION

LEFT: making the most of
the basic structure of your
garden is the first step to
developing its potential.

SURFACES

*I*n the garden, surfaces have both a practical and a visual function. They are used for walking, sitting, or playing on, and they also provide an area of rest for the eye, a space between the profusion of the planted areas.

ABOVE: cobblestones can be used to make odd corners of the garden look attractive.
BELOW: for a patio the surface should be smooth and quick-drying and the materials sympathetic to their surroundings, such as brick.

SURFACES DEFINE the space and layout of the backyard, and their design should be given a great deal of thought. The materials should be chosen with care, taking into consideration color, texture and function; they should be sympathetic to their surroundings, blending with the mood of the garden and the materials of the house and any other buildings or walls. Never employ too many different materials, especially in a small plot, as this will confuse the eye and create a restless effect in an area usually dedicated to relaxation.

The nature and design of surfacing should be assessed carefully for its functional and aesthetic qualities. In functional terms the surface may be used for access (for people, bikes), for children's play, for entertaining, and for sitting and sunbathing.

The materials can vary widely according to function; but whatever it is used for, the best surface for a patio should be hard, clean, smooth, quick-drying and weed-free. And, of course, whatever the material and the use to which it is put, it must be durable and not unreasonably expensive.

See also: Elements of design pages 24–27; Patios pages 68–71

Hard and soft surfaces

THERE ARE two types of surface: soft and hard. Soft surfaces, mainly lawns, are better for occasional use and dry weather, and for covering large expanses, as they tend to be easier on the eye than hard surfaces. Hard surfaces are best for constant use and wet weather, and for smaller areas of the plot. Generally speaking, hard surfaces are expensive to install but cheap to maintain, while soft surfaces are relatively cheap to create but expensive to keep in good condition during bad weather and heavy use.

For a garden to look its best, all surfaces, whether they are soft or hard, should be properly laid and well maintained. As they are such prominent features, any carelessness will affect the whole garden.

HARD SURFACES

Problems such as unevenness, sinking, or breaking up that are encountered once the surface is in regular use are nearly always due to poor foundations or bad drainage; tree roots are another potential source of trouble. Weed growths can be disfiguring as well as damaging, but can largely be prevented if you apply weedkiller before asphalt or gravel is laid.

The key to success is to:

• ensure that the hard surface is laid on a well-drained, stable base; this will avoid problems of sinking and waterlogging.

• remove all topsoil, because it contains organic matter, which will decompose and may settle.

• sometimes lay the surfacing material directly on to well-compacted subsoil, though usually a well-consolidated layer of compacted rubble is needed, covered with sand, ash, or screened gravel.

• plan for effective drainage of rainwater from the outset: under-drainage may be appropriate for some materials.

• always lay the surface with a pitch of about 1 in 40 to prevent rainwater forming in puddles and to help the surface to dry.

Design considerations

FROM THE point of view of appearance, a potentially dull-looking hard-surfaced area can be made interesting and attractive by careful choice of colors, by breaking up the floorscape (for instance, with tubs or small beds of flowers) and by attention to the detailed finishing both within the surfaced area and particularly around the margins. Paving made up of small units, such as brick pavers, can both add character and create an illusion of space within a small plot. If the same type of brick is associated with materials also used in the house or its boundaries, a pleasingly coordinated effect may be achieved.

Colors and textures are very important: bright colors that look attractive in the catalog sometimes look garish on the site, especially if they are mixed, and they tend to attract the eye away from the subtle, natural colors of your plants. Large expanses of light gray cement can cause glare in bright sunlight. Lighter colors can help to reflect light into shaded areas.

ABOVE: paving can be a better choice than grass in small areas.
BELOW: bright yellow *Alchemilla mollis* on gravel.

See also: Paths pages 74–77; Horizontal and vertical surfaces page 20

MATERIALS

There is a wide range of surfaces available now, each with its own advantages and disadvantages. You need to list your own particular requirements in order of importance and then choose the material that suits you best. The materials for surfacing are likely to be the largest single expenditure you will make on your backyard, so it is as well to make the right choice.

Natural stone

LIMESTONE, granite and other kinds of natural rock have one big advantage: once laid they look instantly mellow, as if they have been in place for a long time—a good selling point if your house is an old one. But they are extremely costly, even when bought second-hand, and are not always readily available. If you are buying second-hand from a demolition yard—the cheapest source—you may find that the blocks vary greatly not only in size but in thickness too.

BELOW: natural stone has the advantage of looking mellow as soon as it is laid.

Bricks and blocks

BRICKS ARE not widely used as paving because of the cost involved and the time needed to lay them. However, if they are carefully laid, bricks of appropriate texture and pattern can give a very pleasing appearance indeed, especially on fairly short paths. Hard, dense, impermeable types should be used: they must be frost resistant and not prone to disintegration. Engineering bricks are mostly suitable, but stick to mellow colors. The bricks can be laid either on their side or flat. The latter way is cheaper, but make sure that the top surfaces have a suitable finish: on many facing bricks only the sides and ends are suitable for exposure. A variety of paver bricks and cement blocks is available, and some of them incorporate patterns in their surface.

One of the attractions of using such bricks or blocks is that they can be laid

See also: Combining materials page 72; Laying a brick path page 75

LEFT: paving stones are available in different shapes—square, rectangular, polygonal, circular—as well as in various textures and colors. They can be combined in a red and buff checkerboard pattern to make a large area more interesting.

ABOVE: blue-gray quarry tiles make a smooth formal surface and reflect the sunlight.

RIGHT: bricks come in several different types and can be laid in a variety of different patterns, as seen here: old Tudor bricks *(top)*; natural colors *(center)*; and traditional pattern *(bottom)*.

in a wide variety of patterns to create visual interest, and sometimes also an illusion of extra space, width, or depth. As there is some variation in the size of bricks, it is best not to try a very elaborate pattern, as the bricks might require trimming. Herringbone patterns would entail the cutting of bricks or blocks diagonally at the edges.

Tiles

TILES ARE made of hard-fired clay and, depending on the composition of the clay and the temperature of the firing, they can be very durable. Quarry tiles are popular for paving; these are unglazed, geometric in shape (usually square or octagonal) and regular so they can be used to make formal, smooth surfaces. However, they are very difficult to cut and should be reserved for areas with long, straight edges rather than complicated curved perimeters.

For a more eye-catching effect, use glazed paving tiles which come in different shapes and colors, often with painted motifs or designs. The more decorative tiles look best in the strong sunlight of hot climates. As glazed tiles are both fragile and relatively expensive, they should only be employed in small quantities. Fragments of tiles can be used to make floor mosaics.

Crazy paving

ALTHOUGH CRAZY paving has often been sneered at, there is a great deal to be said for it, provided that the broken stone of which it is constructed is natural and also that it is properly laid. It is those bits of broken cement or synthetic paving, or stretches of cement marked out in a random pattern, or poorly fitted paving with ugly, thick mortar joints that have given crazy paving a bad name. Properly laid random paving can look perfect in a rural setting, although it is inclined to seem out of place in cities or with avant-garde architecture.

If you intend to use natural stone for your crazy paving, bear in mind that the pieces are likely to vary considerably in thickness. Prepare the ground carefully if the paving is to present a flat, even surface.

PREFABRICATED BLOCKS

If you are laying a large area, it pays to use two colors, checkerboard fashion, to avoid monotony. For instance, although gray and honey-beige blocks are uninteresting if used by themselves over a large area, when combined they can look very attractive. However, be careful in your use of combined colors.

• These are now the most commonly used materials for hard surfacing in the garden.

• Prefabricated cement blocks are available in a vast range of colors and textures.

• They vary in shape from the 2 × 2ft common gray block to polygonal and circular forms; most of them are 2in thick or less.

• More expensive types are made of reconstituted stone, and you can even find them in a texture that has the appearance of water-worn stone.

• It is important to make sure that the surface finish is non-slip: a smooth finish encrusted with algae can be treacherous in wet weather.

See also: Crazy paving page 63

Gravel

GRAVEL MAKES a relatively inexpensive and quickly laid surfacing material. Curves are much easier to form with gravel than with paving slabs, and slight changes in level are readily accommodated. Gravel offers the advantage, too, that it can easily be taken up and later relaid if underground piping and other services need to be installed at any time. Finally, if you become bored with it, the gravel is likely to form a good base for an alternative surface. The main disadvantage is that, unless it is carefully graded, the surface will be loose: pieces of gravel spilling on to an adjacent lawn could cause serious damage to a mower, and they are easy to bring into the house on the soles of shoes. Avoid gravel spilling over by creating a firm edge, such as a kerb of bricks on edge.

Gravel is available in two main forms: crushed stone from quarries, and pea gravel from gravel pits. The former is of better quality, but will be very expensive unless the stone is quarried locally. Gravel occurs in a variety of attractive natural colors, and your choice should, if possible, complement any stone employed in the backyard for walling or rock gardens. The alternative, washed pea gravel, comes in shades from near white to almost black. Whichever type is used, ensure that the stones are neither too large (which makes walking uncomfortable), nor too small (they will stick to your shoes). For most purposes the best size is in the range ⅜–¾in in diameter. Be sure that it is all of one grade; a mixture tends to settle out into layers and looks less effective.

Gravel is good at suppressing weeds. The only maintenance it should need is an occasional raking over to keep it looking trim and to remove any bumps or indentations in the surface.

ABOVE: gravel is the quickest surface to lay as it spreads easily around curves and over uneven ground.

RIGHT: examples of different gravel sizes and colorings, blue/gray (left), natural beige (center) and a mixture of gray and white (right).

See also: Wood and gravel paths page 77; Low-maintenance gardens page 30

RIGHT: wood decking is not difficult to construct and it solves the problem of uneven surfaces.

Cement

USED IN mass form as a garden surfacing material, cement is hard, durable, and fairly easy to lay; and once laid it is more or less permanent. Coloring agents can help to relieve the monotony if the cemented area is fairly small and the colors chosen with care, but a more interesting effect can be achieved by modifying the surface texture.

Alternatively, you can mark it out into mock paving squares, although unless this is done neatly, it is likely to look worse than a plain surface. Cement can also be made to look much more acceptable and less harsh if its surface is brushed while still damp to reveal a pebble or gravel aggregate. This mellow, soft appearance is better suited to a garden setting. You may find that the best solution of all is to concentrate on stocking the surroundings with colorful shrubs and flowers.

Cobblestones

THESE SMOOTH rounded stones look very attractive if you use them on a small scale, setting them around a tree for instance, or infilling an odd corner, where it might be difficult to cut larger paving materials. They are not suitable for large areas, as they become dangerously slippery when wet, and they are totally unstable to stand outdoor furniture on. However, they can look very attractive when used to break up a large expanse of cement—set in a circular swirl, for instance, or ranged into a square. Small granite blocks, too, can be used in the same way, to provide patterns on what might otherwise be a dull expanse of paving or cement. Bed them in carefully to achieve a flat surface.

Bark

CHIPPED OR shredded bark is a popular material for creating visually and physically soft surfaces. Its somewhat unruly appearance makes it unsuitable for formal

areas and, because of its natural affinity with wood, it is generally used in wilder parts of the garden. Bark is particularly suitable for woodland areas, where its color and texture blend in well with the trees.

Bark is a good choice in areas where children play, as it is relatively soft. Heavier pieces of bark are better than composted bark, which is more like peat in consistency and can be more difficult to control.

Decking

WOOD DECKING is an alternative to paving and is visually and physically softer than other hard materials. It looks good in rural surroundings or with modern houses, and it is warm to walk on.

HOW TO USE DECKING

• Decking can solve problems as an alternative to paving if you are laying a patio over several different levels or a very uneven surface.

• If you cannot afford to deck the entire area, see if a corner of the patio could be decked.

• You need to use hardwoods (or softwoods that have been really thoroughly treated with preservative) and the very best-quality fastenings.

• Decking is quite easy to construct yourself, unless it has to be built high off the ground.

• Experiment with different patterns by arranging the planks in different designs and at different levels.

See also: Decking pages 64–67

DRAINAGE

There is nothing worse than having to splash your way through puddles of water every time it has rained. Good drainage is absolutely essential.

Draining hard surfaces

PATIOS AND paths can be made impassable by every shower of rain if they are not constructed so that they shed water. When making a paved or cement area, build in a slight slope so that water is shed and does not form pools. A fall of about 1 in 40 will move water quite quickly either onto border soil (where it can be used by plants), or into a shallow gully which can lead to a percolator or drain. Construct the gully from half-round ceramic pipes bedded in cement, or from cement that has been troweled into a similar shape.

If a hidden gully is desirable on a patio or path, lay half-round ceramic pipes down the center of the area and slope the paving or cement very gently toward the gully, overlapping the edges. A ½in gap in the center will allow the water to run into the channel.

Percolator

A PERCOLATOR must be constructed if there is no suitable watercourse for a drainage system to run to. Dig a hole 3–6ft in diameter and at least 6ft deep. The sides should be loosely bricked to allow water to seep through. Leave space for the main pipe to enter. Fill the percolator with coarse clinker or brick rubble. Finish with the topsoil.

CONSTRUCTING A HERRINGBONE DRAINAGE SYSTEM

Make sure the side drains meet the main drain at an angle of 60°. The drains must run toward a ditch or percolator at a gradient of at least 1 in 40.

1 Following the slope of the land, dig V-shaped trenches at the same level as the subsoil, up to 3ft deep and wide enough to take a 4in diameter main pipe. At the same time dig side trenches for 3in diameter drains.

2 Cover the bottom with a 2in layer of gravel. Lay the pipes on the gravel bed.

3 The pipes are butted, not joined. Where the side drains lead into the main drain, break the pipes to fit together and cover them with tiles. Any excess moisture will percolate through the gaps between the lengths of piping.

4 Cover all the pipes with coarse rubble or stones, then finer rubble, finishing with a layer of topsoil.

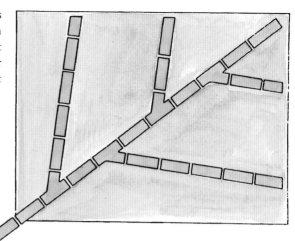

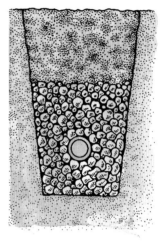

ABOVE: plan for an ideal arrangement of side drains meeting the main drain at the correct 60° angle.

LEFT: a cross section shows the pipe buried in coarse rubble, topped with finer rubble and a topsoil dressing.

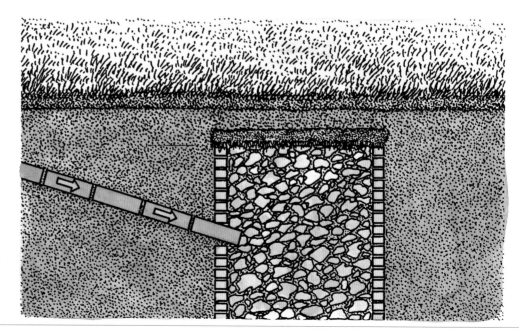

RIGHT: if there is no suitable watercourse for drainage, a percolator can be constructed as shown here.

See also: Surfaces pages 52–53

MORTAR AND CEMENT

Cement paving blocks and mortar are good for most patios and backyard paths, although laying blocks can be quite a strenuous job.

CEMENT

Choosing a cement mix

It is vital that you mix the cement ingredients —sand, cement, and aggregates—in the correct proportion to give the most suitable strength of mix for the job. There are basically three mixes.

A: general purpose for surface blocks and bases where you need a minimum thickness of 3–4in.

B: light duty for backyard paths and bases less than 3in thick.

C: bedding, a weaker mix used for wall foundations and bedding-in blocks.

Mix	Cement No. of 100lb bags	Fine sand plus aggregate	OR	All-in aggregate
A	× 6	17⅔ cu ft + 26½ cu ft		35½ cu ft
B	× 8	17⅔ cu ft + 26½ cu ft		35½ cu ft
C	× 4	17⅔ cu ft + 26½ cu ft		45 cu ft

What to order

When ordering the ingredients to make up twice the amount of the three different cement mixes described above, consult the chart above.

What to mix

Cement mixes are made up by volume, and it is convenient to use a bucket as your measure. For the cement mixes previously listed, mix the following, remembering that each mix requires about half a bucket of water (although this does depend on how damp the sand is).

Mix A
1 bucket cement
2½ buckets fine sand
4 buckets washed aggregate
OR
1 bucket cement
5 buckets all-in aggregate

Mix B
1 bucket cement
2 buckets fine sand
3 buckets washed aggregate
OR
1 bucket cement
3¼ buckets all-in aggregate

Mix C
1 bucket cement
3 buckets fine sand
6 buckets washed aggregate
OR
1 bucket cement
8 buckets all-in aggregate

Mortar ingredients

MORTAR FOR block-laying consists of cement and fine sand mixed together with water to form a self-hardening paste. Mortar mixed in the proportions one part cement to five parts sand is adequate for laying blocks. It is vital to mix the ingredients in the correct proportion. Use buckets as a measure for the ingredients, tipping them on a hard, flat surface or a mixing board.

Plasticizer

OFTEN A "plasticizer" is added to the mortar to aid the workability and flexibility of the mix. Traditionally lime was used but modern science has developed chemical plasticizers, which are easier to mix, and these are now used instead.

These chemical plasticizers usually come in liquid form with the amount you need to add specified on the container.

Ready-mixed mortar

SOME READY-mixed paving mortars have polymer additives, which are designed to enable heavy slabs to be slid into position and held in place while positioning adjustments take place (in a similar way to fixing ceramic wall tiles). Once the mortar has set, the slab will be held permanently.

Each 100lb dry pack of ready-mixed mortar is sufficient to lay about 10 blocks that are 2ft square or about 14 blocks 18in square. The material is used with a fairly dry texture and applied in four generous dabs at the corners of the block: the block is lowered on to the dabs and slid into position. Once you are satisfied with the alignment of the block you can simply tap it down to the required level with the shaft of a drill hammer or any reasonably heavy hammer, compressing the mix by about 1in.

MIXING MORTAR

1 Pile the sand into a pile, form a crater in the top and pour on a bucket of cement.

2 Turn over the sand and cement repeatedly with a shovel until a consistent color shows that it is thoroughly mixed.

3 Add the plasticizer to the water in accordance with the manufacturer's instructions, then form a crater in the center of the heap and pour in about half the water.

4 Collapse the sides of the crater inward to mix the water with the dry mortar. Gradually add more water as the mortar absorbs it, continually turning over the mix until you achieve a really smooth but firm consistency.

5 Draw the spade across the mix in steps: the ridges should remain. If you add too much water you will weaken the mortar mix, but you can stiffen it again by sprinkling on handfuls of dry cement.

See also: Laying paving pages 62–63

TYPES OF FOUNDATIONS

Foundations are necessary for any structure that you build in the garden, in order to support and spread its load to firm ground. Whether you are constructing a solid footing on which to build a brick boundary wall, or laying the base for an outbuilding, the basic principles are similar.

Strip foundations

SMALL STRUCTURES such as brick planters and masonry walls must be built on strip foundations. These consist of a trench filled with a layer of compacted rubble (which comprises broken stones or bricks) topped with fresh cement.

The foundation is built wider than the wall, so that the weight of the wall is spread out at an angle of 45 degrees ("the angle of dispersion") from its base into the foundation and on into the subsoil. To gauge the correct width of foundation for a given wall width you should, as a rule of thumb, allow twice the width of the masonry.

The depth of the cement foundation depends on the height and thickness of the wall and on the condition of the soil, but in general it should be half as deep as it is wide, and project beyond the ends of the wall by half the width of the masonry. For example, a wall over six courses of bricks high would require a trench about 16in deep.

ABOVE: brick boundary walls need firm foundations to give support to climbing plants.

LAYING A STRIP FOUNDATION

1 Fix profile boards at each end of the proposed trench, with nails attached to the crosspieces to mark the trench width.

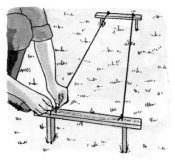

2 Attach stringlines to the width markers, linking both sets of profile boards at each end of the proposed trench, and secure.

3 Sprinkle a little sand along the strings in order to transfer the width marks to the ground, and then remove the strings.

4 Dig out the trench to the required depth, making sure that you keep the base flat and the sides upright in the process.

5 Drive in pegs so that they protrude by the depth of cement needed. Check that the pegs are absolutely level.

6 Soak the trench with water, then add rubble where the ground is fairly soft and ram down well with a sledgehammer.

7 Pour in the cement and work in by slicing into the mix with a spade. This dispels air bubbles which could weaken the foundations.

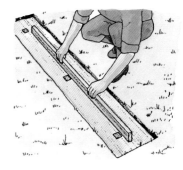

8 Compact the cement by tamping with a straight-edged length of two-by-four and level it to the tops of the guide pegs.

See also: Walls pages 84–87

Paving foundations

PAVING BLOCKS, block pavers and other paving materials must be laid on a surface that is firm, flat and stable. A base of well-compacted subsoil covered with a layer of sand is sufficient for laying paving, but for large, well-used areas, or where the soil is soft, it will be necessary to add a layer of compacted rubble to prevent the paving from sinking.

Compacted rubble contains many depressions, even after consolidation by garden roller. These have to be filled by spreading a layer of sand over the surface and leveling it with the back of a garden rake.

Paving blocks or other small-scale pavers can be laid directly on the sand layer using mortar, although some block pavers can be laid loose on a prepared sand bed without the use of any mortar.

Before doing any excavation work, check where all your service pipes and cables are so as not to damage them.

LEFT: a base of level subsoil with a layer of sand is usually sufficient for laying blocks, but compacted rubble will be needed for large areas that have heavy use.

LAYING PAVING FOUNDATIONS

1 Dig out the topsoil within the stringlines, which are set 2in wider than the finished path. Retain any sod for re-use elsewhere in the garden.

2 Compact the base using a stout wooden post, sledgehammer or garden roller. If using a post, wear thick gloves to protect your hands.

3 Add rubble to the base and ram this down well with a sledgehammer or compact with a roller to a thickness of about 3in.

4 Cover the surface with a layer of sand spread about 2in thick with a garden rake as a means of filling large depressions in the rubble.

See also: Laying paving pages 62–63; Patios pages 68–71; Paths pages 74–77

LAYING PAVING

Paving can be used for both paths and patios; the method used is much the same.

Foundations

FIRST MAKE the foundations as described earlier. Paving blocks can be laid on a sand bed without mortar where there is likely to be minimal pedestrian use. The bed should be about 2in thick: you will need to buy 1.7 cu ft of sand for every 215 sq ft of path. Where patios and paths will receive a lot of heavy traffic, lay the blocks on mortar dabs.

LEFT: this type of irregular pattern also provides space for rock plants.

LAYING PAVING BLOCKS

1 Lightly spread the side of the previously laid flagstone with mortar.

2 Make fine mortar dabs: one at each corner and one in the middle.

3 Carefully position the next flagstone in the correct place.

4 Using the shaft of a heavy hammer, align the flag and tighten the mortar joint.

5 Tap the flag down to the correct level, using a level as your guide.

6 Once you have laid the flagstones, "even" the joints for a good finish.

See also: Mortar and cement page 59; Patios pages 68–71; Edging page 73

PAVING BLOCKS

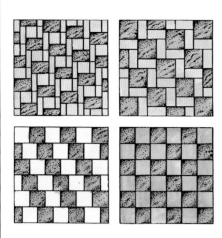

Cement blocks are available in a wide variety of sizes and colors. The simplest designs (*above—bottom left and right*) have the advantage of being easy to lay. They blend in with their setting more readily than complicated and difficult patterns (*above—top left and right*). Detailed patterns can, however, be interesting to look at. It is best to work out the pattern on squared paper before buying blocks so that the exact requirements can be calculated. Lay out all the blocks before securing them, then the whole pattern can be seen. Only cement them into place when you are happy with the effect.

Crazy paving

CRAZY PAVING comprises pieces of broken paving blocks laid to produce a complex, decoratively patterned surface. However, despite the apparently random effect of the paving, the pieces must be laid in a strict formula both for a symmetrical appearance and for strength.

The sides of the paved area are formed by a row of fairly large block pieces which have at least one straight edge, placed outermost. Similar-sized pieces with irregular edges are positioned along the center of the area. Smaller irregular pieces are then used to fill in any spaces remaining between the larger blocks.

Foundations

PREPARE THE base by digging out the topsoil. If the subsoil is not firm, dig this out too and replace with 3–4in of compacted rubble. Top with about 2in of sand, raked and leveled.

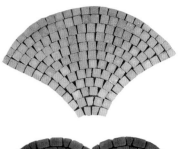

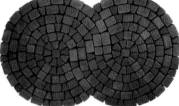

LEFT: a mature path blends in with the foliage and rock plants around it.
ABOVE: materials come in many types—rialtha setts with wedge stones *(top)*; rialta sett circles *(center)*; and tegula cobbles *(bottom)*.

LAYING CRAZY PAVING

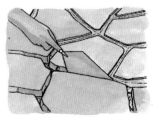

1 Dig out the base and fill with compacted rubble. If soil is loose sand, rake and level. Bed the straight-edged blocks on dabs of mortar at the sides of the path.

2 Lay the larger central blocks and smaller infill pieces in the remaining gaps and tap level using a heavy hammer and a length of two-by-four wood.

3 Point the joints between the crazy paving blocks with mortar, making sure to bevel the mortar. This allows any water to drain away efficiently.

See also: Paths pages 74–77; Low-maintenance gardens page 30

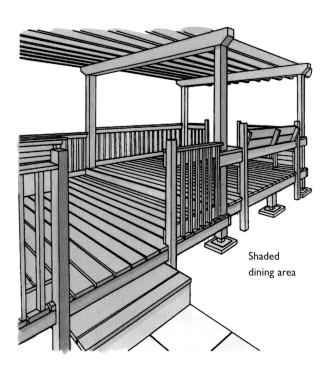

Shaded
dining area

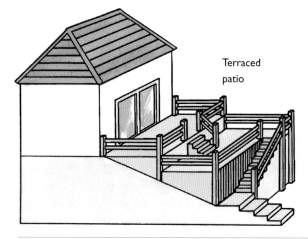

Roof
patio

Terraced
patio

DECKING

A raised wood deck provides you with space outdoors for dozing, dining or soaking up the sun, and can be constructed using just a few specialist carpentry techniques. Decorate the surface with containers.

LEFT: wooden decking can provide a raised, shaded area for outdoor dining, on either built-in or freestanding furniture.

ABOVE: decking combines well with timber trelliswork, outdoor furniture and wooden plant containers.

See also: Decking page 57

Planning the structure

DECIDE WHAT you are likely to use the deck for, as this helps you determine its overall size: if you intend to dine outdoors, it must be large enough for a table and chairs with space for people to pass behind when serving a meal. Where the deck will be used as a sunbathing area, space must be allowed for loungers. Decking combines best with wooden fencing and wooden cask containers.

Consider how the deck will appear when attached to the house wall: if it is fairly narrow—say about 10ft—and projects out from the wall about 20ft, it will not sit easily. A deck of this width running along the wall of the house would probably appear to be in better proportion. A squarer deck, on the other hand, is more in keeping with a corner location, set in the angle between two walls that meet at right-angles.

Draw a scale plan of the garden on graph paper and mark in the intended position and size of the deck, plus access arrangements and other features that might influence the design. Draw a side elevation of the site to illustrate the way the ground slopes: the deck can be constructed on sloping ground by adjusting the length of the wood posts so that the deck surface is horizontal.

Set up stringlines and pegs to mark the perimeter of the proposed deck so that you can imagine the visual impact it will have on the garden and the house.

WOOD REQUIREMENTS

Use the plans you have drawn to work out the amount of wood needed. The main structural components are made from two stock sizes of wood: for the below-deck supports use 5½ x 1½in-profile wood, with 3in-square-profile wood for the above-deck supports. The deck joists should be made from 5½ x 1½in softwood, supporting slats of the same size wood laid flat rather than on their edges.

BELOW: the garden can be made accessible with decking.

THE BASIC BOARDWALK

A basic timber slatted boardwalk platform can be constructed entirely from lengths of preservative-treated sawn or planed softwood measuring about 3 x 1in laid on a cement surface. Assemble the boardwalk on site. It is extremely straightforward to build, consisting of lengths of wood, which form the bearers, spanned by wooden slats.

1 Space lengths of wood about 30in apart and parallel with each other running in the direction of the slope of the surface.

2 Cut slats of the same wood to span the width of the platform and place them across the bearers at rightangles.

3 Set the slats about ¼–½in apart, using an offcut of wood as a spacer so that the gap is constant across the length.

4 Lay full lengths of wood across platforms up to 10ft wide. For wider platforms butt-join the lengths.

5 Stagger the joins at each side of the platform in alternate rows so that there are no continuous break lines.

6 Secure the slats to the bearers with 1½in long floorboard nails, two per bearer position.

ABOVE: a variety of patterns can be formed.

Attractive geometrical patterns can be formed by the decking (right). The more complex, intricate patterns may require more elaborate supports. Some of the options available include checkerboard (top right), angled checkerboard (bottom left), concentric rectangles (top left), and traditional herringbone (bottom right). In some situations it is preferable to consider using a simple arrangement of parallel slats, perhaps laid on a diagonal in relation to the adjacent house wall, to give a dynamic effect.

The raised deck

RAISE THE deck on low brick walls or cement piers about 1ft high and spaced at about 4ft intervals across the site. Make sure there is some form of damp-proof course beneath the supports to prevent damp rising up through the brickwork and attacking the wood.

For neatness, it is a good idea to build a continuous peripheral wall too, so that the underside of the deck is not accessible to pets and inquisitive small children. Make sure the tops of the walls are all level with each other as they provide the supports for the deck's main supporting joists. It is important that the surface of the deck remains at least 6in below the house damp-proof course to prevent damp penetrating the walls.

Simply rest the joists on top of the low walls or cement piers and construct the deck as previously described.

See also: Materials pages 54–57

See also: Outdoor living pages 104–105

LEFT: simple and effective decking formed of single slats.

ABOVE: joists can be laid in a simple square pattern *(bottom)* or a diagonal pattern *(center)*. For more complex designs, use extra strong diagonal joists *(top)*.

PATIOS

Patios can be constructed from many different materials—practically all types of paving are suitable, as is wood—to complement the construction of your house and blend in with the overall theme of your backyard. They can range in style from a simple paved square to a complex "mini garden" on various levels, a built-in barbecue and seating, and even an ornamental pond. The patio treatment can also be extended to a small walled courtyard with great effect, turning it into an outdoor family room.

RIGHT: a patio can be a peaceful green arbor with a host of flowering shrubs positioned around an inviting outdoor seat.

Planning your patio

BEFORE YOU start building a patio you should give a lot of thought to where you will put it. Normally, it will be adjacent to the house so that you can walk directly on to it. However, that may not always provide the best exposure to the sun for most of the day, depending on which way the back or side of your house faces. It may be better to build a separate patio away from the house and linked to it by a pathway.

Sun and shade

The first thing to do is to spend a few days in summer watching how the sun and shade strike various parts of the backyard so that you can select a suitable site. Although you will want the benefit of the sun for most of the day, some shade on your patio will also be desirable, particularly if you want to eat outside regularly.

If your ideal site is shaded by the house for most of the day, there's not much you will be able to do about it; however, if it is in the shadow of a tree or hedge, you may be able to solve the problem by judicious pruning or even complete removal of the offending shrubbery. If a fence is the culprit —assuming you do not need a tall solid barrier to deal with nosy neighbors—then you could replace it with a lower one of open construction such as a trellis.

If your ideal site is always in full sun throughout the day, you can provide the patio with some shade by building a screen wall along one side, by constructing a complex arbor or trellis as a support for climbing plants, or even by fixing a folding awning to the house wall. Alternatively, you can always rely on a large sunshade.

Size and shape

The actual size of the patio will depend on what you intend to use it for and the size of your backyard—you do not want it to overwhelm the rest of your backyard, but if you only have a small walled area at the back of your house, then you can extend the patio construction to take in the entire plot.

As a guide, a patio measuring 12ft square should be considered the absolute minimum. However, there is no reason why it should be square: bear in mind the shape of the backyard and the house, the slope of the ground and the materials you intend to use to pave the surface.

In this instance, a sketch plan of the whole plot is essential for deciding the exact position, size and shape of the patio. Once you have decided on the size and shape of the patio, draw it to scale on tracing paper to make an overlay and try it in various positions on your backyard plan until you find the best spot.

See also: Horizontal and vertical surfaces page 20; Elements of design pages 24–27

Materials

Just about all types of paving materials are suitable for surfacing a patio—bricks, stone or cement blocks, cobblestones, and gravel. However, take care in selecting a surfacing material as you will be laying a wide area and some textures or colors may be too much to bear.

You may want to use the same materials to pave a patio as those used for paths elsewhere in the garden. This helps to give a unified appearance to your garden, or you may want to match materials used in the construction of your house. To provide visual interest in the surface, consider adding sections of other materials which are available—areas of gravel or cobblestones in a patio paved with blocks or bricks, perhaps, or a mixture of pavers and blocks.

ABOVE: shrubs flourish on a sunny but sheltered patio.
ABOVE RIGHT: plant pots with evergreen shrubs make the patio an attractive place all the year around.

DECORATIVE IDEAS

Regardless of the material used to pave a patio, it can still look very stark if the surface is unbroken by decoration. In general, patios also tend to look a lot better if they are linked in one of the ways suggested below to the rest of the garden.

• Leave holes in the surface for planting flowers and small shrubs.

• Simply lay the patio up to the edge of a lawn, making sure it is slightly below ground level to prevent damage to your mower blades.

• Divide the patio from the garden with a low wall of screen blocks or with a low, narrow, raised planter of brick or walling block.

• Plant shrubs to form a low hedge along the garden side of the patio.

• Alternatively lay paving at the edge of the patio with increasingly wider gaps between the individual pieces and allow the lawn to grow in between so that the patio appears to blend into the lawn.

• You can build raised planters as part of the patio, possibly linking them with a seating area or a barbecue, or even incorporate a water feature of some kind—a fountain, perhaps, or a small pool.

• Place pots full of flowering plants at various points around the patio.

See also: Materials pages 54–57; Laying paving pages 62–63

Building a patio

Foundations

Patios and large areas of paving which will receive heavy traffic should always be set on a compacted rubble and sand foundation. Lay a 4in layer of rubble topped with a 2in layer of sand.

Marking out the base

It is essential that you set out the base correctly to ensure the surface has a firm, flat foundation that will not collapse. Use stringlines and pegs to mark the perimeter of the patio. Most patios adjoin the house and it is important that they are constructed so that the level is not higher than the damp-proof course (DPC) of the house walls.

Laying blocks

A large area of paving blocks likely to receive considerable traffic should be bedded on mortar on a prepared foundation. Start to lay the blocks in one corner of the patio and work diagonally across the surface. This makes it easier to ensure that they are laid consistently flat. Place ½in thick offcuts of wood between the blocks as consistent joint spaces, or simply butt up the blocks for finer joints. As you work across the surface, kneel on a piece of board to distribute your weight.

ABOVE: visual harmony— a circular paved patio with stone bench.

LAYING HEXAGONAL BLOCKS

1 Lift the first block and place its outer edge on the sand, then lower it gently on to the mortar dabs. Tap the slab down carefully, with a heavy hammer handle. Place a level on top to check that it is level in both directions.

2 Position the second and subsequent blocks in the same way, checking across the tops with a level. Pack out under blocks that are too low with more mortar, or tap down blocks that are too high so they are level.

3 Mix three parts dry sand to one part cement and brush between blocks. Water in the mixture using a watering can fitted with a fine rose. Once hardened, this filling will help keep the blocks in place and discourage weeds.

USING HALF-BLOCKS

If you lay rectangular or hexagonal blocks, you will need half-sizes for the perimeter. Some manufacturers produce half-size blocks, but you may have to cut others to fit, using a heavy hammer and bolster chisel. Measure the offcut, and score the line with the chisel using a straight-edged length of wood as a guide. Then, resting the block on the length of wood, chop sharply with the hammer and chisel to break along the line.

Lay all the whole blocks first, then cut and fit the ones for the edges.

See also: Urban gardens page 28; Mortar and cement page 59; Types of foundations pages 60–61

DATUM PEGS

A datum peg, made from 1in sq softwood with a pointed end, is used to set the top level of the patio. Drive in the "prime datum peg" so that its top is at the height required for the patio. This must be at least 6in below the level of a DPC to prevent rainwater splashing from the patio surface on to the house wall above the DPC.

1 Stretch stringlines between pegs driven in at the perimeter of the patio, indicating the corners with more pegs set at the ultimate level of the patio.

2 Check the corners with a builder's square to ensure that the stringlines are set at right-angles. Adjust as necessary.

3 Level the pegs by spanning across the tops from a prime datum peg with a level and straight length of wood. Tap down or raise the pegs as necessary.

4 Level the entire base by driving intermediate pegs at 5in intervals across the surface and leveling them to the perimeter pegs.

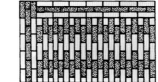
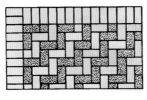
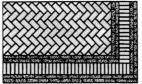

ABOVE: simple or complex, traditional or contemporary, decorative patterns provide scope for adding visual interest.

COURTYARDS

Houses with small walled yards can make great use of the many features of a patio to produce attractive paved courtyards that are easy to construct and maintain.

Different types of paving can be combined to give variations in color and texture. Walkways, for example, can be laid in brick or pavers, while the remainder can be surfaced with paving blocks. Raised planters can be added in strategic positions to add color and a change in level, while a small wooden deck will provide a contrast in surface and possibly a natural link with another feature such as a tree.

Courtyards need careful planning to avoid their becoming overwhelmed by too many clever ideas. Wherever possible, features such as planters, shrubs, and screens that will prevent the entire courtyard being seen from any one position should be incorporated to disguise the yard's small size.

The siting of pots of plants can also add to the illusion of space.

ABOVE: a circular patio with a half-circle of seating is a focal point.
LEFT: trellis climbers and flower-filled stone urns embellish the patio with a riot of color.

See also: Edging page 73

COMBINING MATERIALS

Don't feel confined to one sort of material in your garden. Instead of having a uniform patio area of, say, brick or paving, experiment with more than one type of paving material. You can create many imaginative yet subtle surfaces by mixing materials of different colors, shapes, and textures.

ABOVE: textural variety can be skilfully achieved with combinations of brick and pebble.
LEFT: a path of circular patterns made up of clay cobblestones and fine granular material.

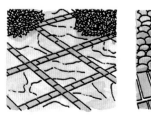
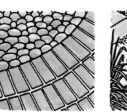

LEFT: making good use of every inch of the garden with combinations of bricks, cobblestones, paving stones, and gravel, with spaces for plants between.

YOU COULD define and soften a patio of square blocks with borders of brickwork or make circular patterns with cobblestones and bricks for a less formal approach. Intersperse areas of gravel within areas of paving slabs and then grow a selection of rock plants in the gravel.

Mixing colors

BY MIXING different-colored paving you can create random or formal patterns. Some ideas include: highlighting diagonal lines across a patio with red slabs contrasted with the overall green or buff ones; picking out alternate rows of blocks in another color; and working from the perimeter of the patio forming squares within squares, finishing with a solid black of blocks at the center.

Mixing shapes

YOU DO not have to stick to either square, rectangular or hexagonal paving stones—you can mix them for a more creative finish. You can mix hexagonal blocks with square or rectangular slabs of different color. With hexagonal blocks, leave some empty units from the overall area to be covered, so allowing you to make any shape you want.

AGGREGATES FOR PAVING

To create an attractive feature within the patio, omit a number of blocks from an area of paving and fill the gap with decorative aggregates. Many types and colors of small-scale stones are available, often pre-bagged.

• Cobblestones are commonly about 2–3in in size, and can be loose-laid within your feature areas, contained by decorative edging or simply by the edges of the paving blocks.

• Alternatively, for a decorative area on which you can walk, bed the cobblestones in a screed of mortar, pressing them down as level as possible with a stout board and a heavy hammer.

• Pebbles measure about 1½–2in and can be used in the same way as the large cobblestones.

• Gravel chippings about ¼in in size and made of rough-edged flint come in various colors, often in mixed bags, and can be scattered over planting areas to reduce evaporation from the soil, or else used to fill isolated areas where blocks have been removed. They will precisely fill any shape of hole in the patio and can be laid right up against plants without doing any harm.

• Crushed marine shell provides a fascinating infill for feature areas on the patio, especially when whole seashells are included in the area for a distinctly seaside look.

See also: Materials pages 54–57

EDGING

In some cases, edging is purely ornamental, but in others it is needed to keep surface materials such as gravel and bark in place, and to keep soil from overflowing from the beds.

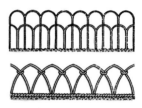

ABOVE: bricks make a simple but very effective edging material.
LEFT: decorative Victorian rope-tile edging.

NOT ALL surfaces need to be edged but it often adds the finishing touch. Use bricks or tiles or, for a more informal, rustic effect, logs. Plants themselves can also be used as edging. Low clipped hedges of box go particularly well with brick or stone surfaces. Lavender is a more decorative choice and it can also be clipped into neat shapes.

Use edging around flowerbeds to stop the soil overflowing on to surrounding areas, especially gravel or paths laid with chipped bark. Edging also helps prevent the edges of hard surfaces breaking away or sinking.

Bricks set in a number of ways are commonly used for edging, as is stone, but you can also use logs in a woodland setting. Tiles also serve the purpose well.

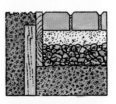

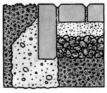

BRICK EDGING

Unless the edge of a brick surface falls against a wall or a similar structure, it must be contained within a permanent restraint in order to stop it moving.

Wood that has been treated with preservative can be used in the form of edging boards. Nail some stakes on to the wood and drive the stakes in until the wood lies flush with the ground. Alternatively, you might prefer to use bricks set on their edges embedded in a 4in bed of concrete. This will create a much more decorative and formal edge.

Various forms of decorative edging (above) can be used for paths and patios. Bricks, for example, can be laid in several different ways: they can be laid either in flat rows or angled for a serrated effect, or you can cement them together to make a low wall. Edging tiles can also be used. There are plain or decorative designs to choose from. Wire edging makes a cheap, versatile alternative and is simply pushed into the soil.

See also: Laying paving pages 62–63; Patios pages 68–71; Paths pages 74–77

PATHS

Although paths have a practical purpose in your backyard, allowing you to move about it without wearing bald patches on the lawn or turning flower beds into mud baths, they don't have to look purely functional. They can be made to enhance the overall design, becoming features in their own right.

AS WITH so many garden projects, a scale plan drawn on graph paper will be of tremendous help in planning the position and width of your path. Draw in all the major features and then try different positions for the path. Another way of doing this is to take a photograph of the site from the house and then use tracing paper to add an overlay showing possible path positions.

If you intend to use bricks or blocks as a paving material, you can sketch these in too and gain a much better idea of how the finished path will look. The pattern in which you lay the paving may require that some pieces are cut, in which case a carefully drawn scale plan of the path will show you just how many will need cutting and allow you to adjust this figure by moving the pattern here and there before actually doing the job.

How much material?

BY DRAWING in the actual pattern, you will be able to work out how many bricks or blocks will be needed to pave a predetermined length of path. Then this figure can be multiplied by the overall length of the path to obtain the total number of bricks or blocks that is required.

Straight or curved?

ALTHOUGH THE shortest distance between one point in your plan and another may be a

ABOVE: changes in direction are more natural if achieved with curves.

straight line, that does not necessarily mean that the path you lay between these two points should be straight. A straight path may fit in with a garden that has a rigid geometric design, but in many cases it will serve only to split the garden needlessly.

Straight or angular paths will tend to segment the area and give a formal appearance, whereas by incorporating curves you can produce a more natural effect. You

should take into account the profile of the ground itself, both for the appearance of the path and for practical considerations: for example, a path sloping toward the house or other outbuilding will create a direct route for heavy rainwater to flow to the house walls rather than soaking into the ground as it would normally.

Where paths need to change direction, in general it is better to make that change in the form of a curve rather than of a sharp angle, unless the latter fits in with the overall design of the garden. However, don't go mad with too many curves and squiggles, as building such a path can be a nightmare.

See also: Laying paving pages 62–63; Edging page 73

MATERIALS AND PATTERNS

Any of the following materials can be used for paths, either on their own or mixed. You can make lots of attractive patterns to give interesting variations in texture and color. In fact, no matter what style of path you choose, you will be able to find a paving material that will suit your needs. Choose from:

- bricks
- cobblestones
- cement pavers
- cement blocks
- gravel
- sawn logs

Marking out

WHEN IT COMES to laying out the shape of the path, use pegs and cords for the straight stretches and lengths of water hose for the curved bits. As a rule, paths should be about 3ft wide, but there is no reason why you can't make them narrower or wider if you wish, provided they are not so narrow that they make you feel that you are walking a tightrope.

Foundations

PATHS THAT are to receive little wear and tear can be laid on a firm, level base formed by the earth itself and a 2–4in layer of sand, without the need for a firmer foundation. Ram down the exposed subsoil with a stout wooden post or compact it thoroughly with a garden roller. Lay the sand and check the base is level using a level placed on a piece of wood. If you live in an area of soft soil, however, or if the path is to support heavier than normal loads, you should lay a foundation of compacted rubble, consisting of about 4in rubble rammed down over a 1–2in thick layer of sand.

Laying a brick path

WHEN LAYING the bricks or pavers, set them out in your desired pattern, keeping the gaps between them uniform and no more than ½in wide. After you have placed a few, lay a wooden straightedge across them and tap it down with a heavy hammer until the faces of the bricks or pavers are all level.

Ideally, if the path does not run downhill naturally, you should arrange a slight drainage "slope" or "pitch" to one side or the other of the path so that rainwater

LEFT: garden paths are usually about 3ft wide, but they can be narrower when they are only lightly used—for example, when working in the flower beds.

will run off. Check this with a level laid on top of a second straightedge held across the path. A small wooden wedge underneath one end of the level will allow you to obtain a consistent slope by keeping the level's bubble in the middle of its tube. Tap the bricks or pavers down more on the side to which the rainwater must drain, but make sure the tops of all the bricks still remain in line.

LAYING A BRICK PATH

1 Place the blocks on the sand bed in your chosen pattern, making sure that the gaps between them are uniform.

2 Set up stringlines across the paving as a guide to laying the blocks symmetrically, especially when creating a diagonal effect.

3 Mark blocks for cutting by holding them over the space and scribing with a bolster chisel against a straight edge.

See also: Laying paving pages 62–63; Combining materials page 72

LAYING PATTERNS

• Herringbone pattern is created by a series of zigzagging rows of blocks laid end to side; it can be laid straight or diagonally.

• A weave pattern comprises staggered rows of three blocks on end alternated with one block laid across their ends.

• Squared design consists of whole blocks laid in a square box pattern with a cut block filling the gap in the center.

• Fishtail blocks laid in a parquet design have the appearance of being underwater due to their wavy interlocking edges.

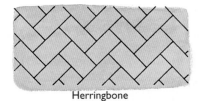

Herringbone

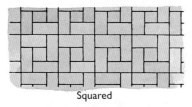

Weave

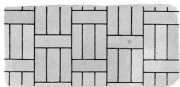

Squared

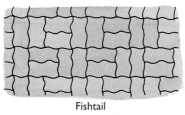

Fishtail

Gravel paths

THE USE of gravel as a paving material can be very effective in many styles of garden. Furthermore, it is easy to lay and easy to maintain. However, you must take steps to restrict the tiny stones to the pathway by providing some form of positive edging, such as bricks laid on edge or cement curb stones bedded in sand or cement, or even stout preservative-treated boards secured by stakes driven into the ground.

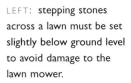

LEFT: stepping stones across a lawn must be set slightly below ground level to avoid damage to the lawn mower.

RIGHT: a flower border can be admired from a path gently curving around its edge.

THE PACE OF A PATH

The arrangement of paving units in a path can subtly affect the speed at which you walk. A uniform grain along the path—for example, that created by bricks laid lengthwise in stretcher bond—can seem to hurry you on, whereas a less directional pattern will encourage a slower pace. The treatment may be chosen to suit the purpose of the path—a "slow" path where there is plenty to admire, a "faster" path where the aim is simply to provide access to another part of the garden.

WOOD AND GRAVEL PATHS

An informal and attractive path can be made from logs and gravel; the wood should be treated with preservative. Make sure all the logs are the same height to ensure that the surface is even. Lay them close together, almost touching, on a sand and gravel base, and firm them down. The gaps between should be filled with a mixture of sand and gravel, and the surface brushed with a stiff outdoor broom.

1 Arrange the logs along the length of the path.

2 Fill in between the logs with shovelfuls of gravel and sand.

3 Brush the gravel over the logs for an even surface.

To lay a gravel path, replace the sand layer in your foundation with a 2in layer of coarse gravel and roll it well to compact it. Then add a 2in layer of fine gravel, raking it out level and rolling it again to make a firm surface.

Stepping-stone path

PATHS DON'T have to be continuous either— you may prefer to make one as a series of stepping stones or rounds of log across a lawn, which will create a less obvious division between one side of the lawn and the other. If you do this, however, give great thought to their spacing. If you don't put the steps in the right place, you may end up walking on the grass in between. Also, make sure the steps are slightly below ground level, otherwise you may find that your lawnmower hits them and then the blades become blunt very quickly.

Simply place the block or log round on the surface and mark around it with a spade or lawn edger. Remove the sod or topsoil and dig out enough for about 1in of sand plus the thickness of the block or log. Allow for the block or log to be sunk beneath the surface of a lawn by about ¾in to enable mowing without damaging the blades. Place the stepping stone in the hole and tap with the handle of a heavy hammer to bed it in firmly.

It can be very effective to continue stepping stones from a lawn across a pond.

LEFT: logs used to make a path should be firmed down on a sand and gravel base.

See also: Gravel page 56

STEPS

Steps give pedestrian access to the various parts of a sloping or split-level garden, while additionally providing a visual link between the separate elements—vegetable area, lawn, planting beds, and so on.

Material options

THE MATERIALS you choose should blend in with their context. There are many types of bricks, blocks, pavers, walling blocks, and paving blocks which are all suitable. You can use bricks and blocks both for the risers and for the treads; face textures may be smooth, pitted or, in the case of decorative cement blocks, resemble split stone. Blocks, although suitable only for the treads, may be smooth-faced, riven, or even geometrically patterned for an ornate appearance.

Step formats

SKETCH OUT the position and shape of the steps on squared paper to help you to determine how they will look and how they will fit in with the existing site plan.

ABOVE AND BELOW: weathered stone or decorative paving slabs can be used to make steps a feature in their own right.

DIMENSIONS

The following dimensions are typical for comfortable, safe walking:

• Risers should usually be 4–5in deep but may be up to 6–7in.

• Treads should not be less than 12in from front to back (sufficient to take the ball of your foot when descending without the back of your leg scraping on the step above).

• Consider who will use the steps: treads 24in wide will accommodate only one person; for two people walking side by side make them 60in wide.

• The nosing is the front edge of the tread, which should project beyond the riser by about 1in to define the shape of the step with an edge of shadow.

See also: Contours pages 20–21

BUILDING CUT-IN STEPS

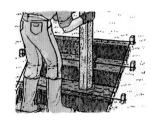

I First of all, measure the vertical height of the slope (see below) to determine how many steps you will need to construct. Mark out the shape and size of the flight of steps.

2 Working from the top of the flight, start to dig out the rough shape of the steps using a spade. Compact the earth at each tread position; take care not to collapse the steps while doing this.

3 Take precise measurements and go back over the surface trimming each step accurately. Dig below and behind the nosing strings to allow for the thickness of the block (or other) treads and brick or blockwork risers.

4 Construct the first riser, following the stringlines. Following basic bricklaying techniques, stagger the bricks in a basic stretcher band. Trowel a layer of mortar about ⅛in thick and furrow the surface.

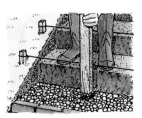

5 Tip rubble behind the riser and ram it down well—but take care not to dislodge the riser in doing so. Add more rubble up to the base of the tread position and ram this down too.

6 Lift a slab into position on the prepared base. If it fits, remove the block and trowel a layer of mortar around the perimeter of the riser. Alternatively, you can stick down the tread using five dabs of mortar (one on each corner and one in the middle) or a bed of mortar.

7 Place a level on the blocks to check they are level with each other; check also that the blocks slope not more than ½in toward the nosing for rainwater run-off. Tap the front edge gently but firmly with the shaft of a heavy hammer so as to give the correct slope.

ABOVE: cut-in steps are used to negotiate a slope or a bank.

CASTING A CEMENT FOOTING

On a large flight—more than, say, about 10 steps—it is advisable to cast a cement footing in a trench at the base to support the bottom riser and prevent the entire flight from sliding down the bank. Dig the trench under the position of the bottom riser, about twice the front-to-back measurement of the riser, about 4in deep. Ram rubble into the base of the trench and top up to ground level with fresh cement. Compact the cement, level it and allow to set overnight before building on the surface.

Perhaps the most important point is to draw a side elevation of the steps, which will show you just how steep they will need to be. You will have to take into account certain safety criteria with regard to the format. If the flight is too steep, it will be tiring to climb. Where it is too shallow there is a danger of tripping.

Calculating the number of steps

TO WORK out how many steps you will need, measure the vertical height you need to scale and divide this figure by the height of a single riser plus tread. With a terraced site just measure the height of the retaining wall. On a sloping site the job is more complicated. Drive a peg into the ground at the top of the slope and a length of pole into the ground at the base of the slope. Tie a length of string between the peg and the pole and set it horizontal using a level. Measure the distance from the base of the pole to the string to give the vertical height of the slope: divide this by the depth of a riser plus tread to give the number of steps that will fit into the slope.

Cut-in steps

THESE ARE used where you need to negotiate a steep slope. The shape of the steps is cut out in the earth itself and various materials used for the treads (the parts of the steps on which you walk) and risers (the vertical parts). Cut-in steps may be formal, regular flights or meandering and informal.

Measuring the slope

WORK OUT how many steps you will need to make by measuring the vertical height of the slope. To do this, drive a peg into the top of the slope and a pole as tall as the slope height at the bottom. Connect the two with string. Set the string horizontal using a level, then measure the pole from ground level to the string. This is the slope height.

Divide the figure by the depth of a riser plus tread of the steps you plan to use. This gives the number of steps you can fit into the slope.

See also: Types of foundations pages 60–61; Basic bricklaying techniques page 85

SAFETY FEATURES

Steep flights should include a handrail—at about hand height, 2¾ft—on each side, which extends about 12in beyond the flight, where it might possibly be linked with existing fencing or railings for a more unified scheme. Alternatively you might prefer to build a wall (at handrail height) at each side of the flight.

Flights comprising more than 10 steps should be broken halfway with a landing which provides a good resting place and can also break a fall. Take this into account when calculating the number of treads that you require.

The treads should slope slightly toward the front—a pitch of about ½in is adequate —so that rainwater will drain off rapidly. This is particularly important in winter, when ice could make the steps slippery and dangerous. For the same reason, choose only block treads with non-slip textured faces.

MAKING LOG STEPS

Masonry steps can appear incongruous in an informal garden and wooden steps are often more appropriate. Cut-in steps are more suitable for this type of garden, and using sawn logs as the risers is a quick and easy way to form an attractive flight.

1 At each step position, drive in stout, rough-hewn stakes to align with the nosing position at each side.

2 Place a log behind the stakes so that they support it, then backfill with rubble. Ram down the rubble with a sledgehammer, then top with fine gravel as the tread surface.

You can also make up a single riser from two or more slimmer logs stacked on top of each other. As an alternative to using round logs you can obtain old railroad ties sold specifically for use in garden construction. Fix the railroad tiess with stakes, as for logs, to create a more formal yet still rustic flight. Turning the flight within the slope is easily done by simply fanning out the logs or ties.

When using wooden steps, be wary of the treads becoming slippery after rainfall. A good way of keeping a gripping surface is to staple chicken wire on top of the wood. Keeping the steps clear of moss and lichen will also reduce the risk of a slip.

LEFT: attractive rustic steps can be made using sawn logs as the risers and gravel for the treads.

See also: Gravel page 56

LEFT: a flight of stone steps edged by heathers and junipers.
RIGHT: log steps in a rural garden setting.

TYPES OF STEPS

Steps can be built of a variety of materials including paving, bricks, wood and sections of tree trunk. If you have a collection of pieces of stone, all different sizes, you can use them to make crazy-paving steps *(top left)*. If using logs, you can either cut them into disks *(bottom left)* or use them whole with stakes in front to keep them firm *(bottom right)*. You can also use planks and lengths of square wood *(top right)*; if you can find them, railroad ties make attractive steps.

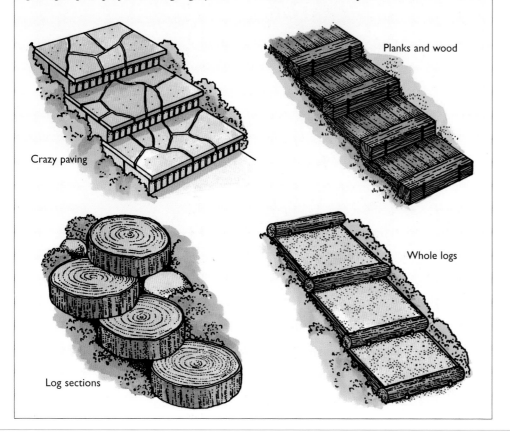

Crazy paving

Planks and wood

Log sections

Whole logs

MAKING CURVED STEPS

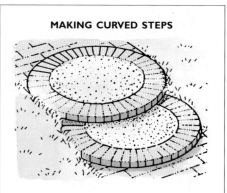

Garden steps need not always conform to a straight format. Where you have enough space, consider creating a flight composed of circular or segmental treads to scale a graceful shallow rise in the ground, perhaps leading to a formal terrace beyond.

Mark out the shape of the steps with an improvised pair of compasses made from a length of wood attached to a stake with string. Cut out the rough shape of the circular treads and cast cement block foundations beneath. There is no need to make the foundation block round; just cover the corners with soil after you have built the steps.

Use bricks or blocks laid on mortar to form the curving front edges of the treads, and fill the circles with gravel or cobblestones. You could even lay turf for a grassy flight of steps, but it is important to bear in mind that these would be very difficult both to maintain and to mow satisfactorily.

See also: Materials pages 54–57; Laying paving pages 62–63

BOUNDARIES

Most urban gardens must have some form of physical barrier around them, partly to keep the world out and partly to keep the garden in. A boundary also defines the limits of a garden and provides a backdrop for displaying plants and other features such as statues and ornamental outdoor furniture. Most forms of boundary can be used to support climbing plants of one sort or another for a decorative effect; you can even grow a climbing rose or clematis up a hedge.

YOUR CHOICE of boundary material will greatly affect the overall appearance of your backyard. Although many fences, walls and hedges are used as screens, they should not always turn the eye inward; any vistas beyond the garden should be framed with well-sited gaps in the boundary.

Walls serve many purposes in the garden: they can provide an impenetrable barrier around the outside of it to stop prying eyes and deter trespassers. Inside the plot, low walls can be used to outline particular areas, such as flower beds and patios, or taller walls can be built to create a safe enclosure for small children, conceal one part from another, or create a "secret" walled garden. Compared to walls, fences are quicker and simpler to construct. But it is well worth taking some time to work out not only what you want yours to look like, but also what you want it to do. Fencing, entrances and gates should always be incorporated into the overall design of your home and garden, whether marking a boundary, partitioning, screening or simply providing a decorative feature.

Hedges make excellent garden barriers where walls and fences are undesirable. They provide a natural backdrop to other plants, and thorny hedges are effective obstacles against domestic and farm animals. Hedges can be either formal and close-clipped or informal and irregular in outline.

RIGHT: curved trellis top to a fence, ideal for climbing plants.

See also: Creating a border pages 121–125; Hedges pages 130–131

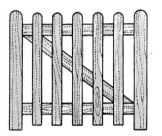

Traditional rural

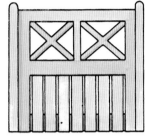

City garden

Wrought iron

Rustic trellis

There are many styles of gate to choose from *(above)*, including the functional ones *(top)*, and the more delicate and rustic *(bottom)*. The choice of gate depends on its proposed function and position: heavier gates should be used in walls, fences and hedges marking the outside property boundaries of a garden, while gates of lighter construction are suitable within the site, used just as much for decoration as for practicality.

Choosing a gate

A GATE is an essential part of a wall, hedge or fence if you want a continuous barrier with access through it. They are commonly made of wood or wrought iron. It is important to choose one that fits in with its surroundings: a very ornate wrought-iron gate would look out of place in a simple rustic backyard, just as a simple picket gate would be inappropriate in a patio garden.

Constructing a gate from scratch is not easy and, if possible, buy a ready-made kit consisting of all the parts that can be glued or screwed together. In general, metal gates should be hung either from metal posts or brick piers, while wooden gates should be used in wooden fences, wherever possible matching the style of the fence.

Gate fittings

ALL GATES need hinges and some form of latch. There is a wide range available to match the style of the gate, many of which are designed to be decorative as well as functional. When buying fittings, select those that are durable and in scale with the gate.

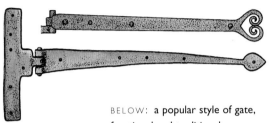

BELOW: a popular style of gate, functional and traditional.

See also: Division page 13

WALLS

Walls are particularly popular with the keen gardener for they provide shelter to delicate plants from prevailing winds and, depending on the site, will give beneficial shade or produce sun-traps.

Planning

PLAN CAREFULLY before you start building your wall. Where will it be sited? How high will it be? How long? What will it be built from? And, most important, why do you want a wall in the first place? It is best to start out by making a scale plan on graph paper. Draw in the outline of the backyard and put in the major features. Then draw in the wall. This will allow you to measure how long it will be and will show you if there are likely to be any problems with its run. Another way of doing this is in the backyard itself, using pegs and cord to outline the wall's position on the ground.

Materials

WHEN IT comes to deciding what material to use to build your wall there are plenty of options, but whatever you choose, make sure it complements the materials from which your house is built and the overall style of your garden. You might want the formality of brick or reconstituted stone walling blocks, the rambling informality of natural stones, or the geometric precision of pierced screening blocks. Whichever you choose, remember that a well-built wall will last you a lifetime, so think carefully before you start. If you are worried, you can always get a professional to do the job instead.

Single or double leaf?

UNLESS YOUR wall is only two or three courses high, a single "leaf" of bricks will not really be strong enough and will need to be reinforced with piers at regular intervals, or built so that the wall appears staggered or stepped when viewed from above. In addition, it will tend to look insubstantial.

A better way of doing the job is to make each course from two rows of bricks laid next to each other and interconnected to produce a very strong self-supporting structure.

Even with a single-leaf wall, the courses must be laid so that the bricks produce an overlapping pattern (known as the "bond"). This locks them together, ensuring great strength. However, you will have to cut some bricks to maintain the pattern, particularly at the ends of walls and possibly at corners.

BELOW: *Ceanothus* enjoying the protection of a substantial wall.

ABOVE: rock plants, such as this pretty *Aubrieta deltoidea,* will thrive readily on a mature stone wall.

See also: Materials pages 54–57

RIGHT: acting as a windbreak to shelter tall plants—like these lovely delphiniums—is an important function of many garden walls.

Bonds

BRICK WALLS can be constructed in several different ways depending on the type of "bond" used. The different bonds are chosen partly for their decorative quality and partly for the strength they give a wall; for example, a retaining wall supporting a hillside must be a double thickness, whereas one supporting a shallow flower bed can be a single thickness. A wall consisting of more than one thickness of brick must have ties through the wall to prevent the two layers from pulling apart. The tie bricks, which show their ends, are known as headers. Those that are laid lengthways are known as stretchers. The various bonds illustrated below are running bond (top), Flemish bond (center), and English bond (bottom), all different combinations of headers and stretchers. The running bond is used for single-leaf walls.

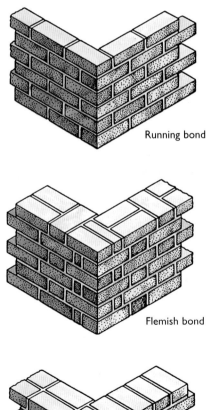

Running bond

Flemish bond

English bond

Basic bricklaying techniques

MIX UP the mortar and tip it onto a 2ft sq-board. Scoop up two or three trowel-loads and transfer the mortar to your hawk (*see Glossary*). Practice slicing off some mortar and scooping it on to your trowel by sliding the blade underneath. Learn how to place the mortar properly: hold the trowel over the site and draw it backward sharply, turning it over at the same time so that a sausage shape of mortar rolls off the blade. Spread a ⅜in thick layer of mortar along the cement strip foundation.

Furrow the surface by drawing your trowel blade back along it in ridges: the furrows will aid the adhesion of the brick to the mortar, and form a suction when the brick is pressed in place.

Transfer the positions of the stringlines fixed to the profile board to the mortar by running a level vertically along each and scribing the mortar with a trowel blade.

To form the brickwork bond, you must overlap the second row of bricks with the first, so that the vertical joints do not align. Check the level of the course with the level, then hold the level along the sides of the wall to check that it too is square.

BUILDING A WALL

Preparing the foundations

• Normally a foundation consists of a strip of cement about three times the width of the wall and varying in depth, depending on the height of the wall. This strip is called the footing.

• For walls up to 2ft high, a 4in layer of cement laid on top of a 4in layer of well-rammed broken brick and rubble will do, but with anything above that height, use 8in of solid cement.

• On light crumbly ground, these figures may need to be doubled, and in this situation you would be wise to seek professional advice from a local builder or surveyor. Always make sure that the cement footing is laid below the frost line to prevent rising/heaving in winter.

To neaten the mortar joints, press the blade of a pointing trowel against the vertical joints, beveling the mortar to one side. Run the blade along the horizontal joints forming a bevel to deflect rainwater from the wall.

See also: Mortar and cement page 59

RIGHT: this stretch of weathered dry stone walling is a perfect setting for foxgloves and roses.

LAYING BRICKS

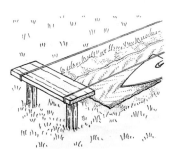

1 Set up profile boards, then spread a ⅜in thick screed of mortar over the cement strip foundation. Furrow the surface.

2 Spread the end of the brick with mortar by drawing the loaded trowel across the end, forming a wedge shape. Furrow the wedge.

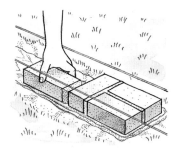

3 Lay the first bricks on the mortar screed, butting the mortared end of the second brick up to the clean end of the first brick.

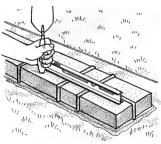

4 Place a level along the course and tap the bricks horizontal, using the shaft of your trowel. Pack under low bricks with more mortar.

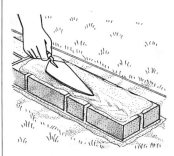

5 Trowel a screed of mortar on to the bricks of the first course, furrow the surface and position the second course on top.

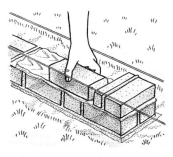

6 Lay the second course as for the first, but insert a brick cut in half across its length in order to maintain the bond.

LAYING PIERCED CEMENT BLOCKS

1 Lay the first block and spread the outer edge of the first block with mortar. Butt the second block up to it. Tap level and square with the stringline.

2 Build intermediate piers as necessary and complete the wall by bedding square capping pieces on top of the piers and bevel coping stones along the top of the screen blocks.

Using pierced cement blocks

PIERCED CEMENT blocks come in a range of geometric patterns *(right)*. They are particularly suitable for screening patios to allow cooling breezes and light to filter through, but they can also be built as a low wall, either on their own or on top of a low brick wall, around a patio, or to divide the garden. Because the cast-in patterns of the blocks are designed to make larger patterns, they cannot be laid in an interlocking bond. Instead, use a "stack" bond, that is to say, one laid on top of the other. To ensure a strong structure, insert a vertical pier every 10ft. These are constructed from hollow precast cement blocks which have slots in their sides to accept the ends of the blocks. The blocks must also be carefully aligned, otherwise the overall pattern will be affected.

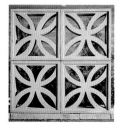

See also: Rock-garden plants page 154

BUILDING A STONE WALL

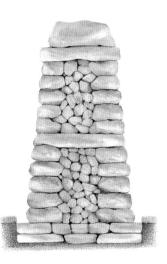

I Lay one layer of large, flat foundation stones on the compacted earth sub-base, interlocking the irregular edges for strength. Build up the ends of the wall by several courses of regularly shaped edging blocks alternated with large, flat through stones.

2 Place small infill stones into the cavity formed between the front and back facing blocks. Ram the stones down firmly. Link the outer leaves of the wall by laying large, flat stones across the wall at random intervals. Continue building the wall with the squarer edging blocks.

3 Fit a row of coverband stones across the top of the wall to close off the structure from rain. Ideally the row of stones should slope slightly for drain-off. Place a row of coping stones along the top of the coverband, setting them on edge with a slight lean to one side, or in decorative buck-and-doe format.

ABOVE RIGHT: tiny rock plants thrive on stone walls, with their good drainage.
RIGHT: walls can provide boundaries, protective barriers, windbreaks, sun-traps, shady areas or scope for decoration, as demonstrated here.

FENCES, SCREENS AND TRELLIS

Like walls, fences have several uses in your backyard, in particular as a barrier around the edge of the property and to divide one part of the garden from another.

A TALL, solid fence will provide privacy, shade, and shelter from the wind, while one of more open construction will allow light and breezes through. Screens and trellis are similar to fences, principally used for concealing or dividing one area from another, and can be decorated with climbing plants for a more attractive finish.

Although not as sturdy and long-lasting as a wall, a fence is much cheaper and quicker to erect, and it makes an ideal temporary barrier while a natural one of shrubs or trees grows to maturity. Even so, a well-built fence can be expected to last for many years, particularly if its wooden structure is treated regularly with preservative.

There are many different styles of fence to choose from, but it is important to choose the style to match the property. Some, such as picket fences, will look more at home with older properties, whereas ranch-style fencing, for example, will be more suited for use with modern buildings.

ABOVE: *Pyracantha* transforms a plain wooden fence.
BELOW: "Masquerade" roses are backed up by fencing.

See also: Horizontal and vertical surfaces page 20

LEFT: a tall fence will provide privacy and shade as well as defining a boundary.

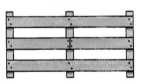

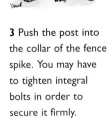

Home-made or ready-made?

MOST TYPES of fence need to be constructed piece by piece on site and can easily be tailored exactly to your needs. However, it is possible to buy ready-made solid fence panels in a range of standard sizes and styles. These speed up construction considerably, but will not be as sturdy as a custom-built fence. In addition, the length of your fence will rarely equal a whole number of ready-made panels, in which case you will have to cut one.

Another type of fence you may find in ready-made form—as a kit of prefabricated parts ready for nailing together—is picket fencing. This, too, will be made to a standard size and may require some trimming to match the length of fencing that you require.

Fence posts and spikes

FENCES MUST have stout posts, and if these are of wood they should be at least 3in square for low fences and 4in square for tall ones. Precast cement posts are also available, some with slots to accept ready-made fence panels, and both these types should be set into the ground by at least 2ft.

Otherwise, use fence spikes. These come in various sizes and support the posts.

CEMENTING A FENCE POST

I Dig a hole and prop the post in it on a brick, with temporarily pinned-on braces. Set it perfectly vertical, checking each side in turn with a level.

2 Ram rubble into the hole around the propped-up post to support it firmly. Stop the compacted rubble short of ground level by about 6in.

3 Trowel in the fresh cement around the post and compact it to dispel air bubbles. Shape the mound so that rainwater will run off quickly.

INSTALLING A FENCE SPIKE

I Drive the spike into the ground at the post position with a sledgehammer and offcut of post (and fixing accessory).

2 Check that the spike is vertical. Do this by holding a level against each side of the spike in turn, and at frequent intervals.

3 Push the post into the collar of the fence spike. You may have to tighten integral bolts in order to secure it firmly.

There are many types of wooden fence to choose from, both solid and open (above). The solid ones are good for privacy, while the open ones provide some kind of boundary with a view of what lies beyond. You can make the fences yourself but they are almost certainly cheaper to buy ready-made. When building your own, however, remember to treat all wooden fencing with a preservative that is not toxic to plants.

See also: Sun, shade and shelter page 12

Buying fencing material

YOU CAN buy ready-made fencing panels and kits from do-it-yourself suppliers and timber yards. The latter will also supply the necessary wood for making your own fencing. In both cases, the wood should have been pressure-treated with preservative—check that the preservative is harmless to plants, as some types are not. For safety's sake never burn scraps of pressure-treated wood or breathe in the dust when cutting it, as it can be toxic. If you are using untreated wood, make sure that the posts are allowed to stand in preservative for a few days before putting them in the ground. This will ensure that their feet are well protected. The rest of the fence can be treated by brush or spray once it has been erected.

When buying nails for fencing work, make sure they are galvanized. This treatment will protect them against rust.

Putting up fences

READY-MADE panels are simply nailed between the posts. Prop each panel on bricks or offcuts of wood so that it is level before driving the nails home. You can prevent the panel edging from splitting by drilling pilot holes for the nails first.

You can also buy U-shaped brackets for nailing to the posts. These allow the panels to be dropped into place and then secured with nails driven through the brackets. Where cement posts are used, the panels simply slot in from the top.

Most ready-made panels are held together by short, thin nails or even staples, so if one needs shortening it is a relatively easy job to prise off the edging, cut the panel to length with a hand or power saw and nail the edging back on.

Finish the fence by nailing wooden posts to protect the endgrain from rainwater. Alternatively, the post top can be cut off at an angle so that rainwater will run off.

With tailor-made fencing, horizontal supporting rails are usually added at the same time as the posts are erected. Known as arris or split rails, they are triangular in section so that water will run off, and their ends fit into slots cut in the posts. The upright palings or boards are then nailed to the faces of the rails.

DECORATIVE PALING

For a more decorative finish, shape the ends of wooden fence palings. The simplest designs are square, pointed or rounded, but more complex ones include intricately carved Gothic and ornate Queen Anne styles.

With vertical close-boarded fences, it is usual to fit a gravel board between each pair of posts at ground level. This should be nailed to two short pieces of wooden batten nailed to the posts. Its purpose is to protect the bottoms of the boards from rotting through contact with the ground.

When horizontal close-boarded fencing is being put up, or some form of post-and-rail arrangement, you can nail the board or rails directly to the posts.

Picket fencing

ALTHOUGH READY-ASSEMBLED picket panels are available, you may prefer to make up this attractive boundary fencing from scratch so that you can vary the design to suit your preferences and your site.

ABOVE: intricately carved paling, painted white, sets off fresh greenery.

Pales are normally spaced about 1½–2in apart, but you may want to fit an arrangement of alternating long and short pales to give a curving or zigzagging top to the finished fence.

PICKET FENCING

I Assemble the picket fence on a flat surface by laying out the arris rails and securing the pales over them. Use a spacer to determine the positions of the pales, usually spaced 1½–2in apart.

2 Nail the picket panels to the fence posts, driving in two nails per arris rail. Ensure that the rails are horizontal and the pales are vertical by checking with a level.

3 When turning a corner, use a corner post and nail the cross rails of the two lengths of fencing to the post at right-angles. Picket fencing is perfect for smaller backyards.

See also: Climbing and screening plants pages 138–139

LEFT: *Clematis alpina* is a climber that needs the support of a trellis.

BELOW LEFT: a screen of trellis and climbing roses.

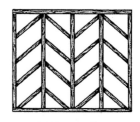

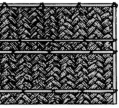

RIGHT: there is plenty of choice when it comes to commercially available screens and trellis. Most are made of wood in a variety of designs. Wood trellis doubles as some kind of screen and a support for climbing plants. It comes in square and herringbone patterns, as well as diamond-shaped patterns. Woven panels make solid screens which can be lightly clad

Screens and trellis

ALTHOUGH SITTING in the sun can be very pleasant, there are times when a shady spot is called for. Some plants do not appreciate being in the sun all day either—in fact, some plants don't like the sun at all. So if your garden does not have any naturally shady areas, it is a good idea to create some. One way is to build some form of screen that will allow sunlight to filter through but create enough shade to provide comfortable conditions for both people and plants. Normally, screens are erected as part of an arbor or similar structure bordering a patio, being fixed between the supporting uprights. There is no reason why they should not be constructed as a form of fence between normal fence posts.

One very popular type of screen is the trellis, a latticework of narrow wooden or plastic slats—about 1 x ½in—forming open squares about 6in in size. Trellis panels can be bought ready-made, but it is not difficult to make them. The slats are simply nailed together and can be attached to a supporting framework of larger-section battens at the edges. These can then be nailed between wooden uprights and plants encouraged to climb up the open framework. In fact, with a trellis screen, it is really the plants that provide the shade since the very open nature of the structure provides very little shade on its own.

The trellis has many uses around the garden as a plant support. It can be added to the tops of fences, fixed to walls or used to build pillars for ornamental arches.

See also: Clematis pages 140–141

GARDEN FEATURES

*T*he framework of a garden is largely responsible for defining its general style, but it is the special garden features like ponds and fountains, rock gardens, arches, and arbors that provide the finishing touch and stamp your garden with your own personal style. Which features you decide to use and how you place them will depend to a large extent on how you use your garden. Once in place, these special features will give your garden its individual character.

IT'S A LUCKY home owner indeed who has a natural stream or spring just waiting to be landscaped into a pond. Most of us have to start from scratch, but it's well worth the effort. Whether it be a formal, regularly shaped pond set in the middle of a paved patio or an informal, irregularly shaped pool at the foot of the garden, water is guaranteed to add another dimension of enjoyment to your garden. A still sheet of water gives a peaceful air to the garden and provides mirror images of the surroundings and the changing sky. Moving water gives varying

patterns and colors as sunlight plays upon it as well as introducing something that no other garden feature can provide—sound.

The well-executed traditional rockery, with its layers of large rocks and colorful plants, can make a very striking feature. It is an ideal way to link the different levels in a garden. It should always be planned in advance as an interesting design feature and not simply plonked there as an afterthought. In this way, it should always be carefully integrated into the overall plan of your garden. The plants in rock gardens, usually

ABOVE LEFT: a modest pond set in a mosaic-patterned patio.

BELOW: flower beds around an outdoor seat and table will make them the centerpiece of your garden.

See also: Ponds 94–96

called alpines, come from the mountainous or rocky regions in the world and their use in the garden recreates a rocky outcrop on a mountain or a cliff face. There are literally hundreds of these pretty little plants, which together form a magical miniature world in a corner of the backyard.

Arches and complex arbors are among the most popular garden features you can build. They can be made in a variety of different styles—very sturdy or more delicate —which should be chosen to complement the overall style and scale of your garden. They may be purely decorative, such as an archway linking one part of the garden with another, or they may have a more practical purpose, such as providing support for climbing plants.

Many people like to use their garden as an extension of their family space—but outdoors. This is where it is important to site carefully chosen pieces of furniture, which will provide not only seating but also something pleasant and welcoming to look at. You may like to barbecue in your backyard and use it as an outdoor kitchen as well as a dining room, in which case the heady aroma of hot charcoal and grilled food will add greatly to your enjoyment—and that of your visitors—of your garden.

ABOVE: a complex arbor adds another dimension to your garden, making a tunnel of greenery and flowers.

LEFT: arches linking one part of the garden with another can be built in a variety of styles.

See also: Arches and arbors pages 102–103

PONDS

Whatever its shape—regular or irregular, round, oblong or square—whatever its size—large or small, grand or more modest—and wherever you put it—slap in the center of the patio or tucked away at the bottom of the rockery—a pond always adds an extra dimension of interest to a garden. Water sets a peaceful atmosphere, while providing added interest in the mirror images it creates of its surroundings and the changing patterns and colors of the sky.

See also: The water garden pages 162–167

IF YOU have a natural stream or spring in your garden, you're one of the fortunate ones. Most of us aren't that lucky and we have to start from scratch. However, the range of equipment and ready-made accessories for the new pond owner is wide indeed. Electrical pumps, underwater lighting and a wide variety of styles and designs of fountains are easy to find.

Waterfalls and fountains can be added to ponds to provide extra interest, and a variety of water plants and fish can make them fascinating features.

Flexible liners

WITH A flexible liner, you have much more choice when it comes to the shape of your pond since the material will stretch or fold to match practically any shape you care to invent. The weight of the water will make it hold its shape, the top edges being retained by paving slabs or stone. A flexible pond liner is supplied as a flat sheet, and all you have to do is add twice the depth of the pond to its width and to its length to obtain the dimensions of the sheet you require. If your dimensions do not quite match those of a standard-size sheet, simply buy the next size up.

OPPOSITE: contrasting ponds: ornamental and stylized (above) and natural and understated (below).

TYPES OF LINER

• Rigid liners are made from fiberglass in a fairly wide range of shapes and sizes. They are very tough and virtually leakproof.

• Semi-rigid liners are made of vacuum-formed plastic. They are cheaper than rigid types of liner but are nowhere near as strong. You would probably be better off using a flexible liner.

• Flexible liners may be made from PVC reinforced with nylon or from butyl rubber. Of the two, the rubber version is the stronger and will often be guaranteed for 20 years, although it may last much longer than that—perhaps as long as 50 years.

SITING YOUR POOL

• A formal rectangular or round pool will probably look best as the central feature of a paved patio rather than a lawn

• An informal, natural-looking pool should be at the lowest point of your garden, since water always drains toward a low point.

• A pool should receive plenty of daylight, so do not put it where it is in constant shade

• Do not put it under trees if you intend to keep fish in it. The falling leaves will sink to the bottom and decompose, giving off a poison that will kill fish.

• A pump for a waterfall or fountain will require running an electrical cable to the house.

• The pool should be on level ground, but if your garden slopes you can overcome this by digging away the ground on the up-slope side and holding it back with a retaining wall.

BELOW: the lowest possible point in your garden is usually the best site for a natural pond.

LINER INSTALLATION

1 Mark out the pool and dig down in even layers. Span the excavation with a plank and measure to the depth of the floor.

2 Using a plasterer's trowel, plaster the excavation with a 1in layer of damp sand, making sure it adheres well to the walls.

3 Lay the piece of liner over the excavation, making sure it is centered. Anchor the liner with rocks around the edge of the pool.

4 Fill the pool with water. The liner will stretch into the shape of the excavation as it fills; gradually lift the rocks in order to release the liner.

POOLS AND CHILDREN

If you have young children or pets, it may be better to build a raised pool. Do not have a pool with an overhanging rim with deep water below. Instead have a shallow "beach" of pebbles in a more natural-looking pool; in a formal edged pool, probably the easiest solution is to place bricks or blocks near the edge just below the surface of the water to form steps.

LEFT: a pool should have a mixture of sunshine and shade—but do not site the pond under deciduous trees, as decomposing leaves can poison fish.

MAKING A BOG GARDEN

The bog garden should be constructed at the same time as the pool, using one large piece of liner for both features.

Excavate a 12in basin next to the pool. Its edges must be the same height or a little higher than the bank of the pool, but the interconnecting lip must be a little lower. Spread a layer of coarse grit or gravel over the soil in order to aid drainage.

When the pool is lined, continue the liner over the lowered bank and across the bog area, and then tuck in the edges in the same way as for the pool. Puncture the liner in a few places and cover the floor with a layer of gravel to prevent the holes becoming clogged up. Add a layer of well-rotted farmyard manure before filling the basin with a mixture of loam and leafmold.

PREFORMED POOL INSTALLATION

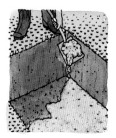  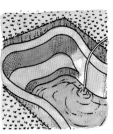 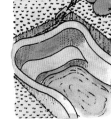

1 Lay a good layer of damp sand on the floor of the excavation. This will serve as a cushion for the preformed pool unit.

2 Once it is installed, check that the unit is level by spanning it with a plank of wood and laying a level on the plank.

3 Using a hose, fill the unit with approximately 4in of water before backfilling around the edges of the unit.

4 Work your way around the pool, feeding in a small quantity of material. After each circuit, check the unit level.

Fountains

ANOTHER ATTRACTIVE water feature is a fountain which, like a waterfall, is operated by a submersible pump sitting on the floor of the pool, or on a platform of bricks or blocks if the pool is deep. Indeed, some pumps combine a fountain with a flexible hose outlet that can feed a waterfall as well.

Choosing a fountain

The important thing is to choose a fountain that will not overpower the effect of your pool. It should not shoot its jets so high that wind-blown spray falls outside the pool, nor should it be over-elaborate if the pool is small. Fountains are ideal for formal pools but should not be included in those that are supposed to look natural—the two just don't go together.

Installing a fountain

In most cases the fountain outlet simply projects above the pump and it can usually be fitted with a range of fountain heads that vary the pattern of the water jets. The pump should be positioned so that the head just projects above the level of the water in the pool, if necessary raised on a piece of paving.

ABOVE RIGHT: fountains can look wonderful in this kind of formal setting. BELOW: a more modest fountain in a simple wooden-barrel pond.

Electric pumps

THE WATER for the waterfall is circulated by a submersible electric pump which usually takes its power from a transformer connected to the normal mains electricity supply.

Water is delivered to the top of the waterfall by a hose connected to the pump. Conceal this underground alongside the waterfall, with its open end hidden by a rock.

The power cable for the pump sits on the floor of the pool. Run it under one of the edging stones, and then take it to a waterproof connector and link it to the transformer with a cable. Although the low-voltage electricity carried by the cable between pump and transformer will not give you a serious electric shock, you should take steps to protect the cable from accidental damage. Do not leave it lying on the ground where, if nothing else, it could trip someone up, and do not run it along a fence which might be blown over.

By far the best idea is to run it through a plastic conduit about 24in underground, making sure it is where you won't be digging in the future. This will provide total protection.

INSTALLING PUMPS

Simple fountains
Place the pump in the pool, on a piece of paving if necessary, to bring it up to the required height.

Ornamental fountains
Connect the pump to the fountain jet. If the fountain plinth is hollow, hide the pump inside it.

See also: Garden ornaments pages 26–27

FOUNTAIN SPRAYS

Make sure the fountain head will create the right effect for the water feature.

BELL: a fountain that produces a sculptural, almost semi-circular sphere of water which falls in a bell shape from a central pipe.

BUBBLE: this head makes a natural-looking, low fountain of water which bubbles up gently as though issuing from a spring.

COLUMN: two or three columns of white water shoot up in a neat and stylized manner. This works well for a modern design.

GEYSER: the geyser fountain forces water up into the air, sometimes to a great height, to give a natural-looking rush of foaming white water and a gushing sound.

PLUME: seething and foaming plumes produced by this head create an architectural feature, best operated from a simple but substantial pool.

TIER: a traditional fountain that produces continuous tiered circles of water gently falling in a pyramid-shaped display.

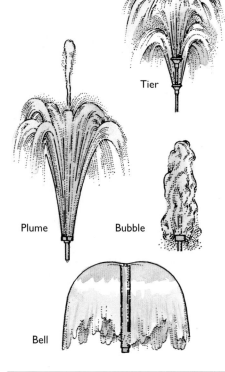

Tier

Plume

Bubble

Bell

Waterfalls and streams

THE SOUND of running water can be particularly restful, whether it is the gentle burble of a tumbling stream or the more insistent rush of a steep waterfall. Both can be incorporated into a pool scene and are especially attractive when combined with a rockery and water-loving plants.

Types of liner

IT IS POSSIBLE to buy rigid liners that comprise a series of small pools with lips that direct the water from an upper reservoir to the main pool. Installing one of these is a relatively straightforward operation, requiring a number of steps to be cut into the slope of your rockery and then the rigid liner to be bedded on them with sand. Rocks can then be placed around the edges to conceal the liner.

Unfortunately, because the water flowing down a rigid waterfall liner will be relatively shallow, the unnatural color of the fiberglass will always be visible and will spoil the effect. A much better solution is to use pieces of flexible rubber liner to make a watercourse with a series of stepped pools feeding one into another.

Another advantage of using a flexible liner, of course, is that you can tailor your waterfall to suit your own ideas. You might want water cascading down a series of steps and flowing along a short channel to the main pool, or you might prefer to have it fall some distance from a small pool directly into the main pool. Both can be arranged with careful digging, placing of the liner, and positioning of rocks and stones.

ABOVE: the construction of waterfalls and stepped pools has been made much easier with the use of flexible rubber liners.
OPPOSITE: rocks and water-loving plants can be positioned to conceal the liner.

See also: Contours pages 20–21

A RIGID LINER

1 Press the unit down into a 1in layer of sand and check that it is level. Backfill around the preformed waterfall shell with soil, packing it down well.

2 Place large, heavy rocks along the lip of the waterfall to create the impression of a rapid water flow. For a smooth flow, use a flat piece of slate.

ROCK GARDENS

A rockery, with its layers of large rocks and colorful alpine plants, can make a very striking feature if executed properly. Resembling a rocky outcrop on a mountain or a cliff face, it is an ideal way to link the different garden levels.

ONE OF the most important features of a rockery is that it should look like a natural rocky outcrop rather than a heap of large stones with plants growing on it. This requires considerable skill in selecting the site and the stones, and in laying the stones so they look as though they belong together.

Very little soil should be visible in a rockery—it should be packed into crevices between and in the rocks, and is even better if covered with a layer of gravel or grit. This will not only disguise its presence but also help to retain moisture during the summer.

Choosing the site

AS WITH so many features in the garden, it is vitally important to choose the correct site for a rockery. Do not forget that you are trying to reproduce a natural setting, so it really should not have a wall, a fence or your house as a backdrop if avoidable, but instead a hedge or trees.

Although you can build a rockery on flat ground, it is much better if you can build it into the face of an existing slope in your garden. This should be a sunny position, although it should not be in full sun all day long. It should definitely not be in shade, nor should it be under trees which will drip rainwater on to your alpine plants. The site and the rockery itself should be well drained and the foundations firm.

Safety: moving stones

ONE OF the important things to watch is that you do not strain your back in attempting to move the rocks. Even apparently small pieces will be very heavy; if you are able to lift them, do so by bending your knees and keeping your back straight.

There are various ways in which you can move the rocks over the ground. Smaller pieces can be moved by wheelbarrow, but larger rocks will need to be rolled along using stout wooden levers or crowbars. You may also be able to move them using wooden rollers on a track made of wooden planks laid on the ground. Rope slings can also be fashioned and fitted around rocks so that they can be lifted between two people.

TOP LEFT: an old trough provides an ideal base for rock plants.
LEFT: site your rock garden in a sunny, well-drained position.

See also: Contours pages 20–21

BUILDING A ROCK GARDEN

1 First of all, mark out the shape of the rock garden on the ground using strings stretched between pegs or a water hose curved to the right shape. Then dig around the perimeter with a spade.

2 Dig out the topsoil within the area of the rock garden and retain the fertile soil for mixing with grit as the growing medium. Compact the base by treading lightly; trampling hard may impede drainage.

3 Next, position the largest rock (the keystone) and build V-shaped arms from it using smaller rocks.

4 Fill the lower outcrop of rocks with a mix of topsoil and grit. Rake out the bedding material and compact it by light treading, but do not dislodge the stones.

5 Build the second outcrop of rocks on top of the first tier, but set back from its edge, leaving adequate space for planting.

6 Remove the plants from their pots and place them in holes dug in the bedding medium between rocks. Introduce plants in crevices between stones.

GROWING ALPINES

Rock plants can be grown in a variety of attractive ways. Old walls *(top)* make an ideal planting position, plants being established by sowing seed. In a well-built rock garden *(center)*, plants can be grown in a much more natural way. Troughs and old sinks *(bottom)* look good on patios.

See also: Rock-garden plants page 154

CHOOSING STONE

• Wherever possible try to use local stone for your rockery as this will be most in keeping with the area.

• If stone is not available locally, choose sandstone or limestone as these weather well into attractive shapes.

• Ask your local do-it-yourself supplier or a nearby quarry for a selection of sizes, telling them that you want the material for a rockery. They may sell it by weight or size, and you will want a lot—several tons for a decent-size rockery.

• Then you must get the rocks to your site. If you have access, you could rent a mechanical digger/backhoe and driver to shift the rock from your driveway (where it will be dumped on delivery).

Scree beds

ROCK GARDEN plants that require extremely sharp drainage are best cultivated in scree beds, designed to simulate the naturally occurring conditions at the foot of mountain slopes where there is a deep layer of finely broken rock and a certain amount of humus.

A scree bed is essentially a raised bed with much of the soil replaced by stone chippings. Retaining walls of sandstone brick or broken paving slabs may be used to support the sides of the bed, and these should be given an inward slant to make them stable. Lay the

lowest stones on a cement foundation; the upper courses may be dry or filled with soil to accommodate plants that enjoy growing in vertical crevices (these should be inserted as building progresses). Leave drainage holes in the base of the wall at frequent intervals. The bed should be at least 2ft high over clay soil to provide good drainage; at least 1ft high over sandy soil. Place a 4–6in layer of broken bricks and rubble in the bottom of the bed and use the following compost to fill the rest of the space: 10 parts stone chippings, 1 part loam, 1 part peat (or peat substitute) or leafmold and 1 part fine sand. Plant up in the fall or spring.

ARCHES AND ARBORS

Plant-clad arches and arbors make perfect ornamental features in any garden. As well as being decorative, they also perform more functional roles: arches are good for linking one part of the garden with another and complex arbors are an attractive means of providing shade.

Arches

WHETHER WOODEN or metal, simple or lightly ornate, arches add considerable charm to any garden. Not only do they form a decorative support for a profusion of climbing plants like clematis, honeysuckle and roses, but they can also be used as an informal division between various areas of the garden, for example, to separate the lawn from the patio or vegetable plot. Built against a hedge, an arch of this construction can be used as a nook; build a series of arches close together and you have a long arbor.

Regardless of type, a wooden arch is relatively straightforward to build, and in most cases the various wooden sections are simply held together with galvanized nails. It is a good idea to sketch out your ideas on paper first. Then take photographs of the archway's position from both sides and use tracing paper to produce overlays that will show what your ideas will look like when built in the garden.

IDEAS FOR ARCHES

You can build various styles of arch, depending on the style of your garden. In fact, whatever the style of your garden, you should be able to devise a style of arch that will fit in with it.

• In a rural setting, build the arch in a lattice-work pattern from rustic poles with the bark still in place.

• For a more formal design, build a less ornamental structure from square-planed lengths of wood.

• For a grand design, build "pillars" made of brick with square sections of wood at their corners and panels of trellis in between.

• A simple arch leading from an Oriental-style part of the garden could consist of large sections of wood with a single crosspiece at the top, its ends cut at an angle sloping upward.

ABOVE AND LEFT: arches can be made of wood (*above*) or of metal (*left*)—both of which look good with climbing roses.

See also: Horizontal and vertical surfaces pages 20–21; Adding the details pages 25–27

When building an arch or arbor, make sure you are working with wood treated with preservative. The joints must be close-fitting and strong; use nails or screws to secure them.

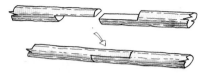

Use this type of joint to join lengths of wood.

To make a right-angle, fix the horizontal and vertical pieces as shown.

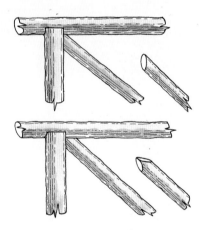

To achieve a decorative effect, use crosspieces in your design. These can be fixed into the corner or on to the upright as shown

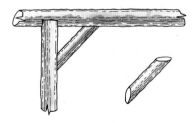

Diagonal corner brackets strengthen the structure.

Arbors

WHETHER ATTACHED to the house or boundary wall or free-standing, arbors are an attractive means of providing shade to a walkway or patio as well as acting as a support for climbing plants. They are invariably built from wood, although some may have brick or block columns supporting thick wooden crosspieces.

As with arches, arbors can be built in many styles to suit varying types of garden, so it should not be too difficult to come up with something that fits in exactly with your own plot. It is a good idea to take photographs of the area where the arbor is to be built and use tracing paper overlays to try out various designs until you find the right one.

Similar sizes of wood should be used for an arbor as for an arch and the minimum width and headroom apply also.

Construction

Erecting a free-standing arbor follows the procedure for a wooden archway. Individual arch frames are nailed together and set in holes in the ground with cement collars. When the cement has set, additional crosspieces and rails can be added to tie the structure together.

You will need surprisingly few tools and materials to construct an arch or arbor using rustic poles. Although the construction must be sound, accuracy is not quite as essential as it would be with wood of uniform section. Slight variations in the sizes and

ABOVE: a well-constructed wooden arbor is an attractive way of providing shade, as well as giving support to climbing plants.

arrangement of the frame's pieces are all part of the attraction of the final appearance.

Materials

IF POSSIBLE, softwood should be purchased already pressure-treated with preservative, but if this is not available you can treat it yourself by brushing preservative on. Make sure you stand the feet of the uprights in buckets of preservative for several days so that it really soaks into the endgrain. Rustic poles with the bark left in place should only be treated on their ends as the bark will prevent absorption of the preservative.

In many cases, no fabrication joints will be necessary to assemble the sections of the arch since there will be little loading on them. The pieces can simply be overlapped and nailed, or their ends formed into halving joints by removing half of the wood for a distance equal to the width of the piece getting joined to it, using a small saw.

Dimensions

AS A GUIDE, an arch should give about 8ft of headroom and be at least 4ft wide. When you are happy with the design, you can order the materials.

As a rule, wood with a diameter or width of 3–4in will be needed for the main supporting framework of an arch.

See also: Climbing and screening plants pages 138–139; Clematis pages 140–141

BELOW: for the perfect seat to suit the location in your garden, it may be best to design and build it yourself.

OUTDOOR LIVING

FURNITURE AND BARBECUES

A garden should be a place where you and your family can relax outdoors whenever the weather permits. It also provides an extra room for informal summer entertaining.

IT IS a place for sitting in and and enjoying wherever possible. After you have laid out your garden and planted it, you should make some provision for using it. An important use is to be able to sit in it in peace—to read a book or follow some other pastime, or just to take in its sights, sounds, and scents.

There is a vast range of ready-made outdoor furniture to choose from, ranging from simple wooden seats to well-upholstered recliners with sun canopies, but often a seat that is tailored to blend in with its surroundings looks best. This usually means making one yourself, using materials that complement the style of the garden.

Designing seats is a complex business, but provided you take care to keep them simple and sturdy you should have no problems. They can be built from wood, from a combination of wood and masonry, or from masonry only, using basic skills.

Barbecues are part of outside living. They may be purchased in a wide variety of designs, or built by hand.

Making a tree seat

CREATE A shady seating area under a favorite tree with a raised planter constructed from interlocking timber logs. These can be obtained in easy-to-assemble kit form. Attractive and practical, this wooden tree seat can be assembled in just five minutes, without the need for any tools. When filled with soil, the same design can serve as a conventional planter which incorporates seating areas round the trunk of the tree.

The logs, which are preservative-treated to ward off rot, have notched edges which interlock to form the

See also: Patio furniture page 27

ABOVE: it is possible to make an attractive wooden tree seat using an easy-to-assemble kit.

Three common kinds of bench are illustrated: an elegant Lutyens-style *(top)*, a simple, attractive teak bench *(center)*, and rustic seating for a rural garden *(bottom)*.

walls of the tree seat and make the structure rigid. No other fixing is necessary.

The principles involved in constructing the tree seat are easy to modify to a home-made unit. Straight-edged wood can be used to construct a planter or tree seat if a more formal appearance is required. If there is no suitable tree in the garden, it may be worth planting one and building the seat around it, leaving room for the trunk to grow as the years go by.

Alternatively, you could use the seat as a planter by filling it with soil and adding small shrubs, or trailing plants.

MAKING AN OUTDOOR BENCH

A simple outdoor bench can be constructed by erecting two piers. The bench top can simply rest loosely on the piers, or can be attached with screws driven into wallplugs.

1 Build the piers using bricks, natural stone, or cement blocks on a strip foundation base. The piers should be no more than about 18in high for comfortable use.

2 Cut four lengths of 6 × 1½in planed softwood or hardwood to fit across the top of the piers with an overhang of 6in at each end.

3 Screw these to three battens of 3 × 2in wood, fixed at right-angles to them near each end and across the middle. Space the planks about ½in apart. Add cushions for comfort.

Barbecues

BARBECUES, ALWAYS very popular adjuncts to the backyard, can offer a versatile summer extension to the kitchen. They may be purchased in a wide range of designs, or constructed for use in a permanent position in the garden.

Siting the barbecue

Although correct design of a barbecue is crucial to its working efficiently and safely, picking the best site for it is of equal importance.

Bear in mind that the spot needs to be accessible from the kitchen for bringing utensils, crockery and food, so avoid a position that is too remote.

Do not position the barbecue below overhanging trees, which could be seriously damaged by the intense heat. Similarly, do not place the unit too close to a wooden fence or trellis.

Avoid siting the barbecue close to open windows, where curtains could billow out and catch light, or where smoke is likely to waft through neighbors' windows or into their laundry.

If the unit is built on an existing lawn the grass will almost certainly become worn by the heavy foot traffic it will receive. It is best, therefore, to surround the barbecue with paving blocks or brick pavers. Ensure that the surface is broad enough to accommodate several people, either standing or sitting, or if it covers a smaller area, that it is set flush with the surrounding turf so that your visitors can move freely in the area.

MAKING A LOOSE-BRICK BARBECUE

A temporary barbecue, which can be dismantled for storage during the winter, can be made by stacking bricks dry, without mortar. Not only is the unit inexpensive and easy to construct in a matter of a few hours, but it is also a very efficient structure: the honeycomb bonding arrangement used to raise the walls ensures a plentiful supply of air to the charcoal for good combustion.

The barbecue can be built in a circular, triangular, square or hexagonal shape, as preferred. A basic circular unit will use about 100 bricks; other shapes need more.

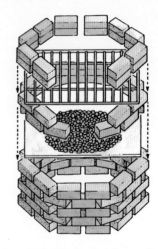

Lay the bricks in the chosen format on the prepared base with 2in wide gaps between each brick. Lay the second course on top, staggering the joints by half the length of a brick so that the bond will be strong. Continue to stack bricks, alternating the staggered bond with each course, until you reach the seventh course. Place a sheet-steel panel across the top of the brick wall as a charcoal tray, then add two more courses of dry-laid bricks before fitting a slatted broiling grill on top. Add another two or three courses of bricks around the back of the unit to act as a windshield for the cooking area.

See also: Outdoor ornaments pages 26–27

USING PLANTS

LEFT: there are plants to suit all places in the garden— the secret is choosing the right ones for your site.

HARDINESS ZONES

Climate, more than any other factor,

determines the success or failure of the

gardener. A garden requires adequate

sunshine and rainfall if plants are to thrive

in it, but it also needs protection against

extremes of weather.

It is the gardener's task to make use of the weather as much as possible. Temperature directly influences the rate of plant growth. The fastest growth will take place at the higher temperature limits of an individual plant's tolerance. A plant classified as tender will not endure temperatures below 32°F (0°C). A half-hardy plant can stand a few degrees of frost, but not a cold winter. By contrast, a hardy plant can tolerate considerable cold. Naturally, the degree of hardiness varies from plant to plant. How well a plant grows in an area depends largely on its native climate and on how easily it can adapt to its new environment.

This hardiness zone map will help you measure the degree of cold that a plant can tolerate in your area. The lower number represents the coldest temperature in which the plant can survive and the higher number refers to the warmest temperature in which the plant will thrive. Some plants, such as hardy bulbs, actually need winter chilling and will lose vigor in a warm zone. No zones have been given for annuals because they do not usually live through the winter.

The plants listed in this book carry a hardiness rating. This indicates that it will flower at the average minimum winter temperature that is given for that zone.

There are eleven hardiness zones, which are defined according to lowest winter temperatures. Zone 1 represents the coldest conditions, with winter temperatures below −50°F (−46°C); zone 11 is the warmest, with a minimum winter temperature of above 40°F (above 4°C). The classification of a plant into a particular hardiness zone means that the plant will normally thrive in that zone and also in any zone which is marked with a higher number.

The dividing line between one zone and the next is not rigid because the weather varies from one year to the next. The variations in landscape can also be an influence, and cities are warmer than rural areas. Also, by utilizing the shelter of walls and evergreen shrubs, plants can be encouraged to survive in zones in which they would normally die. Remember, too, that some plants will not survive in climates that are too hot for them.

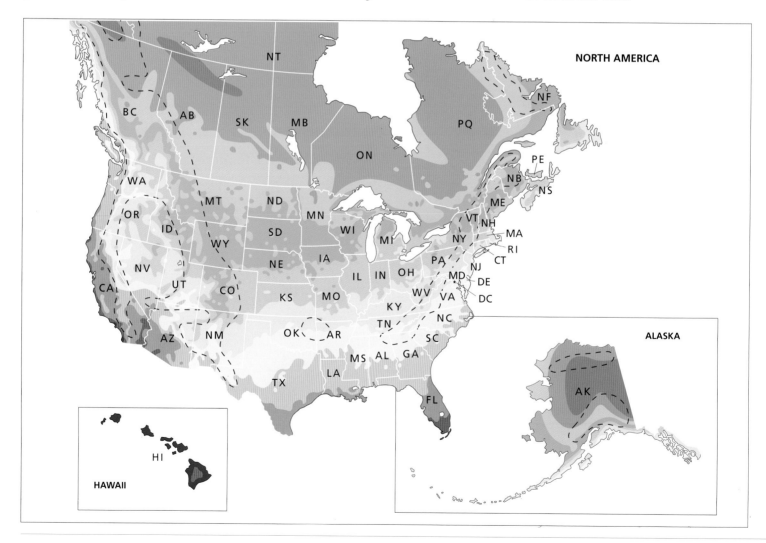

See also: Garden planning pages 10–15; Location pages 110–111

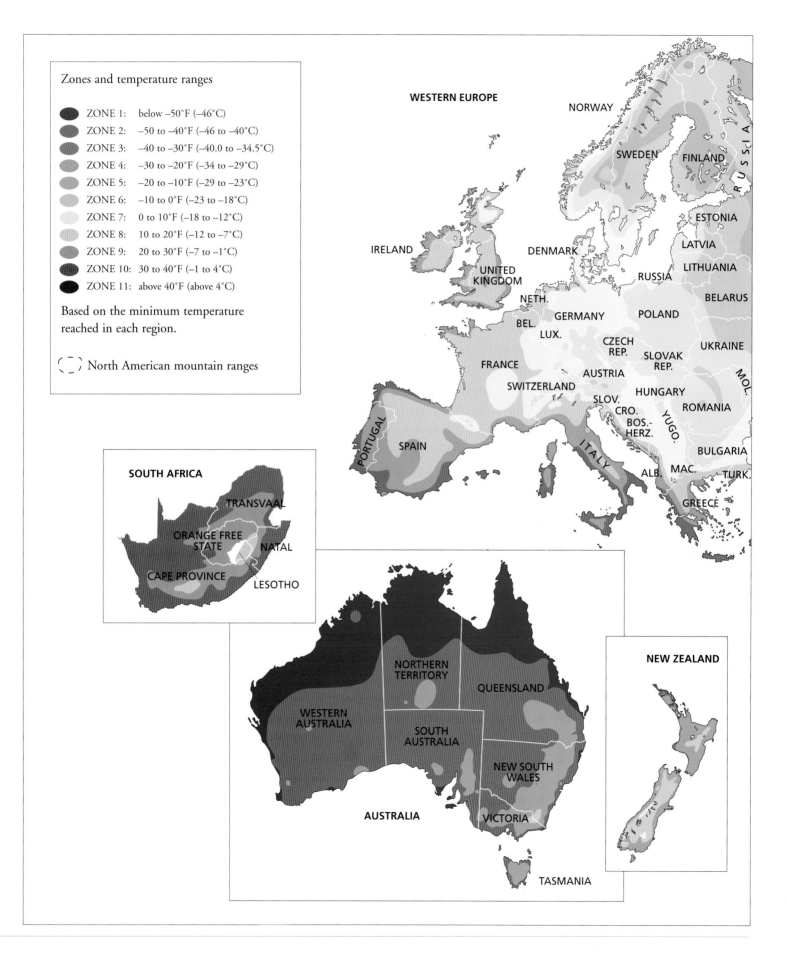

Zones and temperature ranges

ZONE 1:   below −50°F (−46°C)
ZONE 2:   −50 to −40°F (−46 to −40°C)
ZONE 3:   −40 to −30°F (−40.0 to −34.5°C)
ZONE 4:   −30 to −20°F (−34 to −29°C)
ZONE 5:   −20 to −10°F (−29 to −23°C)
ZONE 6:   −10 to 0°F (−23 to −18°C)
ZONE 7:   0 to 10°F (−18 to −12°C)
ZONE 8:   10 to 20°F (−12 to −7°C)
ZONE 9:   20 to 30°F (−7 to −1°C)
ZONE 10: 30 to 40°F (−1 to 4°C)
ZONE 11: above 40°F (above 4°C)

Based on the minimum temperature
reached in each region.

North American mountain ranges

WESTERN EUROPE

NORWAY

SWEDEN

FINLAND

RUSSIA

ESTONIA

LATVIA

LITHUANIA

BELARUS

IRELAND

DENMARK

UNITED
KINGDOM

NETH.

BEL.
LUX.

GERMANY

POLAND

UKRAINE

CZECH
REP.

RUSSIA

FRANCE

SWITZERLAND

AUSTRIA

SLOVAK
REP.

MOL.

HUNGARY

ROMANIA

SLOV.

YUGO.

CRO.
BOS.-
HERZ.

BULGARIA

PORTUGAL

SPAIN

ITALY

ALB.

MAC.

TURK.

GREECE

SOUTH AFRICA

TRANSVAAL

ORANGE FREE
STATE

NATAL

CAPE PROVINCE

LESOTHO

NORTHERN
TERRITORY

QUEENSLAND

WESTERN
AUSTRALIA

SOUTH
AUSTRALIA

NEW SOUTH
WALES

NEW ZEALAND

AUSTRALIA

VICTORIA

TASMANIA

LOCATION

Analyzing the conditions in your garden is one of the first things that you should do when you are planting it. All plots are different; even if they are exactly the same size and in the same road, each condition will demand a different approach. Take time to study your site and to assess both its positive and its negative aspects.

LEFT: assess the advantages and disadvantages of the location before choosing plants for your garden.

BELOW: the ideal conditions for a garden are plenty of sunlight, protection from winds, and good soil.

See also: Elements of design pages 24–25; Patios pages 68–71

Assessing the site

BEFORE YOU start planting your garden, you need to look at your specific plot of land and work out its advantages and disadvantages. Its location will affect many of your planting choices. One plot may be bathed in sun while, next door, a tall tree may plunge part of that garden into deep shadow. Winds may make it necessary to install a windbreak in one garden, while in another breezes may be hardly noticeable. Each plot must be judged on its own characteristics.

The type of vegetation already growing in a plot is often a good indicator of the nature of the soil. If gardens are lush with rhododendrons and azaleas in the spring and there is an abundance of heathers throughout the year, it is certain that the soil is acid. On the other hand, if the surrounding country supports a large population of plants that enjoy alkaline conditions, the soil is definitely chalky. The point to bear in mind is that some plants are lime-haters while others cannot thrive in acid soils. If you are starting a garden from scratch it is a good idea to buy an inexpensive soil-testing kit. Test the soil in several places all over the garden: it is possible that it will prove to be acid in one spot and alkaline at a point only a few yards away.

A preponderance of marsh plants among the wild flora will give a good indication of water-logged soil. If the whole plot shows signs of being wet, the ground will need to be drained. Such a spot in only one part of the site, however, provides the opportunity to have a marsh garden or a natural pool as a special feature. Also take note of any particular places where the soil appears to be exceptionally dry, so that planting can be carried out accordingly.

What grows where

SITUATION AND aspect govern plant selection; so to a lesser extent does the type of soil. Fortunately, most plants are very adaptable: although they may prefer a particular kind of soil, they will usually tolerate most reasonably fertile ones that are neither too wet nor too dry for long periods. Most fussy are the lime-haters. Your garden's situation also affects its exposure to wind and temperature, both factors that influence

ABOVE: *Arum italicum comenatorum* likes shady corners and rich soil.
LEFT: a colorful pot of busy Lizzies and begonias looks wonderful, but make sure that you place it where it will thrive.

growth. There are hillside and seaside gardens in which it is almost impossible to develop a planting scheme until winds have been softened by shelter belts of evergreen trees and shrubs and carefully sited fences that filter the wind. Before you buy any plants, look in neighbors' backyards and note what grows well.

Aspect

HOW THE site is positioned in relation to the sun and shade is the next consideration. The aspect determines how much sun the garden enjoys and at what time of the day certain parts of the area are in sun or shade. In some cases—coastal districts and very exposed inland areas in particular—aspect determines what spots in the garden are exposed to strong winds and so need to be screened.

Ideally, a backyard should have a sunny aspect and receive the maximum amount of sun during the day: if the garden is not over-shadowed, the sun will shine on it from early or mid-morning until evening. The principal drawback to such an aspect is that in some neighborhoods it may be exposed to strong winds, although these are usually relatively warm.

The worst aspects for a garden are when the amount of sun that shines directly on the garden is restricted or where shade prevails during the afternoon. Accompanying winds are often strong and biting, and if the site is in a particularly open position, this could have a damaging effect on plants. Gardens that receive sun during at least the afternoon are much more favorable to plants, as they tend to benefit from a certain amount of warmth, shade and moisture.

Know your soil

SOIL HAS to be improved, modified or manipulated so that the best conditions for plant life can be created. Good soils offer anchorage and support, sufficient food, warmth, moisture and oxygen, and room for plants to develop.

See also: Paths pages 74–77; Horizontal and vertical surfaces pages 20–21

THE ROLE OF PLANTS

There is always plenty of choice when it comes to selecting plants to fill a particular space in the garden. You can choose plants for their decorative flowers, fragrance, evergreen or variegated foliage, colored stems and bark, fruits and berries, their ability to climb or trail, or perhaps their culinary value.

LEFT: plant tulips as "fillers" to provide springtime splashes of color.

BELOW: roses and other shrubs provide the framework of the garden, while herbaceous plants such as irises give it its summer splendor.

See also: Garden trees pages 127–129; Hedges pages 130–131; Shrubs for year-round interest pages 132–135

FOR CULTURAL reasons, some plants need a special environment: many alpines need a rockery, scree bed or sink garden, while bog plants require damp soil and aquatic plants depend on water. In a small backyard, you may not have room for more than a few plants of each type.

Framework plants

TREES, HEDGES and climbers all give an impression of permanence, and are key plants around which many other features can be designed. It is these plants that will provide the vertical dimension and offer contrast. Evergreens and hedges in particular are an essential part of most gardens, and besides possessing beauty in their own right, they provide a natural setting for many of the more colorful subjects. Shrubs also act as a framework to the garden, providing structure against which to grow ornamental flowers.

Trees

Unless you have enough ground to form a small arboretum, trees must of necessity be regarded as background or framework plants. Because trees are so important, they should be chosen carefully and positioned strategically. For a small garden, choose smaller trees, with the emphasis on those that are relatively slow growing. If there are established trees in the garden, try to make use of them, as nothing gives a greater sense of maturity.

Evergreens including conifers

Not only do these provide interesting contrasts of foliage texture and color throughout the year, they also act as a foil for many deciduous shrubs.

Hedges and screens

There are many excellent hedging plants, some with attractive foliage, others that make ideal informal flowering hedges. Whichever is chosen, it is worth bearing in mind that a hedge provides shelter as well as beauty. Careful positioning in an exposed garden can make all the difference when it comes to growing some of the less robust plants. So always consider hedges in relation to the other plants you intend to grow.

Shrubs

Once garden trees have been chosen and plotted on a plan, use shrubs to build up the framework of the planting. Distribute those that have evergreen leaves over the whole of the garden. This is advisable for two reasons: first, it will give a certain amount of form to the entire plot, and second, it will prevent one particular corner from becoming heavy and unchanging, which might be the case if the evergreens were all planted together. In very small gardens where there is no room for trees, shrubs must take their place, creating focal points and structure.

Climbers

There are many small gardens where the potential growing space on the walls is greater than the ground area available. This space should never be wasted; climbers not only increase the range of plants that you can grow in your garden, they also screen what can otherwise be rather bleak walls and fences. Although some, such as wisteria, are planted with the long-term in mind, there are many that will grow rapidly. Make the most of walls and fences, poles and arbors and clothe them with climbers.

Decorative plants

ONCE YOU have created your framework planting, add some seasonal color and interest using a range of perennials, annuals, biennials and bulbs.

Perennials

No garden would be complete without herbaceous plants, for they act as fillers around the framework trees and shrubs. In most gardens the two types of plant are intermingled in mixed borders, the best solution where year-round interest is required. They can also be planted on their own in island beds, used as ground cover or grown in containers; indeed, their diversity makes them suitable for every garden.

Perennials are valued for both flowers and foliage. Not only are they a major source of color, but they also add shape and texture, sometimes even scent, to the garden.

Annuals and biennials

These plants play a valuable role in border and container planting. They can either be used on their own for a spectacular display, as in bedding schemes, or they can be used to fill in any unsightly gaps in the garden. They are particularly useful for providing splashes of instant color and they can bring life to any planting within a few months. Being short-lived, they can also be replaced the next year with something different to change the look of the garden, although if left in the ground they will self-sow. It is difficult to find any other plants that will transform a bare patch of ground into such a riot of color in so short a time. They are especially useful in a newly constructed garden, but certainly merit inclusion at any time.

Bulbs

Bulbs are ideal "fillers" in the garden, and are useful for providing seasonal splashes of color before disappearing into the soil to make way for other plants. Easy-to-grow favorites include crocuses, grape hyacinth, snowdrops, winter aconites and tulips. Some bulbs are also suitable for naturalizing in large patches, notably daffodils and bluebells.

LEFT: tall and vulnerable plants such as delphiniums thrive in the protective shelter of a hedge.

See also: Climbers pages 138–139; Perennials pages 142–145; Annuals and biennials pages 146–147; Bulbs pages 152–153

PLANT ASSOCIATIONS

Whichever plants we choose to grow, they must be displayed well if they are to look their best. The easiest way to group is to make a series of small feature "pictures" and create clusters of plants, sometimes only two or three, each adding to the others' beauty and effectiveness.

Shape, height and texture

PLANT ASSOCIATION is not just a question of putting together plants that flower at the same time. Instead, look for plants that complement each other in terms of habit and size, texture and color.

Shape

All plants fall into one of a number of basic shape categories, the plants in each category fulfilling a similar role in the overall scheme. There is the tall upright shape of fastigiate trees and conifers which leads the eye upward and commands attention, especially when used repeatedly in a group or row. The effect is the same whatever the scale. Low rounded shapes or domes are equally arresting, but in a more earthbound way. They sit heavily upon the ground and fix the eye. Fans or fountain shapes offer a softer touch, lifting the eye but in a gentler, lighter way than a conifer. A more extreme version of this effect is the weeping shape, less visually static than the sphere and less busy than the fountain. Finally, there are the horizontal shapes. They keep the eye peacefully arrested, moving neither up nor down. There are endless variations within and between these categories, but when

RIGHT: color and shape complement each other in this match of pyrethrum and foxgloves.

See also: Location pages 110–111; Hardiness zones pages 108–109

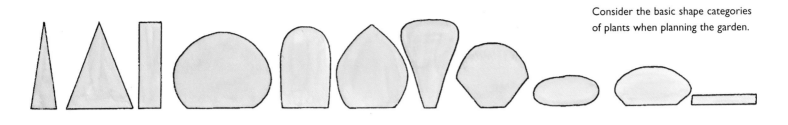

Consider the basic shape categories of plants when planning the garden.

LINKING SHAPES

Different shapes are linked to lift the eye or to give a special focus.

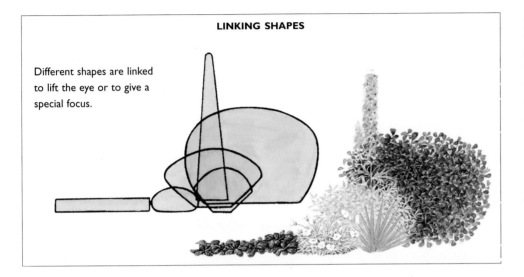

planning a layout they are very useful devices. As well as looking at the overall shape of a plant, do not forget to focus in on the form of its flowers. Choose flower shapes that complement one another in some way, either a combination of pleasing contrasts or harmonious similarities. Remember, too, the shapes of individual leaves, and even the branch patterns of trees and shrubs.

Height
A variation in levels and a variation of plant heights all help to add interest to a border planting. The regularity of a border planted with tall plants at the back and low-growing ones at the front can be much more interesting if you introduce a few tall plants midway, to create some interest at intervals.

Texture
Plants not only have form, they also have texture: coarse or fine, solid or filigree, and so on. Some are velvety soft to touch while others are hard and unyielding; some absorb light and some reflect it.

ABOVE: the circular shape of *Allium giganteum* adds visual variety to any group of plants.

RIGHT: the unusual combination of penstemon and *Eryngium alpinum* makes a vivid contrast.
FAR RIGHT: *Euphorbia marginata* is grown for its unusual form and cactus-like texture.

See also: Climbing and screening plants pages 138–139

ABOVE: the bold ornamental *Eryngium alpinum* is a handsome sight in a large garden.
RIGHT: color, texture and foliage are all elements that are skilfully combined in this mixed border.

See also: Shrubs for year-round interest pages 132–135

Texture is perhaps best appreciated from a distance. Create patterns using different textures: plant a misty open plant against a dense, solid plant; try mixing hostas and ferns, for example.

Year-round interest

A GARDEN CAN never be as colorful in winter as in summer, but there is no reason why it should not be just as interesting, though in different ways. This is simply a matter of planning so that your garden has some framework plants (preferably evergreen) to give year-round interest and there is always something attractive to look at. Each season needs thinking about in terms of the color of flowers, foliage and fruit, form, texture, perfume, and the uses to which the garden will be put. Even if summer color is desired, it is still possible to underplant and interplant for other times of the year using bulbs and annuals.

Bulbs and annuals are invaluable for spring and early summer color, while herbaceous perennials are the most colorful summer contributors. In many places herbaceous perennials can be found in flower for most of the year, and by planting a good cross section it is possible to get a long flowering season.

Fall color can be found in trees like maples and rowans, but there are vines of equal brilliance and even herbaceous plants such as euphorbia and gillenia. Fruits and berries need not just be a fall feature.

LEFT: the spare outline of branches can be an attractive counterpoint to other plants.

BELOW: a cool backdrop for colorful plants is provided by the soft green shapes of ferns.

Many roses carry their hips and *Mahonia aquifolium* bears its blue berries in late summer. Later come the reds, yellows and oranges of holly (*Ilex*), rowans (*Sorbus aucuparia*), cotoneasters and pyracantha. Usually the paler the berries, the later the birds will descend to eat them.

Color in the garden in winter may seem impossible, until you realize that there are plants for which winter is the natural time of flowering. Certainly you will not get a great deal of bloom, but you will find a surprising variety of plants that will take up where the summer plants left off, and flower in succession through the otherwise dormant months of the year. Such shrubs as witch hazel (*Hamamelis*), some of the rhododendrons, corylopis and *Mahonia* "Charity," and herbaceous perennials, hellebores, snowdrops, *Iris reticulata*, bergenias and some of the violets are all winter-flowering.

To add to winter color, there is a great variety of textures and colors to choose from including: the glossy spiny leaves of holly, the soft gold of some variegated yews, or the blue of spruce needles. The interest supplied by colored bark is also invaluable. Stooled dogwoods offer scarlet, purple and yellow bark; while that of willows is orange, gray or glossy brown. Some species of birch have brilliant white or coppery-pink bark and there are cherries with the glorious, dramatic bark of purest polished mahogany.

In winter a garden falls back on its structure to make itself interesting, and it is then that the most benefit is gained from light and shade and the clarity of the design. With careful plant choice, your garden can continue to be clothed in winter—in fact, a

really well-designed and thought-out garden will look just as good, though in a different way, as in summer.

Scent

HAVING SATISFIED the eye by planting subjects of good form and color, do not forget to include some scented plants. Aromatic plants add an extra dimension. Scented carpet plants like thyme and chamomile can be planted in the gaps between paving and will release their fragrance when brushed against. Lavender alongside paths will scent the air, as will perfumed roses and certain border plants.

USING FOLIAGE

Foliage plays a vital role in the garden, for not only does it create a neutral backdrop against which colorful flowers will show up, but it has a much longer period of interest than flowers and berries and so forms the framework of your planting. Indeed, evergreen leaves are a good way of providing year-round interest.

Foliage is particularly useful for texture, and there is no better way of breaking up blocks of color than by introducing leafy plants. There are many types whose leaves are handsome in shape, agreeable in color and pleasing in texture.

See also: Perennials pages 142–145; Annuals and biennials pages 146–147

Color

COLOR IS without doubt the most obvious part of an ornamental plant's attraction, and the most important to the majority of gardeners. A dazzling, riotous display of color from spring to the fall is generally the ideal for beginner gardeners. But as time goes on and experience accumulates, this aim gradually changes as you realize that more subtle but more satisfying blendings can be obtained, in which colur is mixed with white, or cool grays and silvers, or with plants grown for the shape and texture of their leaves.

A blaze of all the colors of the rainbow is difficult to absorb all at once: much better to group the plants in types of color, and merge each into the one adjacent to it. Pink, purple, rose, gray, lavender, blue, and lilac make one group; and yellow, cream, orange, bronze, brown, and light red another. The reds will graduate into shades of rose, lavender and so to blue; or on the opposite side into scarlet, vermilion, flame, and finally yellow. Gray-leafed and white-flowered plants will calm down the brighter colors, and mix beautifully with muted shades.

Another way of breaking up blocks of color is to introduce leafy plants. There are many species whose leaves are handsome in shape, agreeable in color and pleasing in texture. These deserve a place in the garden in their own right.

LEFT: a bold color scheme of scarlet "Toronto" tulips, blue muscari and pink rhododendrons.

BELOW: the green and white foliage of hostas makes a cool color combination together with white tulips.

LEFT: a modern pink shrub rose, "Rosy Cushion," cascades over a pink and blue border.

RIGHT: the bright yellow of *Hypericum* "Hidcote" has a bold summer presence.

See also: Bulbs pages 152–153; Choosing plants pages 180–181

Color wheel

ALTHOUGH THE PERCEPTION of color and taste is a personal and subjective matter, there are basic guidelines that can help you plan the color schemes of your garden.

The theory behind color combinations, both harmonies and contrasts, can be most readily understood by visualizing a chart known as the color wheel. This is based on the colors of the spectrum and consists of the primary colors red, blue and yellow, separated by the secondary, blended colors violet, green and orange. Colors adjacent to each other on the wheel, such as yellow and orange or blue and green, are generally considered to go well together—in other words they harmonize. Colors opposite each other, however, such as red and green or blue and orange, can be seen as contrasting colors, known as complementary colors. There are, of course, infinite nuances of color between each of these rather artificial subdivisions of the wheel. Colors can be pale or intense depending on the colors they are mixed with and, technically speaking, they become shades, tints and tones of the original base color. A shade, for instance, is created by adding black to the base color, while a tint is made by adding white, and a tone is the result of a color being either lightened or darkened by the addition of gray.

RIGHT: the glorious reds of Virginia creeper enrich the fall garden.
BELOW: the rich purple of clematis is a summer favorite.

LEFT: adjoining colors on the wheel blend happily, as with these yellow/red tulips and (below) the bright yellow of *Zinnia elegans*.

ABOVE: purple-blue violas at ground level harmonize with the heavenly blue of the climber *Ipomoea* or morning glory (right).

LEFT: the handsome ornamental foliage of the hardy evergreen *Ilex* "Golden King" makes a telling contrast with bold primary reds.

See also: Bedding plants pages 148–149

TOP RIGHT: shades of pink and blue combine happily— a mixture of *Allium sphaerocephalon* and phlox.

ABOVE: use bright colors in small touches of brilliance for the best effect.

Such variations make a huge difference to the effect of color combinations; different intensities of one basic color create a completely different feel. Take an apparently simple association of blue and yellow. Pale blue and pale yellow is a soft, unchallenging combination with a restful and airy feel to it. Now consider a mixture of golden yellow and violet blue and you have a far more vibrant and challenging effect which makes much more of a statement. However, both combinations have a place in the garden, the pale planting being particularly appropriate in a corner of an old walled garden for a timeless, relaxed atmosphere, and the stronger scheme being perfect as part of a mixed planting along a path to promote the feeling of movement.

Colors can also be loosely divided into warm and cool effects, with greens and grays providing a neutral buffer zone in between.

Reds, oranges and golden yellows seem warm, while purples and blues seem cooler. Furthermore, warm shades appear to advance toward the eye, making an area seem smaller than it really is, while cool colors seem to recede, thereby providing the illusion of space. In practice, if you clothe a garden in cool and light colors it will seem bigger than in reality, which is useful in small gardens, and to make large gardens more intimate, you can interrupt a view and bring the eye up short with a strong display of bright, warm colors.

Experimenting with these effects is immensely enjoyable and the only way of developing your individual garden style. Do not be afraid of making mistakes, but it can be a good idea to try out color combinations with bulbs or bedding plants first, before investing time and money in planting shrubs and perennials.

See also: Colorful perennials pages 142–145

CREATING A BORDER

The wonderful thing about gardening is that you are free to create as you wish. Lovers of shrubs can establish a shrub border, while wonderful spot beds can be made with annuals; and roses can be really spectacular when they are grouped together. But surely the most interesting sight of all in the backyard must be the flower border that provides a little bit of everything—annuals, perennials, shrubs, bulbs and roses.

MOST PEOPLE call it the mixed border, although "versatile" might be a far better word because it suggests both colorful flowers and attractive foliage right through the year. Certainly the mixed border must rank as the most rewarding feature of the small to average-sized garden. The possibilities are enormous. Just consider growing sweet peas side by side with an elegant group of regal lilies, or having dramatic large-flowered delphiniums towering over old-fashioned pinks, all close beside the soft-colored bearded iris.

RIGHT: a well-established cottage garden border— a mixture of achillea, campanula and scabiosa.

A border of mixed or herbaceous plants will provide flowers and foliage for cutting, and plants that can be left in position for a number of years. Apart from pruning and dividing, they demand little work. However, it has to be said that these benefits will only be reaped by those who put the initial work into the planning, designing and preparing. That might sound horrifying to the new gardener, but it can be a pleasure.

Such a border can be planted anywhere, even in open lawn, although where it can be viewed from each side there will be more restrictions on the types of plants you can use. Most usually a background wall, fence or hedge will provide the necessary frame, and will also provide a windbreak, which is important when taller plants are being grown.

The dedicated planner can devise a highly scented border devoted to one type of plant (such as the rose), or a theme—delphiniums, dahlias, chrysanthemums and roses, among those that immediately come to mind, but there are so many others that the gardener can be spoilt for choice.

A scented garden has its own obvious pleasures, and despite the cries that scent is being lost by modern flower breeders there are many different types of flowers that can be used effectively in this way. The heady scent of wallflowers *Erysimum*, the lovely mignonette and, of course, night-scented stock are all excellent choices. There are many more that can be appreciated from spring to winter, and they include the white *Nicotiana* (tobacco plant) and many forms of lilac, lavender, lily-of-the-valley, honeysuckle, viburnum, sweet peas, and jasmine.

ABOVE: long-flowering petunias—equally at home in the garden or in pots and baskets.

Size and shape

A BORDER needs a certain amount of space to be effective. The minimum requirements are 4 x 12ft. If the border is any smaller than this you should restrict the number of plants used to six or seven different types, ensuring that they provide a good mix of flowers and foliage over a long period of the year.

If you have more space it is possible to create one of a wide range of borders, incorporating varying widths and curves, which will be far more interesting than a border of straight lines. One of the great

advantages of a mixed or herbaceous border is that you can change it from year to year. And as you become more adventurous and knowledgeable, it will be possible for you to create bolder and ever more spectacular border displays.

Introducing plants

WHEN DESIGNING a border, never think of a plant in isolation: judge it as a companion for its neighbors. Plants should always be positioned to show one another off, not simply planted in the soil. Rely on leaf shape, color and texture even more than on flowers. The leaves are in evidence for most of the year (all year if they are evergreen), whereas flowers are fleeting. You will find that almost all flowers have more impact if they are shown off by a backdrop of handsome foliage than if they have to sit in mid-air. Also choose your plants with seasons of interest in mind. Make sure there is at least a handful of flowers, fruits and bright foliage to see you through the winter until the colorful spring show begins once more and the garden comes alive.

Flowering shrubs can be used to provide a permanent framework in the border and a setting for perennials, annuals and bulbs with their more flamboyant flowers. Many will also create year-round interest with fruits following flowers, silver or evergreen foliage and fiery color in the fall. The choice of perennials is almost without bounds but once you have selected your favorites, and once they are established, they will go on growing and flowering for several seasons, giving pleasure year after year.

ABOVE: during this border's first year, annuals and tender plants complement the permanent planting.

ABOVE: by late spring, the peony and barberries are in full bloom, and white arabis flowers in the foreground.

See also: The role of plants pages 112–113

PRACTICALITIES

Some of the rules for creating a mixed border are:

• All borders, whether shrub or mixed, need sun, so must be sited in the sunniest part of the garden.

• Careful soil preparation is vital. There is nothing to beat a well-dug, fertilized bed.

• If planting against a wall, hedge or fence, leave at least 18in between the back of the border and the "frame." If you can, lay some sort of path. This will make it easy for you to tend to the back of the border and to repair the wall or fence, or trim the hedge.

• Soggy land or a sunless position are the two great handicaps. Try for good drainage and full sun.

• When selecting plants make sure that you have allowed space for those that are rampant growers and which may suffocate slower-growing plants placed near them.

• Place taller-growing plants (such as weigela or fuchsia) at the back of the border, with the lower ones in front. The middle area is reserved for the iris, lupin, stocks and other average-sized flowers.

• Try to keep the ground between plants open by hoeing and weeding.

• A mulch of organic material—peatmoss or well-rotted compost, for instance—will keep down weeds and also conserve water. On the edges of beds a mulch of small forest bark can be very effective.

• When cutting flowers for house decoration be gentle on new plants. The loss of stems and greenery can harm next year's growth. This will be obvious on perennials and even newly-planted roses. If you want a flower from a first-year plant, then cut it with as little stem as possible.

• Remove flower heads once they have faded, which will give the plants a chance of repeat flowering later in the season. Remove them with sharp scissors, shears or pruners.

• If you wish to move a plant in the border wait until the fall, but identify where to place it.

• Wear gloves. These can be awkward to work in but they are safer.

See also: Elements of design pages 24–27

ABOVE: a subtle border combination of rose, phlomis, lily, and *Allium caeruleum*.

RIGHT: this spring border contains bulbs supplemented by wallflowers and forget-me-nots.

BELOW: in summer perennials take over from the bulbs and harmonize with the foliage of the juniper and euphorbia.

Annuals are superb for bringing color into mixed borders. Either use them boldly spread in drifts, so that their color is not diluted, or mix them with other plants and perhaps plant them by scale rather than by color. There is a wide range of bulbous plants that can be grown in a mixed border, from the stately gladiolus to the perfumed lily. Make sure that you know the eventual height that the flower will reach before planting it.

Putting your thoughts on paper

IT IS OFTEN helpful, in the planning stages of a border, to make simple sketches that block in the most important shapes and lines (as well as the main color effects). This will enable you to envisage the composition in advance and allows the main refinements to be made before planting begins. It is also useful for considering the mature aspect of the garden at different seasons, which should include appropriate spacing of trees and large shrubs at their ultimate size. This is an

ABOVE: the splendid golden yellow *Achillea filipendulina* is ideal for border planting.

excellent tool for clarifying your ideas; on paper, the imagination can run riot, but once planting begins, changes become much more difficult. A plan can bring you that much closer to your ideal, well-balanced garden. With the outline in hand, start filling in planting details on the plan— shapes, colors, texture and scent, leaving the choice of most plants until last.

The next stage is to ensure that the planting line-up is going to provide color and interesting shapes right through the year. Use four different-colored pens (signifying winter, spring, summer and fall) to mark blocks of plants on the plan and, if possible, grow one spectacular plant for every season in each area. (When planting, leave space around the young specimens to accommodate their ultimate spread. Annuals and bedding plants can be used to fill the gaps temporarily.)

Planning a border

THE BEST WAY of planning a border is to work with small groups of plants so you can

See also: Drawing up your plan pages 16–17

concentrate on the relationship between the subjects, and so gradually build up the groups into a whole border planting. Choose plants with shapes that complement each other and which make an interesting and varied effect.

You will notice that different plants create a variety of effects. Spiky plants, for example, are active and lead the eye upward and onward to neighboring plants, while gentle hummock-forming plants are calming and bland, and lead the eye horizontally along the border.

At the same time think of height. Either use a tier system with tall plants at the back and shorter ones at the front, or use tall plants in the middle of the group to create peaks of interest, with shorter-growing plants leading the eye upward toward them. This will divert the eye and prevent it from traveling straight down the border, taking it all in at a glance. However, if tall plants are used toward the front of a border, they should be wispy enough to allow the eye to pass through them, yet substantial enough to break the line.

LEFT: a brilliant border of narcissi, blue *Anemone blanda* and tall *Fritillaria imperialis*.

BELOW AND BELOW LEFT: planting plan for a mixed border containing a combination of plant heights and shapes.

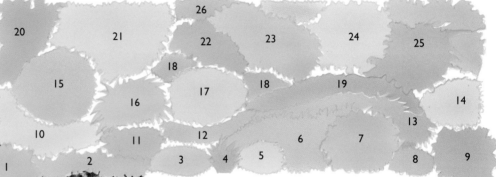

KEY

1. *Alchemilla mollis* (z4–8)
2. *Ajuga reptans* "Atropurpurea" (z3–8)
3. *Dianthus* "Mrs Sinkins" (z4–8)
4. *Iris pallida* "Argentea Variegata" (z4–9)
5. *Lavandula angustifolia* "Munstead" (z6–9)
6. *Sisyrinchium striatum* (z7–8)
7. *Sedum spectabile* (z4–9)
8. *Geranium clarkei* "Kashmir White" (z4–8)
9. *Heuchera micrantha* "Palace Purple" (z4–8)
10. *Salvia nemorosa* "Ostfriesland" (z5–9)
11. *Achillea* "Moonshine" (z4–8)
12. *Aster thomsonii* "Nanus" (z5–8)
13. *Catananche caerulea* (z5–8)
14. *Lavandula* x *intermedia* "Grappenhall" (z8–9)
15. *Santolina chamaecyparissus* (z6–9)

16. *Agapanthus* Headbourne hybrids (z8–10)
17. *Spiraea japonica* "Goldflame" (z4–9)
18. *Aster novi-belgii* "Marie Ballard" (z4–8)
19. *Aster novi-belgii* "White Ladies" (z4–8)
20. *Anemone* x *hybrida* "Queen Charlotte" (z6–8)
21. *Euphorbia characias wulfenii* (z7–10)
22. *Delphinium* Pacific hybrids (z2–9)
23. *Cotinus coggygria* "Royal Purple" (z5–9)
24. *Echinops ritro* (z4–9)
25. *Berberis thunbergii atropurpurea* (z5–9)
26. *Aster novae-angliae* "Harrington's Pink" (z4–8)

See also: Design guidelines pages 18–23; Hardiness zones pages 108–109

PLANT SELECTOR

The plants that you choose to put in your garden depend on a number of things, including the size and scale of your backyard and the effect and atmosphere you are trying to achieve.

THE FIRST basic question you need to ask yourself is what, in the main, do you use your backyard for? Is it somewhere you spend relatively little time and do you use it principally to provide a view from the house? Or do you spend a great deal of time in it—every free moment you have available, in fact? Are you looking for somewhere to sunbathe, read a book and relax? Or do you do a lot of entertaining and want the garden to be an extension of the house? Do you have children and need to provide a play area? And perhaps most important of all, do you want it to be somewhere you spend hours tending to your plants or are you after a low-maintenance garden that looks wonderful for minimum effort?

Then, of course, there's the not inconsiderable matter of your own personal preferences. Everyone has their own favorite plants. Think about what it is that attracts you most about them. Do you like them to be exotic, dramatic, pretty, colorful, graceful or unusual? Do you want them to provide a peaceful relaxing background or do you want attention grabbers?

These are all considerations that will greatly influence your choice of plants. The pages that follow look at all the different types of plant that are available to you, including trees, hedges, shrubs, climbers, perennials, annuals and biennials, bedding plants, bulbs and rock-garden plants.

RIGHT: a rustic garden style is a favorite choice for those who like traditional plants.

GARDEN TREES

Trees can make or mar a garden. Too many of them, or unsuitable kinds, can rob the garden of light and the soil of food and moisture, making it impossible to grow anything else well. However, a few well-planned and well-chosen trees can give a garden distinction and provide welcome summer shade.

Site considerations

SITE TREES where they will have room to develop unhindered and avoid planting specimens that will outgrow available space. Consider the habit of the trees as well as their flowers, foliage and berry color, and plant them where their form can be appreciated. In confined spaces fastigiate (columnar) trees are best, but where space needs to be filled those with spreading branches are ideal. For small backyards, select trees with several attractive features which can be enjoyed for much of the year, rather than those that have only a spectacular but brief blossoming period. Evergreen trees provide form and interest all year around although many deciduous trees are attractive even when bare.

Trees can affect nearby buildings, creating shade and extracting water from the subsoil, which brings the risk of subsidence. Plant large trees away from buildings if possible. The ground under deciduous trees will have to be cleared of leaves in the fall. For this reason, do not position pools or sandboxes under their canopies.

BELOW LEFT: a blend of color all the year—red berberis, silvery-blue spruce and dark-green pine.
BELOW: fastigiate, or columnar, trees add another dimension to gardens where space is at a premium.
LEFT: vivid yellowy-greens contrast well with more mellow coppery leaves.

Conifers

CONIFERS, OF WHICH cypress, cedar, juniper, fir, larch and pine are familiar examples, differ from other trees in having narrow, sometimes needle-like leaves. Though naturally green leaved, some conifers produce varieties with leaves of a different color, ranging from silver, gray, blue, and green to bronze and gold.

Most, but not all, are evergreen. There are not many other evergreen trees, so conifers do play a rather special role in the garden as framework plants, accentuated by the fact that many are conical in habit in contrast to the more rounded shapes of broad-leaved trees. Most conifers are allowed to branch from ground level but other trees are often grown on a bare trunk and are known as standards.

See also: Hedges pages 130–131; Shrubs for year-round interest pages 132–135

Which tree?

LARGE TREES such as oak (*Quercus*), lime (*Tilia*), poplar (*Populus*), beech (*Fagus*), willow (*Salix*), cedar (*Cedrus*), and pine (*Pinus*) are only suitable for large gardens, but there are sometimes dwarf, upright-stemmed or fastigiate forms of large trees that can be planted in quite small backyards.

Some trees have bright and colorful bark and are particularly spectacular in winter, when there is little else of interest in the garden. *Acer griseum* (paperback maple) (z6–8) has polished, orange-brown peeling bark, while *Betula papyrifera* (paper-bark birch) (z2–8) has smooth, silver-white, brown-banded bark. *Prunus serrula* (Tibetan cherry) (z6–8) has smooth bark the color of polished mahogany, with peeling rings running around it and *Rubus cockburnianus* (whitewashed bramble) (z5–9) has whitish-purple arching stems.

Acer palmatum (Japanese maple) (z5–8) is a useful tree for shady areas. It grows in dappled shade. *Aucuba japonica* (z7–10) is another shade-loving specimen and, being evergreen, is an ideal framework plant. *Prunus lusitanica* (Portugal laurel) (z7–9) also tolerates shady conditions.

Another member of the acer family, *Acer negundo* (box elder) (z3–9), is a quick-growing tree, reaching up to 30ft in 20 years. Similarly, *Liriodendron tulipifera* (tulip tree) (z4–9), grows up to 40ft in 20 years, and *Populus* x *canadensis* "Aurea" (golden poplar) (z4–9) grows up to 30ft in 20 years.

LEFT: liquidambar's glorious foliage.
BELOW: brilliant golden laburnum makes a stunning feature in any backyard.

See also: Climbing and screening plants pages 138–139

RECOMMENDED ORNAMENTAL TREES

Amelanchier lamarckii—
SNOWY MESPILUS Z4–8
This round-headed tree has bronze young leaves turning crimson in the fall and masses of tiny white flowers in late spring.

Ginko biloba—
MAIDENHAIR TREE Z5–9
This tree is slow-growing so is suitable for a small garden, though it can reach up to 90ft. The fan-shaped leaves are pale green in spring, turning to yellow in the fall.

Laburnum x *watereri*
"Vossii"—GOLDEN CHAIN TREE Z6–8
This favorite form reaches up to 20ft but it can be trained to grow over arches and arbors. It has long trails of bright yellow, fragrant, pea-like flowers.

Liquidambar styraciflua—
SWEET GUM Z6–9
This tree has maple-shaped leaves which turn to rich shades of crimson before they fall. It grows into a shapely, pyramidal tree, rather narrow in proportion to its height.

Prunus x *subhirtella*
"Autumnalis"—WINTER-FLOWERING CHERRY Z6–8
The mid-green leaves of this cherry turn a shade of orange-bronze in that fall and the flowers, pink in bud, open out white.

Robinia pseudoacacia
"Frisia"—GOLDEN FALSE ACACIA Z4–9
This has ferny leaves and white pea-like flowers in clusters in summer.

Sorbus aucuparia—
MOUNTAIN ASH OR ROWAN Z4–7
This is an excellent garden tree of small to medium size, making a neat, pyramidal shape. The leaves are rather ferny and the white, summer flowers are replaced by orange-scarlet berries in the fall.

ABOVE: scarlet foliage brightens the dullest of fall days.

ABOVE LEFT: spreading a cool shade, trees with wide branches need the space of large gardens.

LEFT: blossom is an additional delight of trees in the *Prunus* species.

TREE FORMS

It is important to know the habit of a tree before planting it. Trees can be spreading (a), weeping (b), fastigiate (c), or conical (d). Check the eventual height and spread of the tree and allow it adequate space when planning the garden.

See also: Hardiness zones pages 108–109; Location pages 110–111

HEDGES

Hedges serve both a decorative and a utilitarian role in the garden. They can be used to give privacy and to keep out intruders, to separate one part of the garden from another or to provide a fine background for a border of flowers. They can be clipped in simple or elaborate shapes or left to grow freely—an informal treatment that suits flowering shrubs, including shrub roses.

Conifer hedges

THE THREE principal kinds of conifer used for hedging are cypress, thuja and yew. All are evergreens which stand frequent clipping and yew, like box, is much used for topiary.

The most popular hedging cypress, *Chamaecyparis lawsoniana* (Lawson cypress) (z6–9), has rather ferny, green foliage and will make good hedges up to 10ft high. It's quick-growing, hardy and tolerates most soils. There are numerous varieties of this

LEFT AND ABOVE: evergreen and deciduous hedges offer differing interest throughout the year. BELOW: small box hedges make edgings to beds.

See also: Garden trees pages 127–129; Shrubs for year-round interest pages 132–135

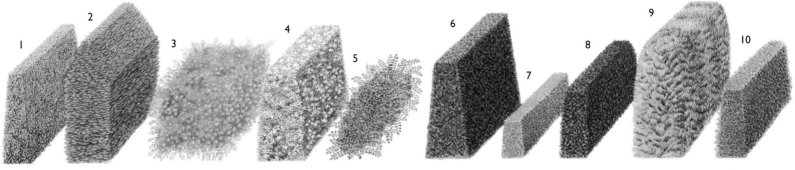

1 *Ligustrum ovalifolium*
2 *Fagus sylvatica*
3 *Rosa rugosa*
4 *Crataegus monogyma*
5 *Berberis thunbergii*
6 *Taxus baccata*
7 *Buxus sempervirens*
8 *Ilex aquifolium*
9 *Thuja occidentalis*
10 *Lonicera nitida*

ABOVE: evergreen and deciduous hedges after eight years' growth.

cypress, some with lighter green foliage, some blue-green and some golden, all suitable for hedges either by themselves or in mixtures. Leyland cypress, x *Cupressocyparis leylandii* (z6–9), resembles Lawson cypress but grows almost twice as fast. *Thuja plicata* (z6–8) and *T. occidentalis* (z3–8) grow well in heavy soils and may be treated as for Lawson cypress.

Yew (*Taxus*) (z6–7) is available in dark green and gold-leaved varieties which may be planted separately or in a mixture. It's slow-growing and so does not need frequent clipping, is very durable and will grow in most conditions including both chalky and limy soils.

Deciduous hedges

THESE ARE hedges made of shrubs that do not retain their leaves all the year. Their appearance changes with the seasons and this can add interest to the garden.

Beech (*Fagus sylvatica)* (z4–7) is the most popular deciduous garden hedge. It grows rapidly, has such strong stems that it can be used to make a tall yet narrow hedge, and, when trimmed, retains its reddish-brown dead leaves throughout the winter. Beech grows in all well-drained soils, and especially well in chalky and limy soils. For a tapestry effect, copper and purple beech may be mixed with green-leaved beech.

Hornbeam (*Carpinus betulus*) (z5–9) closely resembles beech and is better in clay and other wet soils. Plant in the same manner as beech.

Prunus x *cistena* (z4–8) is a purple-leaved plum which makes an excellent small hedge of up to about 4ft high. Hawthorn (*Crataegus monogyna*) (z5–7) makes a strong outer barrier and is very cheap.

ORNAMENTAL SHRUB HEDGES

Many flowering or fruiting shrubs make excellent informal hedges. The shrub rose, *Rosa rugosa* (z3–8), grows quickly to make a dense, prickly hedge. Bright red hips follow the fragrant flowers. *Berberis darwinii* is neat, evergreen and prickly and has orange flowers in late spring; *B. x stenophylla* is yellow-flowered and less tidy. *Cotoneaster simonsii* is deciduous and has scarlet berries in autumn and winter; *C. henryanus* is evergreen, scarlet-berried, looser in habit. Laurustinus (*Viburnum tinus*) is evergreen, with pink and white flowers.

Small-leaved evergreens

Lonicera is the most popular small-leaved, fully evergreen hedge shrub. Two kinds are commonly used, *Lonicera nitida* (z7–9) with very slender stems and little round leaves and *L. nitida* "Yunnan" (z7–9) with stiffer stems. Both thrive in most soils and situations and will make good hedges up to 5ft high.

POPULAR HEDGING PLANTS

Buxus sempervirens—common box (z6–9)

Crataegus monogyna—hawthorn (z5–7)

Fagus sylvatica—common beech (z4–7)

Ilex aquifolium—holly (z7–9)

Taxus baccata—yew (z6–7)

Box (*Buxus sempervirens*) (z6–9) also has small, round, fully-evergreen leaves. It is much favored for topiary specimens. "Handsworthiensis" is best for hedges up to 8ft high and for topiary; "Suffruticosa" is most suitable for low box edgings to beds.

Privet *Ligustrum ovalifolium* (z6–10) is only fully evergreen in mild winters. The best varieties are "Oval-leaf," which is all green, and "Aureum" which has bright yellow leaves and is slow-growing. Both will grow practically anywhere and are excellent for hedges 4–8ft high.

Large-leaved evergreens

Common laurel (*Prunus laurocerasus*) (z7–9) has large, shining, dark green leaves, will grow well in most soils in full sun or dense shade and is excellent for large, broad hedges. Portugal laurel (*Prunus lusitanica*) (z7–9) has smaller, darker green leaves and is also excellent for a big, thick hedge. Neither is recommended for small backyards.

Aucuba has large, light-green leaves, heavily spotted with yellow in the most popular species, *Aucuba japonica* (z7–10), sometimes called spotted laurel. It will grow anywhere, succeeding especially well in the shade even in grimy industrial surroundings, and is excellent for large hedges.

Holly (*Ilex*) (z7–9) makes a dense, impenetrable hedge. There are dark green-leaved, golden-variegated and silver-variegated varieties which may be planted separately or in combination. *I. opaca* (American holly) (z5–9) is often used for hedging and comes in many variegated forms. Holly will make good hedges about 5–10ft in height. It is very hardy and long-lived, but rather slow-growing.

See also: Hardiness zones pages 108–109; Climbing and screening plants pages 138–139

SHRUBS FOR YEAR-ROUND INTEREST

Shrubs of all kinds make a year-long contribution to the garden scene. They can be planted on their own, in groups or with herbaceous plants.

LEFT: *Hydrangea quercifolia* gives good value with its long-lasting flowers.

BELOW: shrubs, deciduous and evergreen, can be mixed to provide continuous color and variety in the backyard.

See also: Annuals and biennials pages 146–147; Bedding plants pages 148–149

EVEN THE deciduous kinds of shrub (for example, *Buddleja davidii* and *Hydrangea macrophylla*), which lose their leaves in the fall, have interesting branch patterns. These are sometimes given added attraction by virtue of having a particularly distinctive bark color.

Evergreen shrubs (like *Viburnum tinus* and *Ceanothus impressus*) retain their leaves all winter and then stand out in sharp contrast to the deciduous kinds, which should be taken into account when deciding where to locate them. Evergreens that have leaves variegated with white or cream (*Euonymus fortunei* "Silver Queen") or yellow (*Aucuba japonica*) can be particularly valuable in the winter months because they add a touch of color.

Some shrubs are grown primarily for the beauty of their flowers (*Syringa* x *persica*), some for their berries or other falltime fruits (*Cotoneaster* x *watereri*), some for the color of their foliage (*Cotinus coggyria* "Royal Purple"), and a few combine two or more of these attractions. There is also great variety in height and habit, from completely prostrate shrubs such as some species of cotoneaster, to almost tree-like specimens, such as the lilacs.

LEFT: color and fragrance combine perfectly in syringa (lilac), which thrives in a sunny position.

Using shrubs

SHRUBS ARE commonly grouped either with other shrubs or with herbaceous plants and annuals, but some kinds look their best planted as isolated specimens and some can be trained against walls. *Magnolia stellata* is an excellent example of the former type and pyracantha, Japanese quince (*Chaenomeles japonica*), and ceanothus all do well against walls, where their stiff branches may provide support for genuine climbers, such as the less rampant varieties of clematis.

Most shrubs take several years to attain their full size. In the meantime, temporary plants, such as dahlias, annuals and herbaceous perennials, can be used to fill the space until the shrubs require it all.

LEFT: there are many excellent reasons for choosing shrubs: for their flowers, their berries and—perhaps most of all—for the beauty of their foliage.

FAVORITE SHRUBS
Abelia x *grandiflora* (z6–9)
This shrub has arching branches of pointed, deep green leaves and small, very fragrant pink-tinged, white flowers. This is a useful shrub since it flowers well into the fall when little else is of interest. "Goldsport" is a yellow-variegated form.
Buddleja davidii—
Butterfly bush (z5–8)
A favorite plant for attracting butterflies, buddlejas have long, conical spikes of flowers ranging in color from deep purple ("Black Knight") to mauve ("Empire Blue") and white ("Peace").

Chaenomeles speciosa—
Ornamental quince (z5–9)
This colorful shrub produces bright vermilion-colored flowers in early spring, sometimes followed by yellow fruits in the fall. "Nivalis" has white flowers, "Moerloesii" has pink and white flowers, while "Simonii" has semi-double crimson flowers, which are ideal against walls.
Ceanothus impressus (z8–10)
This evergreen bush produces clusters of beautiful deep blue flowers from late spring right through to fall.

See also: Hardiness zones pages 108–109; Colorful perennials pages 142–145

Cornus alba—RED-BARKED DOGWOOD (z2–8) The young shoots are bright red in winter, while the dark green leaves turn vivid shades of orange and red in the fall. Creamy-white, star-shaped flowers are produced in spring. "Elegantissima" has white-edged, gray-green leaves; "Spaethii" has yellow-edged, green leaves.

Cotinus coggygria—SMOKE TREE (z5–9) This neatly mounded shrub has rounded or oval leaves which turn red or yellow in the fall, and plumes of pale grayish-brown flowers.

"Royal Purple" has purple leaves and pink flowers.

Cotoneaster frigidus (z7–8) Cotoneasters are grown primarily for their red falltime berries, but they are also fine evergreens. They are very hardy.

Cytisus* x *praecox— WARMINSTER BROOM (z6–9) In mid-spring this broom is covered in a cascade of yellow flowers.

Daphne odora (z7–9) Daphnes are popular plants, known for their rich heady perfume and for their beautiful pink, lilac and white flowers.

LEFT: viburnum is a hardy deciduous and evergreen shrub. Some varieties of viburnum have a pronounced fragrance.

BELOW: in summer cytisus is a brilliant display of yellow, with other varieties yellow/red and white.

ABOVE: striking an unusual blue note in the garden.

See also: Hardiness zones pages 108–109; Climbing and screening plants pages 138–139

CAMELLIAS (Z7–9)

These evergreen shrubs are grouped according to flower type: single, semi-double, anemone-form, peony-form, rose-form, formal double, and irregular double. These are produced above glossy green leaves. *C. japonica* "Alba" has single white flowers with yellow centers; *C. j.* "Rubescens Major" is a formal double with deep pink flowers; *C. j.* "Mathotiana" has formal double red-pink flowers, *C* x *williamsii* "Donation" is a semi-double with mid-pink flowers; *C.* x *w.* "Clarrie Fawcett" has pale pink, semi-double flowers; and "Anticipation," a peony type, has dark-pink flowers (pictured below).

ABOVE: yellow-centered *Camellia japonica* "Alba."

Kerria japonica (Z5–9)
This graceful shrub has golden-yellow flowers on green shoots.

Magnolia stellata (Z5–9)
The sweetly scented flowers of this magnolia are white, star-shaped and many-petaled. The leaves are narrow and deep green.

Syringa vulgaris (Z3–8)
Lilacs have trusses of highly scented flowers, which can be white, cream, purple, mauve, or pink.

Viburnum* x *burkwoodii (Z4–8)
This shrub produces fragrant pink then white flowers above glossy, dark-green leaves. "Park Farm Hybrid" is very fragrant, with dark-pink buds.

ABOVE LEFT: pale-pink *Camellia* "Clarrie Fawcett."
LEFT: red peony-flowered *Camellia* "Anticipation."

See also: Hardiness zones pages 108–109; Location pages 110–111

Rhododendrons

At the height of their flowering season in early and mid-summer, rhododendrons are the most spectacular of all flowering shrubs.

Hardy hybrids

FOR SHEER display none surpasses the group of varieties known as hardy hybrids. These are also the easiest to grow, for, as their name implies, they are quite hardy and will thrive in either sun or shade and in almost any soil that is not chalky or limy. If chalk or lime is present, they can be grown in specially prepared beds of lime-free loam and peat and they will benefit from an annual spring feeding with iron and manganese sequestrols.

All hardy hybrid rhododendrons are evergreen and make dome-shaped shrubs eventually 6–10ft high and as much across. Pruning is not necessary, but overgrown bushes can be cut back in spring, one year's flowers being sacrificed.

Other varieties

In addition to the hardy hybrid rhododendrons there are a great many other kinds which are excellent garden shrubs, all evergreen and all disliking chalk or lime. They succeed best in loamy or peaty soils and though some will grow in full sun most prefer a partially shaded place. Many are first-class shrubs for planting in thin woodland.

LEFT: "Elizabeth"—a bright red and highly recommended variety.
BELOW: "Pink Pearl," which has rosy pink blooms.

RECOMMENDED HARDY HYBRIDS

- "Betty Wormald"—deep pink (z7–8)
- "Britannia"—scarlet (z7–8)
- "Cynthia"—rose red (z7–8)
- "Doncaster"—deep red (z7–8)
- "Fastuosum Flore Pleno"—mauve; double flowers (z5–8)
- "Gomer Waterer"—blush white and gold (z7–8)
- "Loder's White"—pure white (z7–8)
- "Mother of Pearl"—blush turning white (z7–8)
- "Mrs Furnival"—rose and maroon (z7–8)
- "Pink Pearl"—rose pink (z6–9)
- "Purple Splendor"—deep purple (z6–8)
- "Sappho"—white and maroon (z7–8)

Azaleas

AZALEAS ARE deciduous rhododendrons and their hybrids. The name is also given to a range of compact evergreen shrubs. They are prized for their vibrant colors in late spring and for their fine foliage.

Deciduous azaleas flower in early and mid-summer. They are immensely showy with good-sized flowers in fine clusters and a wonderful color range, including yellow, orange, pink, scarlet, crimson, and many intermediate shades. The flowers of some varieties are very fragrant. In some varieties, the leaves turn copper and crimson before dropping in the fall. *Mollis* varieties have larger and earlier flowers than the Ghent varieties.

The evergreen azaleas are low, densely branched spreading shrubs with neat leaves and small to medium-sized flowers, very freely produced in early and mid-summer. Their color range is from white to crimson, but with none of the yellow shades that characterize the taller, more open-branched deciduous azaleas, and with greater emphasis on pinks, carmine and scarlet. They are among the most showy of all shrubs when in flower and, being evergreen, give the garden a well-furnished appearance even in winter.

Some good varieties are: "Addy Wery" (vermillion); "Benegirl" (deep magenta); "Christmas Cheer" (crimson); "Hinomayo" (pink); "Hinodegirl" (carmine); "Malvaticum" (mauve); "Orange Beauty" (orange); "Leonora" (lemon); and "Palestrina" (white).

OTHER RECOMMENDED VARIETIES

- *R. augustinii* (z7–8)—light blue
- "Blue Diamond" (z6–8)—lavender blue
- *R. cinnabarinum* (z7–8—orange-red; hanging tubular flowers)
- "Dairymaid" (z7–8)—cream and red
- "Electra" (z7–8)—violet blue
- "Elizabeth" (z7–8)—bright red
- *R. impeditum* (z6–8)—deep blue
- "Lady Chamberlain" (z7–8)—red and orange hanging; tubular flowers
- "Loderi" (z7–8)—white to pale pink; very large, fragrant flowers
- "May Day" (z7–8)—scarlet
- "Naomi" (z7–8)—various shades of lilac pink and greenish yellow
- *R. racemosum* (z6–8)—small rose-pink flowers
- "Temple Belle" (z7–8)—pink flowers; bell-shaped
- *R. williamsianum* (z7–8)—pale pink flowers; bell-shaped
- "Yellow Hammer" (z7–8)—yellow

ABOVE: azaleas come in striking colors such as this luscious "Pucella."

LEFT: the lovely "Hinodegirl," like all rhodoendrons, hates lime or chalk soil.

CLIMBING AND SCREENING PLANTS

Climbers fulfil an essential part in the furnishing of a well-organized garden and can even play a dominant role in determining its character. It is quite possible, even in the very limited space of a small city yard, to create an air of jungle-like profusion by the lavish use of some vigorous climbing plants.

BELOW LEFT: *Lonicera americana* is an excellent, vigorous, sweet-smelling honeysuckle.
LEFT: the hanging blue trails of wisteria can completely cover a house front.

BELOW: candy-striped clematis, "Nelly Moser," festooned on a trellis.

Different types of climber

CLIMBERS MAY be shrubby, with more or less permanent woody stems, as in honeysuckle (*Lonicera*), roses and wisteria; they may be herbaceous perennials with soft stems dying to ground level each winter, as in the everlasting pea (*Lathyrus grandiflorus*); or they may be annuals, completing their growth in one season and then dying, as in nasturtiums (*Tropaeolum*) and sweet pea (*Lathyrus odoratus*).

Some kinds, such as honeysuckle, twine themselves around anything available, even quite large objects such as trunks of trees. Others, such as

See also: Shrubs for year-round interest pages 132–135

clematis and sweet pea, climb by tendrils which cling most readily to string, wire or trelliswork. Yet others, such as ivy (*Hedera*) and ampelopsis, will attach themselves securely to walls and other smooth surfaces by means of aerial roots or adhesive disks. Roses and various brambles (*Rubus*) sprawl through other plants and gain some support from their thorns.

Choosing plants

CLIMBING FOLIAGE is particularly useful for clothing unsightly buildings and blending them into the backyard scene. Types of ivy (*Hedera*, z6–9), vines (*Vitis*, z4–9), and species of *Parthenocissus* will all quickly grow and cover the building or wall they are grown up. Virginia creeper, *Parthenocissus quinquefolia* (z4–9), and Boston ivy, *P. tricuspidata* (z5–9) have the added advantage of stunning crimson foliage in the fall, as does *Vitis coignetiae* (z5–9), aptly named the crimson glory vine.

Other recommended foliage climbers include *Actinidia kolomikta* (z4–9), with its startling pink- and white-tipped leaves. It also produces cup-shaped, white flowers in summer which look good against walls.

For a spectacular show, the passionflower *Passiflora caerulea* (z8–10) produces truly exotic-looking flowers consisting of white, sometimes pink-flushed, outer petals and a circle of fringed inner petals which are white coloring to pale blue or purple at the tips.

The center of each flower is surrounded by a band of dark blue or purple. *Fremontodendron californicum* (z8–10) is another spectacular climber with bright yellow, saucer-shaped flowers from late spring to mid-fall. It is also evergreen. Also yellow, *Laburnum* x *watereri* "Vossii" (z6–8) produces long, drooping panicles of deep yellow, pea-like flowers in early summer. It can be trained over an arch or arbor to create a dense tunnel of shimmering color.

There are many scented climbers to choose from, perfect for warm alfresco evenings. Wisterias (z4–10) have beautiful perfumed, pale mauve or white flowers in

long, hanging panicles in early summer, and the jasmine *Jasminum officinale* (z9–10) produces clusters of very fragrant, pink-tinged white flowers from summer to fall. Another favorite, honeysuckle, *Lonicera* (z4–10), produces delicately scented clusters of flowers. These range in color from yellow and orange through to white and pink.

Training wall plants

SHRUBS SUCH AS firethorn (*Pyracantha*), *Hydrangea anomala* ssp. *petiolaris*, ceanothus, Japanese quince (*Chaenomeles japonica*), and fishbone cotoneaster (*Cotoneaster horizontalis*) can readily be trained against walls and, by reason of their stiff stems, are almost self-supporting. All the same, trellis or wires can greatly facilitate the training of such plants, since young growths have a natural tendency to grow forward away from the wall or fence and they can then be drawn back toward it. All supports should be fixed 1in from the wall so that the growth, tendrils and ties can go round them.

BELOW LEFT: climbing hydrangeas are slow starters but then become very vigorous.
ABOVE LEFT: *Ceanothus purpurens*—"Ray Hartman" variety—seen here in lustrous blue bloom.
LEFT: *Parthenocissus*—the popular Virginia creeper, seen in so many gardens.

ASPECT

When choosing climbers for planting against houses or high walls, the direction that they will face must be considered since climbers on shaded walls will get little direct sunshine; those on some sunny walls may get too much; and those on walls with sun for part of the day may be exposed to cold winds. The problem hardly arises with fences, since plants quickly rise above them. The soil close to house walls can be dry, and until climbers become established they may need regular watering.

See also: Hardiness zones pages 108–109; Garden trees pages 127–129; Hedges pages 130–131

Clematis

Clematis are among the most valuable of all garden climbers. This is because there are a great many varieties, differing in vigor of growth, time of flowering and the size and color of their blooms. Thanks to the enormous choice, something can be selected for almost every possible purpose. Clematis may be broadly divided into small- and large-flowering kinds.

ABOVE: a popular choice: the striped, pale-pink "Nelly Moser."

BELOW: the magnificent purple of the Jackmanii group of clematis.

Small-flowered types

Of the small-flowered species *Clematis armandii* (z7–9) is one of the first to flower, opening its clusters of small white flowers in mid-spring and continuing throughout late spring. The leaves are evergreen.

Clematis alpina (z6–9) and *C. macropetala* (z6–9) both have little nodding bell-shaped blue or soft mauve-pink flowers in mid- and late spring.

Clematis montana (z6–9) has masses of small white or pink flowers in early summer. It is one of the most vigorous of all clematis, but can be kept in check by shortening side growths in the early fall.

Clematis viticella (z5–9) has medium-sized, purple or red flowers in late summer and early fall. There are several varieties of it, all very showy.

Clematis tangutica (z6–9) and *C. orientalis* (z6–9) have small yellow flowers from early to late fall.

Large-flowered types

The large-flowered clematis are divided into several groups according to their parentage. These groups are Florida, flowering mainly in early and mid-summer; Jackmanii, flowering mainly in late summer and early fall; Lanuginosa, flowering at different times between mid-summer and the early fall; Patens, flowering mainly in early to mid-summer; Texensis, flowering mainly from late summer to mid-fall and Viticella, also flowering mainly from late summer to mid-fall.

ABOVE RIGHT: the massed white flowers of *Clematis montana*—vigorous and easy to grow.
RIGHT: purple, pink, mauve and white are the most familiar colors, but there are also some brilliant carmine—"Ville de Lyon."

COLORFUL PERENNIALS

Hardy perennials are very valuable in the garden and play a major role, as most of them are relatively cheap, grow quickly, and can readily be increased in several ways, including by seed, division, or cuttings. Most of them, like trees and shrubs, live for many years. In addition, most of them, unlike trees and shrubs, are herbaceous as they have soft stems which die down in the fall and grow again the following spring. A number of them have evergreen leaves, and one or two grow in the winter and die down in the summer. Not all herbaceous perennials are in fact hardy, but here we are concerned only with those that are.

Using perennials

Herbaceous perennials may be used in a variety of ways in the backyard. Where space permits, whole borders or beds may be devoted to them or they can be used with shrubs, annuals or bedding plants, or as isolated plants or groups of plants. An open, sunny position is best for beds or borders devoted exclusively to herbaceous perennials since this will suit the majority, but there is no shortage of kinds that will grow in shade that is not too dense.

Most herbaceous plants flower for three or four weeks each year, so if a bed or border devoted exclusively to them is to remain interesting, plants with differing flowering periods must be chosen and placed with regard for their color, height and flowering time. As a rule they are planted in irregular groups of a variety, with the taller kinds at the back of a border or in the middle, and the shorter ones in front or around the edge. It is better to make individual groups long and narrow rather than broad since they will be less conspicuous when not in bloom.

BEST PERENNIALS

Acanthus spinosus
(Bear's breeches) (z5–9)
This is a tall, stately perennial, as popular for its foliage as for its summer flowers. The arching leaves are deeply cut with pointed ends, while the flowers above the leaves are pale mauve and white.

Achillea filipendulina
"Gold Plate" (z4–8)
For a splash of summer color, include a clump of this cheerful plant in your border. It has bright golden-yellow flowers above fern-like leaves.

Anemone x *hybrida*
"Honorine Jobert" (z6–8)
A good choice for early fall interest, this anemone produces simple, single white flowers with yellow centers from summer until fall. The dark-green leaves are deeply divided. There are forms with single, semi-double and double flowers; "Bressingham Glow" has semi-double, pinky-purple flowers.

Aster x *frikartii* "Mönch" (z5–9)
This is one of the best-loved fall-flowering perennials and lasts well into the late fall. Its daisy-like flowers are mauve-blue in color and scented.

Astilbe x *arendsii* (z5–8)
This has feathery plumes of delicate flowers in summer and finely cut,

fern-like leaves. The green leaves have a bronze tinge to them. There are many forms to choose from, including "Bridal Veil" (white), "Venus" (soft pink), "Federsee" (salmon pink) and "Fanal" (a deep, rich crimson).

Delphinium Pacific Hybrids (z2–9)
These familiar perennials are the mainstay of many summer borders. They have spires of flowers which range in color from white and pale blue to deep blue and purple.

Euphorbia polychroma (z5–9)
Good for spring interest, this plant has bright acid-green flowers produced above bright green leaves in spring. The whole plant forms pleasing cushions of bright color.

Hosta sieboldiana elegans
(plantain lily)
(z4–9)
An excellent foliage plant, this hosta has huge, heavily veined leaves. These come in a variety of colors, from deep blue-green to acid green-yellow, including white- and yellow-variegated ones.

ABOVE LEFT: Oriental poppies love sunny positions. The fact that these vivid flowers are so short-lived makes them all the more valuable.
BELOW: peony blooms are big and showy. They come in a range of colors, from the purest white to deep red.

See also: Hardiness zones pages 108–109; Annuals and biennials pages 146–147

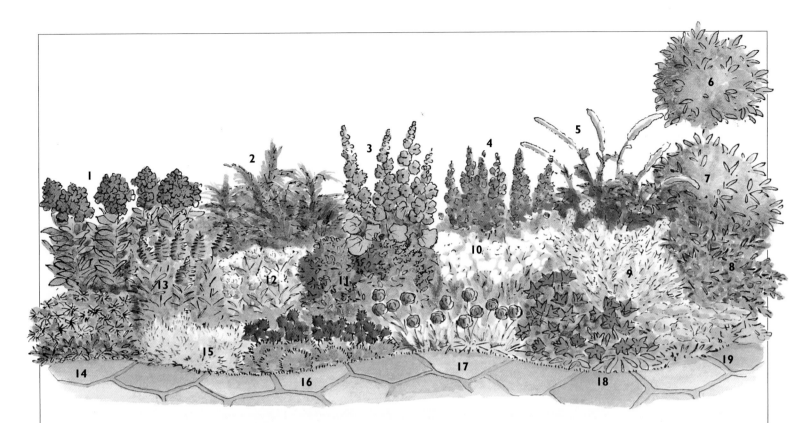

HERBACEOUS PERENNIALS AND EVERGREENS FOR A MIXED BORDER

This planting will suit any sunny border with a sheltered yet fairly open aspect and light, well-drained, slightly alkaline soil. The herbaceous plants may die down in winter, but the evergreens provide winter interest.

1 *Phlox* "Sandringham" (z4–8)
Perennial; cyclamen-pink flowers are produced from mid- to late summer.

2 *Foeniculum vulgare* "Purpureum" purple fennel (z4–8)
Perennial; this has feathery, dark purple fronds and umbels of yellow flowers in summer.

3 *Alcea rosea* cultivars (syn. *Althaea rosea*) hollyhock (z5–9)
Perennial; the upright spikes of funnel-shaped flowers are borne in summer and are cream, pink, apricot or red, single or double.

4 *Sidalcea* "Rose Queen" (z5–8)
Perennial; silky-pink, mallow-shaped flowers are produced from mid-summer onward.

5 *Cimicifuga simplex* "Brunette" (syn. *ramosa* "Brunette") bugbane (z4–8)
Perennial; this has deep purple leaves with white cats'-tail-like flower heads in late summer.

6 *Prunus* x *sargentii* sargent cherry (z5–8)
Deciduous tree; the leaves are coppery-red fading to green for summer, coloring well for the fall. The single, pink flowers are borne in the spring.

7 *Elaeagnus* x *ebbingei* (z7–9)
Evergreen shrub; the foliage is grayish-green in color.

8 *Abelia* x *grandiflora* (z6–9)
Semi-evergreen shrub; the leaves are green, tinged red, and the flowers are pink from late summer through to early fall.

9 *Helichrysum italicum serotinum* (syn. *H. angustifolium*) curry plant (z8–10)
Semi-evergreen shrub; this has silvery, aromatic foliage and yellow flowers are borne in summer.

10 *Achillea ptarmica* "The Pearl," bachelor's buttons (z4–9)
Perennial; this has bright green leaves and small white buttons of flowers in late summer.

11 *Campanula lactiflora* bellflower (z4–8)
Perennial; the lavender-blue flowers are produced in mid-summer.

12 *Anaphalis triplinervis* pearl everlasting (z4–9)
Semi-evergreen perennial; this has grayish-white leaves and white, papery flowers which are borne in late summer.

13 *Physostegia virginiana* "Bouquet Rose" obedient plant (z4–8)
Perennial; the foliage is bright green and pink, tubular flowers appear in the late summer.

14 *Aster thomsonii* "Nanus" Michaelmas daisy (z5–8)
Perennial; the foliage is gray-green and lavender-blue flowers appear from summer to the fall.

15 *Artemisia pontica* Roman wormwood (z4–8)
Perennial; this has feathery, silver-gray and aromatic foliage.

16 *Armeria maritima* "Ruby Glow" sea pink, thrift (z4–7)
Evergreen perennial; evergreen foliage forms clumps of pompom flowers, from mid-summer right through to the fall, which are small and deep pink.

17 *Dianthus* "Doris" garden pink (z4–8)
Semi-evergreen perennial; this has semi-evergreen, grass-like, gray leaves and pink scented flowers which are prominent from mid-summer onward.

18 *Platycodon grandiflorus mariesii* (z4–9)
Perennial; the deep-blue and cup-shaped flowers are produced in late summer.

19 *Solidago* "Queenie" (syn. *S.* "Golden Thumb") dwarf golden-rod (z4–9)
Perennial; plumes of yellow flowers are produced in late summer.

See also: Bedding plants pages 148–149

Kniphofia "Little Maid"
(red hot poker) (z5–9)
Useful for height and color
in the border, the red hot
poker has spikes of bright
red and yellow flowers in
summer. "Little Maid" is
one of the more delicate
types, with pale yellow
flowers. There are many
colors to choose from,
including deep-red to
peachy orange and golden
yellow. All these plants
boast border color.

BELOW: *Phlox paniculata*,
suitable for sunny or
partially shaded beds.

LEFT: the spectacular
Oriental poppy—as well as
the traditional bright
scarlet, it also comes in
pink or white.

papery, brightly colored
petals. These appear from
late spring to mid-summer.
They come in a range of
colors, from pure white and
pale yellow to pale pink,
deep pink and crimson red,
with single, semi-double,
double or anemone-form
flowers.

Papaver orientale
(Oriental poppy) (z4–9)
For a truly spectacular early
summer display, this poppy
has large flowers of papery
petals. These range in color
from bright scarlet ("Marcus
Perry"), and pink ("Mrs
Perry") to grayish-white
("Perry's White"). The hairy
leaves are dissected.

Penstemon
"Snowstorm" (z5–8)
There are many types of
penstemon ranging in
flower color from deep red
to white, with several shades
of blue. They flower from
early to late summer,
sometimes into the fall.
"Snowstorm" is white.

Phlox paniculata
hybrids (z4–8)
Phlox have very colorful
flowers produced in late
summer, ranging from
white and orange to pink,
purple and lilac.

Salvia x *superba*
(sage) (z5–9)
This ornamental sage has
deep violet and crimson
flowers in summer, which
are held on spikes above
oval, dull green leaves. "May
Night" has violet-purple
flowers.

Leucanthemum maximum
(Shasta daisy) (z4–8)
This reliable perennial has
daisy-like flowers in the
fall, in colors ranging from
pale yellow ("Cobham
Gold"), right through to
white ("Aglaia") and pink
("Talbot Jo").

Liatris spicata (z4–9)
This plant has leafy stems
topped with bottlebrush
flowers in summer:
"Kobold" is rosy-mauve,
and "Alba" white.

Nepeta x *faassenii*
(catmint) (z4–8)
This is a good scented
choice for the border. The
soft foliage is grayish-green
in color, and the flower
spikes are covered with
purple-blue flowers in late
spring and early summer.

Paeonia (peony) species
and cultivars (z4–8)
There are many types of
peony, all prized for their
luscious, droopy, glove-
shaped flowers made up of

MIXING PERENNIALS

These three plants have been carefully chosen for
their complementary coloring, shape, texture and
height. The grouping is best in summer, when the
hemerocallis is in full flower, but fall interest is
created by the eryngium and salvia.

Hemerocallis "Pink   *Eryngium* x   *Salvia* x *superba*
Damask" (z4-9)   *oliverianum* (z5-8)   (z5-9)

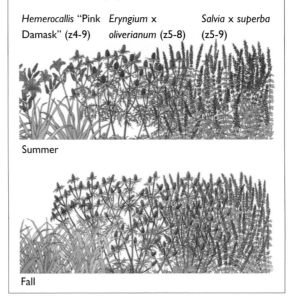

Summer

Fall

See also: Shrubs for year-round interest pages 132–135

Sedum

"Autumn Joy" (z4–9)
This delightful perennial is
a must for any planting
scheme. The attractive
fleshy leaves are grayish-
green in color and provide
spring interest, while the
flat, saucer-shaped flower
heads or unopened green
flowers of the sedum
provide summer interest.
Toward late summer, these
open out into bright pink
flowers to create an eye-
catching patch of color in
the garden. By fall, they
have turned a deep
coppery-red.

LEFT: border species of
penstemons are tall and
graceful and combine well
with deep-blue eryngiums.

LEFT: peonies have
handsome, showy blooms
of many petals in varieties
ranging from deep red to
white flushed with pink.
ABOVE: the tubular
blooms of penstemons
are delightful in bicolors.
They have a particularly
long flowering season.

See also: Hardiness zones pages 108–109; Bulbs pages 152–153

ANNUALS AND BIENNIALS

Annuals are plants with a short life but a merry one. In the space of a few months they grow, flower and die, leaving the ground free for further cultivation, if necessary, and for other plants. Biennials are plants which must be renewed annually from seed, since they die after they have flowered and set seed. In this they resemble annuals, but biennials take over a year to complete their cycle of growth. Seed sown one year will produce plants that will flower the next year, ripen their seed, and die before the second winter.

Annuals

THESE PLANTS are among the cheapest flowers to grow and the quickest to give a return. They are invaluable for furnishing new plots before more permanent plants have been put in or have become sufficiently established to require all the space. They are also excellent for filling any vacant spaces that may occur in the flower beds.

There are many different kinds of annuals and innumerable varieties of some of the most popular ones, such as marigolds and petunias. They vary greatly in height and habit as well as in the color and form of their flowers. Some sprawl over the ground and make colorful flower carpets beneath taller plants. Some are bushy, some erect, and a few, such as the sweet pea (*Lathyrus odoratus*), the canary creeper (*Tropaeolum peregrinum*), the nasturtium (*Tropaeolum majus*), and the morning glory (*Ipomoea hederacea*), are climbers. There are also annuals, such as mignonette (*Reseda*), stocks (*Matthiola*) and the tobacco plant (*Nicotiana*) with sweetly scented flowers.

TOP LEFT: speckled blooms of *Digitalis* (foxgloves).
CENTER: zinnias—a riot of color.
LEFT: *Dianthus barbatus* (sweet Williams).

See also: Colorful perennials pages 142–145

Biennials

MANY BIENNIALS flower in early and mid-summer, thus usefully filling an awkward gap that can occur between the spring and summer flowers. Like annuals, they are temporary plants which should be pulled up and put on the compost pile when they have finished flowering. Also, as with annuals, though it's easy enough to save seed of most kinds it is usually impossible to prevent cross-fertilization of different varieties, as a result of which home-saved seed produces only a mongrel population. The distinction between annuals, biennials and herbaceous perennials is not always clear-cut since sometimes varieties of one group can be treated as if they belonged to one of the other groups; hollyhocks (*Alcea*), for example, can be grown as annuals, biennials or short-lived perennials. However, to be sure of a regular succession of biennials it is necessary to sow seed every year at the correct season.

LEFT: multi-colored annuals and biennials. BELOW: *Tagetes* or marigolds—bright, dainty, easy to grow in many different forms.

Salvia splendens (A)
This annual has bright flowers ranging in color from scarlet and salmon pink to white produced in summer and early fall.
Tagetes (marigold) (A)
There are many types of marigold: *erecta* (African marigold) and *patula* (French marigold) being very popular. They produce

FAVORITE ANNUALS AND BIENNIALS

Antirrhinum majus (snapdragon) (A)
This annual has spikes of tubular or trumpet-shaped flowers in many colors including white, yellow, orange, red, pink and purple, from spring through to summer.
Brachycome iberidifolia (Swan River daisy) (A)
The small, daisy-like flowers are fragrant and come in colors ranging from blue, mauve and purple to pink and white. They flower in summer and early fall.
Chrysanthemum carinatum (A)
In summer, this chrysanthemum produces daisy-like flowers in many color combinations, for example, red with yellow centers or white with red.
Coreopsis "Sunray" (A)
Double, bright yellow, daisy-like flowers are produced in summer.
Cosmos Bright Lights Series (A)
This group of annuals has single or semi-double, yellow, orange or red, daisy-like flowers in summer and early fall.
Dianthus barbatus (sweet William) (B)
In early summer, these plants produce flat heads of brightly colored, bi-colored flowers in shades of pink, red or white, each with a different-colored central zone.
Digitalis purpurea (foxglove) (B)
The tubular flowers in shades of pink, red, purple and white are produced on tall spikes in summer.
Erysimum cheiri (syn. *Cheiranthus cheiri*) (wallflower) (B)
In spring to early summer, this biennial produces heads of fragrant, four-petaled flowers in colors ranging from deep red, yellow, bronze and orange to white.
Helianthus annuus (sunflower) (A)
In summer, the sunflower produces very large, daisy-like flowers with bright yellow petals and brownish-purple centers.
Impatiens Duet Series (busy Lizzie) (A)
From spring to fall, this plant produces many flowers in white, red, pink and orange.
Nicotiana (tobacco plant) (A)
This has trumpet-shaped flowers in late summer, in colors ranging from shades of pink and purple to white. There is also one with lime green, fragrant flowers called "Lime Green."
Lathyrus odoratus (sweet pea) (A)
A climbing plant, the sweet pea has delicate, scented flowers in many colors, from white to mauve, purple, pink and red.
Lavatera trimestris (A)
In summer and early fall, shallow, trumpet-shaped flowers appear.
Nigella damascena (love-in-a-mist) (A)
The flowers of this plant are many-petaled and either blue or white, and are produced in summer amid feathery, bright green leaves.
Petunia (A)
These produce trumpet-shaped flowers, some double, in summer. Colors range from white, purple and pink to striped purple-and-white and pink-and-white.
daisy-like flowers in a range of oranges and yellows in summer and early fall.
Tropaeolum majus (nasturtium) (A)
This trailing plant has trumpet-shaped flowers in bright yellow, orange and red produced in summer through to the fall.
Viola x wittrockiana (pansy) (B)
The velvety blooms come in many colors, from creamy white and yellow to pink and purple, each with a black eye in the center.
Zinnia (A)
Zinnias have large, dahlia-like flowers in summer and the early fall.

See also: Creating a border pages 121–125; Containers pages 174–192

BEDDING PLANTS

Bedding displays can be simple or elaborate according to taste, and the patterns may be given permanent form by being edged with small shrubs such as box or lavender.

BEDDING OUT means putting plants in the garden for a limited period only, while they are able to contribute most to the display, and then replacing them with other plants. Spring bedding plants are those that make their display from early to late spring; summer bedding plants are those that are at their peak from early summer to early fall.

Beds can be filled with a number of plants of differing habits and, usually, mixed colors. Carpeting plants are used as a base planting, with taller plants employed to produce a second or third tier of flowers.

Recommended bedding plants

THE BEGONIAS used in bedding displays are from the semperflorens hybrids (z10), fibrous-rooted perennials grown as half-hardy bedding annuals. This type is particularly suitable for bedding displays because all the plants in the group have a neat habit and continuous flowering. They have a succession of small white, pink, or red flowers and green or bronze, slightly fleshy leaves. "Organdy," with green leaves, and "Coco Mixed," which has bronze foliage, are good varieties to give a contrast of colors.

Dahlias of all kinds can be used for summer bedding, but the most useful and adaptable are the bedding varieties, such as the single-flowered "Coltness Hybrids" and various other strains of dwarf hybrids with their semi-double or double flowers in mixed colors.

Other plants include dwarf varieties of *Impatiens*, such as the "Super Elfin" series (z10). These are available in white, rose, carmine, scarlet, orange, and purple, and in mixtures of these colors. They grow to a height of 9in and make excellent summer bedding plants. Heliotropes are also popular pot plants which are excellent for summer bedding displays. *Heliotropium arborescens* "Marine" (z10) is an excellent variety with violet-purple flowers. It is compact, well branched and grows up to 15in high.

FAR LEFT: a pink-flowered, silver-leaved display of cineraria, impatiens and salvias.
CENTER: the rich colors of begonias and impatiens with campanulas.
LEFT: it is a good idea to draw up a plan of your bedding displays.

See also: Colorful perennials pages 142–145

ABOVE: the variegated leaves are an additional attraction of some pelargonium varieties.

ABOVE RIGHT: a pretty mixture of white pansies with lobelia.

RIGHT: brilliant dahlias brighten the late summer garden.

Pelargoniums
(perennials in z10 although treated as annuals)

THE GERANIUMS used for summer bedding are correctly named pelargoniums.

There are two main types of pelargoniums: zonal-leaved which have round, slightly downy leaves and strong stems, and ivy-leaved which have smooth, angular leaves and weak stems.

Some good bedding zonal pelargoniums are: "Gustav Emich" (double scarlet); "King of Denmark" (semi-double pink); "Maxim Kovalevski" (single vermilion); "Paul Crampel" (single scarlet); "Queen of the Belgians" (double white); and "Vera Dillon" (single magenta).

Good ivy-leaved varieties are: "Abel Carrière" (soft purple); "Galilee" (pink); "Jeanne d'Arc" (white); "Mrs W. A. R. Clifton" (scarlet).

Ornamental-leaved varieties are: "Chelsea Gem" (green and silver); "Crystal Palace Gem" (green and gold); "Mrs Henry Cox" (green, yellow and red).

Foliage

PLANTS WITH silver or gray leaves are useful in summer bedding schemes as a foil to the colors of the flowers.

Calocephalus brownii (z9) is silvery, with wiry stems and narrow leaves. It can be grown as a small column and as a dot plant, or the growing tips can be pinched out frequently, making it into a dwarf, spreading plant suitable for carpet bedding. *Senecio cineraria* (z6–9) is a bushy, fairly hardy perennial with deeply divided silvery-white leaves.

Centaurea cineraria (z4–9) and *C. rutifolia* (z6–9) are similar in appearance. *Senecio repens* (z9) is a creeping plant only a few inches high, with blue-gray leaves, useful for outlining carpet bedding.

Colored foliage can be as useful as silver and gray foliage in diversifying the effects in summer bedding displays. *Kochia scoparia* f. *trichophylla* (z10), for example, is an annual known as summer cypress, because it makes a 2ft column of fine leaves and looks rather like a miniature conifer; the leaves are green at first, turning to purplish-red in late summer. *Abutilon pictum* "Thompsonii" (z8–10) is a shrubby plant with light-green leaves heavily mottled with yellow, and with orange, dropping, trumpet-shaped flowers. Particularly useful as a dot plant, it will quickly grow to a height of up to 3ft and can be used as a background or a centerpiece. *Tanacetum parthenium* "Aureum" (z4–9) is also known as golden feather because it has bright yellow feathery leaves. It is good for carpeting or groundwork.

See also: Hardiness zones pages 108–109; Location pages 110–111; Annuals and biennials pages 146–147

Fuchsias

*Many varieties of fuchsia make excellent summer
bedding plants. They can be grown as bushes or trained as standards,
and they can be raised from cuttings or bought in late spring or early
summer ready for planting out. They are beautiful and decorative flowering
shrubs. They are particularly valuable in pots and hanging baskets.
Their natural colors are purple and carmine-red, although
there are also variants of white, all shades of pink, lilac,
red and crimson. Some are even orange.*

ABOVE: the fuchsia's bell-like flowers.
BELOW: vivid scarlet "Mme Cornelissen."

ABOVE: the upright character of "Lena" makes it an ideal fuchsia for growing as a standard.

BELOW: the small-flowered "Tom Thumb" is an excellent fuchsia to use as an edging plant.

FAVORITE FUCHSIAS

The following are some of the hardiest and best fuchsia species and varieties. All flower from summer well into the fall.

F. "**Alice Hoffman**" (z9)
This compact shrub has bronze-colored foliage and small, semi-double flowers. These have pinky-red tubes and sepals and milky-white, red-veined petals.

F. "**Brutus**" (z9)
The single or semi-double flowers of this vigorous plant are either crimson-red or deep purple.

F. "**Corallina**" (z8–10)
The scarlet and purple flowers of this fuchsia are medium-sized and are freely produced. The foliage has a bronze tint. Growth is arching and spreading.

F. "**Lady Thumb**" (z8–10)
A dwarf, upright shrub, this fuchsia is very bushy and can be used as an edging plant, in a hanging basket or trained against a support. It has small, semi-double flowers: the white petals are pink-veined and the sepals and tubes are reddish-pink.

F. "**Lena**" (z9)
This fuchsia makes a good standard. It has double, pale-pink flowers with pink-flushed purple outer petals.

F. "**Mme Cornelissen**" (z8–10)
This fuchsia has large scarlet flowers, with scarlet-veined, white inner petals. The flowers are small and the growth is strong and upright.

F. **magellanica** *var. gracilis* "Versicolor" (z7–8)
This upright shrub has small flowers. The leaves are gray-green, tinted pink when young and variegated creamy white. This is not as hardy as its green-leaved parent. Both have long, slender, red and violet flowers.

F. "**Mrs Popple**" (z8–10)
In sheltered areas, this upright fuchsia may be grown as a hedge. Large scarlet and violet flowers are profusely produced.

F. "**Riccartonii**" (z8–9)
The small red and purple flowers of this fuchsia are very striking and are produced from mid-summer to mid-fall.

ABOVE: the large scarlet and violet flowers of "Mrs Popple" variety are borne on arching stems.

BELOW: popular for summer bedding plants as well as containers, "Marin Glow" has white sepals and pink petals.

BULBS

Many of the most familiar and attractive flowers in our backyards are produced from bulbous plants, a large and varied group of plants consisting of true bulbs, corms, tubers and rhizomes.

Using bulbs

TULIPS AND hyacinths are particularly useful for spring bedding displays and for cultivation in pots, window-boxes and other containers. Daffodils (*Narcissus*), crocuses and snowdrops (*Galanthus*) are usually planted more informally and may be naturalized in grass, provided it is not mown until their leaves are beginning to ripen and to turn yellow in early summer. Small bulbs such as grape hyacinths (*Muscari*) and scillas are often grown in rock gardens or used to make carpets of spring color beneath taller plants. Because spring-flowering bulbs die down in summer they can be used effectively

ABOVE AND LEFT: tulips, cyclamens, snowdrops, and grape hyacinths are all ideal garden bulbs.

with deciduous shrubs, which are bare of leaves when the bulbs are growing and flowering, or with herbaceous plants, most of which will hardly have started to grow so early in the year.

Winter aconite (*Eranthis*), snowdrops, crocuses, scillas, chinodoxas, muscaris, and daffodils are all particularly recommended for this kind of two-tier planting, as they do not have to be lifted every year but can be left undisturbed for several years until they become overcrowded.

See also: Hardiness zones pages 108–109; Colorful perennials pages 142–145; Fuchsias pages 150–151

TOP BULBS

Crocus (z3–8)
This bulb has funnel-shaped, long-tubed flowers, both plain and striped, in colors including white, yellow and purple.

Cyclamen hederifolium (z5–9)
Pale to deep-pink flowers are produced among ivy-shaped, silvery-green leaves in the fall.

Fritillaria meleagris (snake's head fritillary) (z3–8)
Bell-shaped, checkered flowers appear in spring. These range in color from pinkish-purple to white.

Galanthus nivalis (common snowdrop) (z3–9)
The small white flowers have delicate green markings and appear in spring.

Gladiolus (z9–10)
This produces spikes of funnel-shaped flowers, some double and frilly, in summer. Colors include white, yellow, red and pink.

Hyacinthoides hispanica (Spanish bluebell) (z4–9)
Pendent, bell-shaped blue flowers are produced in spring. Some types have pink or white flowers.

Lilium (lily) (z4–8)
These beautiful summer-flowering bulbs are grown for their fragrant, brightly colored flowers.

Narcissus (daffodil) (z3–9)
The trumpet- or cup-shaped flowers come in a range of colors from cream, through yellow to orange plus mixed colors.

Tulipa (tulip) (z3–8)
These bulbs produce cup-shaped blooms in spring. There are single, double, frayed or striped flowers in a variety of colors.

LEFT: plant crocuses as soon as the corms are available. They look their best in groups in the rock garden, under deciduous trees or in the lawn.

BELOW: in protected corners crocuses will flower very early in the year. They can be white, yellow, purple or striped.

NATURALIZING BULBS

One of the most popular ways of growing bulbs—snowdrops, daffodils and crocuses, in particular—is to naturalize them in drifts so they spread at will. This is usually done in grass, but those bulbs preferring shady woodland conditions can be naturalized in soil under trees and shrubs. It is also possible to establish bulbs beneath a planting of ground cover like scrambling ivies.

• When choosing a grassy site, remember that the grass cannot be cut for up to six weeks after the bulbs have flowered.

• If naturalizing in established grass, choose your bulbs carefully as not all types can compete with turf, especially the more vigorous grasses already growing.

• Aim at creating an area that looks as natural as possible.

• Plant the bulbs at random.

• Either grow a single type or plant a mixture of bulbs to create the effect of an alpine meadow.

• Bulbs can be naturalized in lawns, meadows, around trees and shrubs, or on grassy banks.

BELOW: the essence of the spring garden—drifts of dancing narcissus.

ROCK-GARDEN PLANTS

Most rock-garden plants are relatively small in size and so a considerable variety can be satisfactorily grown in quite a limited space.

THEY ARE immensely varied in character, some being tiny shrubs, some herbaceous plants, others bulbs, corms, or tubers. Though the majority enjoy open sunny places and well-drained soils, suitable rock plants can be found for almost any situation in the garden, including those that are moist and shady. The fact that rock plants have developed from wild plants brought from many different lands accounts for their fascination with collectors, who can grow a wide variety of plants with different origins in a small area.

It is not essential to have a rock garden in order to grow rock-garden plants. Many will grow just as well in ordinary beds, provided the soil is suitable and they are not overrun by larger plants. Dry walls and raised beds are also satisfactory substitutes for rock gardens and may fit more appropriately into the design of small gardens, including even those of formal design.

Yet another possibility is to grow rock-garden plants in pots, pans or other containers. Old stone troughs and sinks are excellent for this purpose provided they have adequate drainage holes through which surplus water can escape. Trough or sink gardens can make beautiful and interesting ornaments for patio gardens and, if each container is restricted to plants with similar requirements, exactly the right kind of soil can be supplied and the best aspect can be chosen.

To carry this system of individual treatment a stage further, a rock-garden plant grown in a pot or pan can have its special soil mixture, can be placed in a frame when normally in its mountain home it would be protected by a deep carpet of snow, and can be brought into a light, airy greenhouse when it is about to flower so that its blooms are not damaged by rain.

Some rock-garden plants prefer acid soil and can be grown most successfully in special peatmoss beds, which have been built in shallow terraces and retained by low walls of peatmoss blocks. A cool, partially shaded position is best and it is usually necessary to mix some coarse sand with the peatmoss filling in order to improve its porosity. Provided the peatmoss beds are built above the surrounding level, lime-hating plants can be grown even in limestone districts.

TOP: aubrieta takes naturally to rocks and walls.
ABOVE: a stone trough can be attractively planted with numerous miniature alpine plants and bulbs.
BELOW: *Phlox douglasii*— popular for its leaves as well as its white flowers.

TOP ROCK-GARDEN PLANTS

Aubrieta (z4–7) is a trailing and mound-forming plant with blue, mauve or purple flowers which appear in spring. Also spring-flowering, *Aurinia saxatilis* (syn. *Alyssum saxatile*) (z4–7) has large spikes of bright yellow flowers. *Viola cornuta* (horned violet) (z5–8) is a delicate-looking plant with pale to deep bluish-purple flowers and *Primula* "Wanda" (z6–8) is a neat, clump-forming plant with crimson-purple flowers. Both flower in spring.

Cerastium tomentosum (z4–7) is a ground-covering rock plant, with silver foliage and star-shaped, white flowers in late spring and early summer. Once this is over, there are many choices for summer flowers, including *Campanula cochlearifolia* (z5–7). This mat-forming plant has tiny white or pale blue bells, while *Dianthus* "Pike's Pink" (z5–8) has fragrant, double pink flowers.

Phlox douglasii (z5–7) produces masses of saucer-shaped, white flowers in summer and is as popular for its leaves as its flowers; *Sempervivum giuseppii* (houseleek) (z5–9) is good for carpeting. The leaves of this plant form mats made of rosettes of leaves and clusters of star-shaped flowers.

See also: Rock gardens pages 100–101; Hardiness zones pages 108–109; Location pages 110–111

THEME PLANTS

There are certain plants that instantly provide a garden with a ready-made theme. If you like the idea of a themed garden, perhaps you should try one of these. The advantage is that you don't actually have to plan very hard—once you've made the initial decision, the plants take over and do the rest for you.

THE MOST obvious theme garden, perhaps, is the herb garden. This not only looks lovely—so fresh and green—but it also smells fragrant and is always a delight to sit near or walk through. Most important of all, it also has a practical use, particularly if you are a keen cook as well as gardener. Develop your interest in herbs and extend your collection to include some of the more unusual ones. Like your gardening, your cooking will soon know no limits.

Water gardens provide the opportunity to experiment with aquatic and moisture-loving plants. As well as those plants that actually grow in water, there are also those that are happiest on the edge near water. Choose from ferns, water lilies, irises, and many more for a dreamy, magical quality.

A rose garden is always a delight which appeals to the romantic side in us all. Roses come in a great many different shapes and colors. They can be standard or climbing, delicate or brash, scented or not. These pages look at the many different types of rose that you can plant to achieve stunning effects. You will not only be impressed—you will also be inspired!

LEFT: an herb garden is one of the easiest and most delightful theme gardens to create.

GARDENING WITH HERBS

A herb can be defined as any type of plant—annual, bulb, perennial, evergreen or shrub—grown for its culinary and medicinal qualities as well as for its aromatic and decorative contribution to the garden.

MOST HERBS thrive in the same conditions, despite their diversity in size, shape and habit. So they can be grouped together in a special herb bed, formal or informal, which will delight all year round.

Variegation is an attribute of many herbs, adding a further visual dimension to these invaluable plants. Golden marjoram makes splendid little tussocks, but is apt to scorch in full sun. Thymes come in both silver- and golden-edged forms. But do not forget the flowering ability of many herbs: chives produce fluffy pink flower heads, borage has deep blue flowers, nasturtiums and marigolds have flowers ranging in color from golden-yellow to dark orange and, of course, lavender has spikes of highly scented purple flowers which are attractive to insects.

A B O V E : many herbs, such as chives, which produce handsome rose-pink flowers, can be grown in a border or rock garden.
R I G H T : versatile, sweet-smelling lavender can be planted to edge a flower border or as a low-growing hedge. Lavender also attracts butterflies.

IDEAS FOR GROWING HERBS

• For an impressive formal feature use symmetrical beds of herbs divided by paths, perhaps in gravel or brick, and edged with chives, box, santolina or lavender.

• Instead of a fullscale herb garden, plant a selection of herbs in an herb wheel.

• Make a truly tiny herb bed by lifting three or four flagstones from a patio for an easy-maintenance herb bed.

• On a still smaller scale, a window-box will hold a surprising amount of herbs.

• Grow some of the more decorative herbs in an ornamental border.

• Herbs such as lavender and thyme can also be used to edge patios or paths, or to enliven areas of paving by planting them in the cracks between the paving.

• Consider using a half-barrel, an old sink or trough, a strawberry pot, a window-box or even a hanging basket.

See also: Garden features pages 92–93

ABOVE: the **attractive pink flower heads of chives.**
RIGHT: **a well-stocked herb garden.**

Making a herb wheel

An attractive and novel way of growing herbs is to construct an herb "wheel" using either brick, which tends to look rather formal, or stone, which is more natural in appearance. The individual compartments between the "spokes" help to confine the more invasive herbs.

First, mark out a circle by hammering in a peg in the center of the site and marking the circumference with a stick and length of string.

Then dig out the soil inside the circle to a depth of about 6in and remove the earth. Tread the surface flat.

Lay a row of bricks or stones on the inside of the circle, keeping the tops level. Cement the bricks or stones. Place a short length of drainage pipe in the middle of the circle and mark out the "spokes" leading from this center to the outside of the wheel. Lay bricks or stones along these lines and cement them in.

Fill the segments with potting compost and gently firm, bringing the level to the top of the edging. Plant the herbs and water them thoroughly.

LEFT: an herb bed can be created in any number of settings. It might be a special feature, as here, enclosed by a hedge with flagstones for accessibility. Equally successful herb beds can be made in old sinks or troughs, strawberry pots, half-barrels, window-boxes and even hanging baskets.

LEFT: an herb "wheel" is an excellent way to display a collection of different herbs. Simply form a circle of bricks, placing a drainage pipe at the center and lay out the spokes with more bricks. Different herbs, especially the more invasive types, are confined to the spaces. Stones can also be used as part of the construction.

See also: Edging page 73; Walls pages 84–87

Ornamental herbs

HERE ARE some favorite herbs that are grown more for their decorative appeal than for culinary reasons.

Lavandula angustifolia (z6–9), commonly known as lavender, is a well-known herb used mostly in the flower garden. It has spikes of purple flowers and small, gray-green leaves, and is highly fragrant.

For a splash of color, the pot marigold, *Calendula officinalis* (annual), is a good rustic-style backyard plant with vivid orange-yellow flowers, each with a dark eye. Tansy, *Tanacetum vulgare* (z3–9), is another favorite plant for rustic-style backyards. It has deeply cut leaves and small yellow flowers held on tall stems.

There are many other colorful ornamental herbs to brighten up the flower garden, including the nasturtium, *Tropaeolum majus* (annual). This has bright heads of scarlet, red, orange and yellow trumpet-shaped flowers and leaves that are rounded in shape. Bergamot, *Monarda didyma* (z4–8), has spectacularly colorful flowers of red, pink, white or purple and the whole plant has a delightful fragrance.

ABOVE: flowers and leaves of peppery-tasting nasturtium are attractive.
LEFT: the red whorls of the delightfully fragrant bergamot are always eye-catching.
BELOW LEFT: vivid orange-yellow *Calendula* (pot marigold) is a firm favorite in rustic-style gardens.

Mostly grown for its foliage, rue, *Ruta graveolens* (z5–9), has blue-green, deeply divided leaves and acid-yellow flowers. Known as the curry plant, *Helichrysum serotinum* syn. *angustifolium* (z8–10) is a bushy plant with attractive, narrow, silvery leaves and clusters of small dull yellow flowers.

Lad's love, *Artemisia abrotanum* (z6–9), is a shrubby plant which bears spherical yellow flowers in panicles, but it is grown mainly for its silky, gray-green, fine foliage. Lovage *Levisticum officinale* (z4–9) is another handsome choice with large but delicate light-green leaves.

Chamomile, *Chamaemelum nobile* (z6–9), has small, daisy-like flowers of white, cream, yellow or orange, and caraway *Carum carvi* (annual) is a graceful plant with flat, lacy heads made up of many tiny white flowers. Chamomile is a good border plant, flowering all summer. Attractive gray-green foliage makes it a popular plant for flower arrangements indoors.

See also: Hardiness zones pages 108–109; Rock-garden plants page 154

Culinary herbs

Allium schoenoprasum (z3–9) Chives
Chives are one of the most important culinary herbs, with a mild onion flavor. The chopped leaves can be used to garnish soups, salads and cooked vegetables, in omelettes or mixed with cream cheese. The narrow grass-like leaves grow in clumps up to 15in high. Pink pompon-shaped flowers appear in summer, pretty enough to qualify chives to be used as edging plants in a rustic-style garden. For the best flavor, however, flower heads should not be allowed to form on the plant.

Propagation and growing: chives may be raised from seed sown in shallow drills in spring and transplanted in early summer, or you can start with young plants and set them out in light, moisture-retentive soil. Water well in dry periods. Every few years, in the

ABOVE: the anise flavor of fennel is strong in both the leaves and the seeds.

fall, divide the clump into several sets and replant them in fresh soil. Chives do well in window-boxes or small pots, which can be kept indoors for a winter supply.

Artemisia dracunculus (z5–9) Tarragon
There are two species of tarragon for the kitchen garden: *A. dracunculus* (French tarragon) is far superior to *A. dracunculoides* (Russian tarragon), which is somewhat lacking in aroma. The sharp pointed leaves can be used in egg and chicken dishes.

Propagation and growing: set out groups of young plants in good, well-drained soil in spring or the fall. Full sun is essential, and it is advisable to feed the plants during the

growing season to achieve a good flavor. Pinch out the growing tips to encourage leaf development. Tarragon is a perennial: cut down the plants in the late fall and cover with straw to protect from frost. Divide and replant every three years in fresh soil, or treat as annuals.

Foeniculum vulgare (z8–10) Fennel
Fennel is both highly decorative, with feathery bluish-green leaves, and very useful in the kitchen. The anise-like flavor is even stronger in the dried seeds than it is in the fresh leaves.

The leaves are best used to accompany fish, vegetables, and salads, while the seeds add flavor to bread or soups. At 7ft high, this herbaceous perennial makes a stately addition to the border.

Propagation and growing: sow seed in late spring, in well-drained, rich soil. If seed is not required, remove the flower stems as they appear. Self-sown seedlings will grow freely if the plants are allowed to flower; if not, propagate them by dividing the parent plants approximately every three years or so. The seeds are ready to harvest when they have turned a gray-green color and have hardened. Cut off the whole flower head and dry slowly indoors.

TOP: chives—a pretty as well as useful edible plant, mixing well with salads and cream cheeses.
ABOVE: there are French and Russian varieties of tarragon—plant the French.

Laurus nobilis (z810) Bay
As a culinary herb, bay is indispensable, whether in a bouquet garni, added to the poaching liquid for fish, in stews and soups or even in creamed rice. An evergreen, its leaves have as much flavor in winter as in summer, a rare quality among herbs.

Propagation and growing: set out your plants in spring on any type of soil. A sunny, sheltered spot is preferable—leaves are easily damaged by sharp winds. Most trees will reach about 12ft in maturity if left alone. Specimens grown in tubs of about 18in in diameter should be pruned to shape during the summer. Propagate from cuttings taken in late summer, or by layering low-growing shoots.

See also: Containers pages 174–179

BELOW: the essential fresh parsley, best sown annually when the weather is warm.

LEFT: thyme, an invaluable aromatic herb, likes a sunny position.

BELOW LEFT: the purple-crimson flowers of the culinary herb, marjoram.

Mentha spp. Mint

The popularity of the mint family is undeniable, but all the mints are to varying degrees invasive, and will eventually take over the herb bed if left unchecked. Confine mint to tubs or boxes. If you want it in the ground, grow it in a submerged bucket with the bottom knocked out, or restrict the roots with slates buried vertically around them. Mint is used with many vegetables, in yogurt as a dressing, with fish and salads, and with fresh fruit. *Mentha spicata* (common mint or spearmint) (z4–9) has pointed leaves; *M. rotundifolia* (apple mint or Bowles' mint) (z4–9) is a round-leaved variety and the cook's favorite. Decorative mints include *M. citrata* (bergamot mint) (z4–9) which has almost heart-shaped lemony leaves and *M. requienni* (z7–9), a prostrate, spreading species with tiny, round, scented leaves.

Propagation and growing: set out rooted runners of this hardy perennial in spring, in rich, moist soil. Water well during the growing season and pinch out the tips to encourage a bushy shape. Plants are easy to raise by division in spring.

Origanum spp. Marjoram

Marjoram belongs to the mint family, and the small, rounded leaves have an aroma like thyme, but sweeter. Primarily a culinary herb, *Origanum majorana* (sweet marjoram) (annual), is the best for flavor and good with meat and stuffings for vegetables. *O. onites* (pot marjoram) (z8) is a hardy perennial with a strong aroma, *O. vulgare* (common or wild marjoram or oregano) (z4–8) is a hardy perennial, and the decorative variety "Aureum" has leaves splashed with gold.

Propagation and growing: treat sweet marjoram as a half-hardy annual. Sow seed under protection in early spring. Set out hardened-off plants in early summer in light but fertile soil in a sunny position. Sweet marjoram is useful for edging herb beds or raised beds of aromatic plants. Perennial species can be increased by cuttings of basal shoots taken in spring.

Petroselinum crispum Parsley (annual)

Parsley is one of the half-dozen most popular herbs and one of the few that good cooks insist on using fresh. It is an essential component of a bouquet garni, and in traditional rustic gardens parsley was often used with alyssum as an edging plant. It attracts bees and is thought to repel greenfly, making it doubly useful.

Propagation and growing: sow seed outdoors in early spring in moist, rich soil. Parsley is notoriously slow to germinate; delay sowing for a few weeks and the warmer temperature will speed things along. Thin the seedlings to 8in. Water well in dry weather and cover with clear plant covers if frost threatens. Later sowings, especially in pots that can be brought indoors, will provide leaves well into the winter. Although biennial, parsley is best grown as an annual and raised from fresh seed each year.

See also: Bedding plants pages 148–149

Rosmarinus officinalis (z7–9) Rosemary
Hardy almost everywhere, *Rosmarinus officinalis* reaches 3–6½ft or more in height, making a dense, semi-erect bush of small, narrow, dark-green leaves which are intensely aromatic. Pretty pale-blue flowers appear in early summer; if you are prepared to forgo them, rosemary can be clipped to make a hedge. Because of its powerful aroma, rosemary should be used sparingly when cooking.

Propagation and growing: set young plants in a dry, sunny spot where they can be left to achieve full height. Cut back mature plants to half their height in the fall to keep the shape neat. Increase by tip cuttings taken in summer. No regular pruning is needed but the shrub should be kept under control.

BELOW LEFT: sage or *Salvia officinalis*—a vigorous, bushy culinary plant also excellent in borders.
LEFT: prized as an herb, rosemary can be clipped to make a hedge.
BELOW: round-leaved apple mint is the favored culinary choice.

Thymus spp. Thyme
Thyme predominates in the kitchen. It is included in bouquets garnis, in stuffings, with vegetables, in omelettes, and on pizzas. Place a sprig underneath a roasting joint or fowl. Dried thyme keeps its flavor well. *Thymus vulgaris* (common thyme) (z6–9) has dark green narrow leaves and a good flavor. *T. v.* "Aureus" is an ornamental golden-leaved form. *T.* x *citriodorus* (lemon-scented thyme) (z6–8) has broader leaves; silver and gold-leaved forms are available. *T. herba-barona* (caraway thyme) (z4–7) is a mat-forming species, not fully hardy.

Propagation and growing: plant in spring in a sunny position in well-drained soil. Thyme is excellent in troughs, as an edging plant and for ground cover. Replace the plants when they become leggy. Propagate by division in spring.

Salvia spp. (z6–9) Sage
The green-leaved garden sage, *Salvia officinalis* is grown primarily for its culinary uses, and has a number of decorative forms equally useful in the kitchen which often feature in scented gardens. All are hardy, evergreen sub-shrubs of attractively bushy habit, reaching about 24in. The slightly bitter oval leaves can be used in any number of dishes, including meat, fish, eggs, or vegetables. They retain their flavor well when dried and in combination with onions are used as a stuffing for roast pork.

Propagation and growing: sow seed in the open in late spring in a sunny position in well-drained soil. Remove flowers as they appear. Trim plants two or three times during the summer; they become leggy after a few years and should be replaced. Propagate from cuttings taken in the early fall.

THE WATER GARDEN

Water can be used in many ways in a garden. It provides a medium in which plants of a special kind—the aquatics—can be grown. It can also be stocked with fish which bring life and movement to the garden. Plants and fish combine well, as the latter benefit from the protection that floating and submerged leaves provide. But if the fish are to be enjoyed to the full, planting must not be too dense or they will be screened almost completely from view. One advantage of having both fish and plants in a pool is that the plants will help keep the water fresh.

Water plants

THERE ARE various types of water plant: water lilies, deep-water aquatics, floating aquatics, submerged plants, marginal plants and bog plants. Water lilies, deep-water aquatics and, to a lesser extent, floating aquatics all provide cover for fish and insects, and also shield the water from sunlight, so helping to keep algae under control. Submerged plants and floating aquatics also play an important role because they feed off the nutrients in the water that algae need in order to live, and in this way they help to reduce their proliferation.

LEFT: aquatic plants are not only decorative but can also control algae and provide oxygen in the pond.

See also: The role of plants pages 112–113

Once you have your quota of functional plants, use marginal and bog plants as decoration. Choose those that suit the design of your pool.

An informal pool should include a variety of plants that have been positioned at random. They should complement the surrounding area to make the feature look as natural as possible. Since the bog area helps merge the pool into the landscape, the bog plants should match groups of nearby plants. For formal pools it is best to select three or five specimen plants and place them in some kind of definite pattern.

Year-round interest

WHEN PLANTING an ornamental pool it is important to take into account the flowering seasons of the ornamentals. Most water lilies are at their peak during the summer months, so try to supplement these with marginal and bog plants that provide spring and falltime interest. Since foliage plants have a longer period of interest than flowering plants, they should form the backbone of your planting.

ALGAE CONTROL

Although a pool should receive plenty of light, direct sunlight will encourage the growth of algae which will turn the water to "pea soup." However, you can counteract this by adding submerged and floating aquatics which consume the nutrients in the water that the algae feed on. You can also starve algae of sunlight by shading the water surface. About one-third of the surface should be covered by water lilies and other deep water aquatics.

RIGHT: *Iris laevigata* looks its best when growing at the water's edge.

LEFT: adding an exotic touch to a garden pond.

PLANTING DEPTHS

It is important to grow each plant in the correct depth of water: grow water lilies, deep-water aquatics and submerged plants in the deeper parts of the pool according to their depth requirements, leaving the shallow areas for marginals and the marshy areas for bog plants.

See also: Annuals and biennials pages 146–147; Bedding plants pages 148–149

Water lilies

WITH THEIR startling flowers and rounded, leafy pads, water lilies, *Nymphaea*, are a familiar sight in most garden pools. They come in a wide array of colors, including white, yellow, pink and red, and there are different types to choose from including single and double; some have star-shaped flowers and some cup-shaped, while others have incurved petals or petals which are papery to touch.

Most water lilies will provide color from early summer until early fall. They do not, however, tolerate moving water. Plant them in planting baskets at the correct water depth.

LEFT: glowing in a sea of green, "James Brydon" is a fine example of a water lily or *Nymphaea*. Water lilies have a long flowering season, are long-lived and require little attention.

ABOVE AND RIGHT: these striking water lilies come in a range of colors, from white to brilliant red.

PINK- AND RED-FLOWERING WATER LILIES

N. **"American Star"** Star-shaped; semi-double; deep pink (z8–10)

N. **"Attraction"** Cup-shaped; semi-double; garnet-red (z5–10)

N. **"Escarboucle"** Cup-shaped; semi-double; deep crimson (z5–10)

N. **"Firecrest"** Star-shaped; semi-double; deep pink (z5–10)

N. **"Froebelii"** Open tulip-shaped; deep blood-red (z5–10)

N. **"James Brydon"** Peony-shaped; crimson (z8–10)

N. **"Rose Arey"** Star-shaped; semi-double; deep pink (z8–10)

N. *laydekeri* **"Fulgens"** Miniature; star-shaped; semi-double; bright crimson (z5–10)

See also: Ponds pages 94–96

LEFT: "Gladstoneana," which is white with a yellow center.
RIGHT: "Chromatella," a stunning canary yellow water lily.

RIGHT: the beautiful pure white *N. alba*.

YELLOW-FLOWERING WATER LILIES

N. x *helvola* Star-shaped; semi-double; canary-yellow (z5–10)

N. odorata "Sulphurea Grandiflora" Star-shaped; semi-double; fragrant (z5–10)

N. pygmaea "Helvola" Star-shaped; semi-double; pale yellow (z5–10)

N. x *marliacea* "Chromatella" Cup-shaped; semi-double; canary-yellow (z5–10)

N. "Sunrise" Star-shaped; semi-double (z8–10)

WHITE-FLOWERING WATER LILIES

N. alba Cup-shaped; pure white (z5–10)

N. caroliniana "Nivea" Star-shaped; semi-double (z5–10)

N. "Gladstoneana" Semi-double; papery petals (z8–10)

N. marliacea "Albida" Cup-shaped; semi-double; scented (z5–10)

N. tetragona Miniature; single (z5–10)

N. "Virginia" Star-shaped; semi-double; papery petals (z5–10)

See also: Fountains pages 98–99

Other water plants

The largest and most colorful groups of plants for the water garden are those known as marginal plants and bog plants. Not all pools have a moist, marshy area for bog plants, but bog gardens contribute greatly to the overall look of the pool since they help merge it into the rest of the area.

Marginals

Marginal plants grow around the edge of pools in shallow water up to about 6in deep. They are decorative and adaptable plants and are useful for masking the edge of the pool where it meets the land. These plants also provide the main flowering interest in the pool. Grow them in planting baskets on the marginal shelves of the pool.

Acorus calamus (sweet flag) (z4–10) This has greenish-yellow, horn-like flowers and fresh-green iris-like leaves.
Butomus umbellatus (flowering rush) (z6–10) Umbels of pink or red flowers grow among grass-like leaves.
Calla palustris (bog arum) (z3–8) This delicate-looking plant has white spathes and heart-shaped, glossy green leaves.
Caltha palustris (kingcup or marsh marigold) (z4–9) A popular sight in informal-looking pools, this has cup-shaped, bright yellow flowers.
Iris laevigata and *I. versicolor* (z5–9) *I. laevigata* is a lovely blue iris with many attractive hybrids including soft pink, white and violet and white, with fine variegated types; *I. versicolor* has strong violet-blue flowers which are veined purple and splashed gold.
Juncus effusus "Spiralis" (corkscrew rush) (z5–9) A curious-looking plant, this has twisted, curled stems.
Lysichiton camtschatcensis and *L. americanus* (z7–9) These two plants have bold, eye-catching,

LEFT: *Pontederia cordata* displays spikes of blue among glossy leaves. This hardy aquatic perennial thrives as a marginal plant in ornamental pools.

ABOVE: *Lysichiton camtschatcensis* is very much at home in moist places beside ponds and in bog gardens. The plant is notable for its large shiny green leaves and its arum-like flowers.

white and yellow spathes respectively, amid oblong leaves.
Menyanthes trifoliata (bog bean) (z5–8) An attractive marginal plant, this has fringed white flowers and mid-green leaves.
Myosotis scorpioides (z4–10) Small, blue forget-me-not flowers spring up above mounds of mid-green leaves.
Pontederia cordata (z4–9) Spikes of blue flowers rise above lance-shaped, glossy leaves.
Schoenoplectus lacustris ssp. *tabernaemontani* "Zebrinus" (zebra rush) (z4–9) This spectacular marginal has green and white striped stems.

TOP: marsh marigolds or kingcups are a cheerful sight at the side of the pool.
ABOVE: the stately *Iris laevigata* can be violet, blue white or pink.

See also: Colorful perennials pages 142–145

Bog plants

Bog plants enjoy very wet conditions but, unlike marginals, they do not actually like to stand in water. They are planted directly into the soil of a marshy area.

Ajuga reptans (bugle) (z3–8)
This creeping plant has bronze-colored ("Atropurpurea") or creamy-variegated, pinkish ("Multicolor") leaves.

Astilbe hybrids (false goat's beard) (z5–8)
The feathery plumes of flowers are available in many colors including bright crimson, salmon pink, pale pink and white.

Filipendula ulmaria (meadowsweet) (z4–8)
Frothy spires of creamy white blossom rise above deeply cut, dark-green foliage.

Gunnera manicata (z7–10)
This is a large plant resembling a giant rhubarb, with hairy leaves and a reddish flower spike.

Hemerocallis (daylily) (z4–9)
The brightly colored, trumpet-shaped flowers are available in many colors including bright orange and lemon yellow with strap-like leaves.

Hosta sieboldiana (plantain lily) and *H. lancifolia* (z4–9)
H. sieboldiana has bold, heart-shaped glaucous leaves; *H. lancifolia* has long, lance-shaped leaves with sprays of lilac blossom.

Iris ensata (z5–9) and *I. sibirica* (z4–9)
I. ensata has clematis-like flowers in a range of colors including purple-blue, pale rosy lavender and deep violet, and broad, grassy foliage; *I. sibirica* is an iris with flowers ranging from pale blue to deep violet and white with grassy leaves.

Lysimachia nummularia (creeping Jenny) (z4–8)
An evergreen plant, this forms a carpet of yellow, star-shaped flowers.

Osmunda regalis (royal fern) (z3–9)
This tall, statuesque fern has feathery, bright green fronds.

Primula species and hybrids (z6–8)
Clusters of brightly colored flowers including white, yellow, red, crimson, and purple are held in either drumsticks or candelabras above soft green, oval leaves.

Deep-water aquatics

Plants that have their roots on the bottom of a pool and their leaves floating on the surface are known as deep-water aquatics. These plants are of less ornamental value than water lilies, with their large exotic blooms, but they help keep algae at bay.

Aponogeton distachyos (water hawthorn) (z9–10) has very fragrant, "forked" white flowers and oblong-shaped leaves, and *Hottonia palustris* (water violet) (z5–9) has white or lilac-tinted flowers and large whorls of bright green leaves. There is a range of plants with yellow flowers, including *Nuphar lutea* (yellow pond lily) (z5–10), which has small, bottle-shaped, yellow flowers and leathery, green leaves, and *Nymphoides peltata* (water fringe) (z7–10), which has delicately fringed, buttercup-yellow flowers and round, purple-mottled leaves.

Floating aquatics

Along with the leaves of water lilies and deep water plants, floating

LEFT: the plantain lily or *Hosta sieboldiana* makes a valuable contribution to pond areas.

See also: Bulbs pages 152–153

ABOVE: the vast primula family includes species that flourish in damp conditions and are, therefore, excellent for planting beside pools. Colors include white, yellow and crimson.

plants help to cover the water's surface to reduce the amount of sunlight that algae thrive on.

These plants do not need planting as they float around the pool. They are prized primarily for their foliage. *Azolla mexicana* (water fern or fairy moss) (z7–10) has divided leaves varying in color from red and purple to green, and *Hydrocharis morsus-ranae* (frogbit) (z7–10) has kidney-shaped leaves and small, white flowers. The leaves of *Pistia stratiotes* (water lettuce) (z8–10) form rosettes; the foliage has purple markings.

Submerged plants

For the most part, these plants have totally submerged foliage and emergent flowers. They play the vital role of maintaining water clarity by starving the algae of their life-giving food.

Eleocharis acicularis (grass hair) (z7–10) has fine, grass-like leaves which form underwater colonies that cannot be seen from above, while *Myriophyllum aquaticum* (parrot's feather) (z6–10) is a feathery plant with spreading, blue-green foliage. The foliage of *M. spicatum* (spiked milfoil) is much-divided and held on long, slender stems, coppery-green turning bronze, and *Potamogeton crispus* (curled pondweed) (z7–10) has seaweed-like bronzed and green shiny foliage.

WAYS WITH ROSES

There are few places in a backyard, however small, that cannot be enhanced by roses. Ground-cover types brighten the soil with flowers, pillar roses stand like sentries and create color throughout much of summer, standard roses add height to rose beds, while miniature and patio types can be introduced into even the smallest area of courtyard or balcony. Climbers and ramblers cover walls and fences, and some are ideal for growing as flowering hedges.

ABOVE: everyone loves red roses—like the intensely red *R. gallica* "Duc de Guiche."

ABOVE: enveloping trelliswork, pink blooms of the Bourbon climber, "Old Rectory."
RIGHT: in the foreground, the shrub rose "Pink Grootendorst," which is highly recommended for cutting and including in your flower arrangements.

See also: The role of plants pages 112–113

Bush roses

BUSH ROSES usually form the main part of a rose garden. The term refers to Hybrid Teas (correctly known as Large-flowered roses) and Floribundas (correctly known as Cluster-flowered roses).

Hybrid Teas produce the largest and most beautifully formed blooms of all and they have a color range that lacks only blue and deep black. They are also highly scented, but their greatest glory comes from their ability to produce continuous crops of flowers from early summer to mid-winter. Where they grow in the garden is best decided by you. Grow them in a group on their own or in a mixed border.

Floribundas have clusters of flowers which look much more informal than Hybrid Teas. For impact, they are best grown in beds of one type although they can also be placed in mixed borders.

Climbers and ramblers

CLIMBERS CAN transform a garden with flourishes of color. They are superb for covering house walls, framing windows and doors, climbing up pillars, arches and arbors, as well as scrambling into trees. Climbers have a more permanent framework than ramblers, and their flowers range from small to those as large as Hybrid Teas. Ramblers have huge trusses carrying hundreds of generally small blooms, but there is only one truss of flowers. They are excellent for growing in tall trees.

Shrub roses

SHRUB ROSES is an all-embracing classification that covers a huge range of roses including Species and Old roses, such as Bourbon, China, Damask, Moss, and Tea types. These roses are mostly big, heavy-petaled and perfumed, available in wonderful colors.

Miniature and patio roses

THESE FASCINATING roses have small flowers and a miniature stature suitable for, among other things, edging borders, planting in rock gardens and planting in containers. There are also dwarf polyantha roses characterized by their bushy, compact habit.

See also: Shrubs for year-round interest pages 132–135

ABOVE: the rampant rambler "Félicité Perpetué" dominates an arbor.

Flower colors

TERMS USED to describe the colors of flowers include:
• Single color: one color
• Bi-color: the colors on the inside and outside of each petal are different
• Blend: two or more colors on each petal
• Multi-colored: colors change with age
• Hand-painted: center is light-colored and delicately feathered merging with other colors toward the outside
• Striped: two or more colors positioned in bands or stripes

KEY PLANNING POINTS

• With bedding roses, plant the taller varieties in the center.

• Stagger the planting within a bed.

• Keep the roses at least 18in from the outside edges of the beds to avoid problems when trimming the grass.

• Do not make the bed any deeper than 5ft, otherwise you will have difficulty reaching and cutting off dead heads.

• The same points apply to borders and to beds, except that as the roses are not being seen from all sides the tallest (like "Queen Elizabeth" and "Alexander") should be at the back, medium-sized growers in the center, and low growers in the front row.

• Try to plant roses in batches of three to five to form a group of one color.

• Some roses make good hedges, but do check the height and color before you place your order.

• There are many different roses, such as the patio types "Sweet Dreams," "Sweet Magic," and "Cider Cup," and the older "Ballerina" with its five-petaled blooms of light pink and white eye, which are ideal for planting in tubs and urns.

Flowering times

GROWTH TYPES

Prostrate rose
12–15in (or less)

Miniature bush
15in (or less)

ROSES FLOWER over a surprisingly long period during summer, some just once, others repeatedly.

Single flush, also known as "once flowering," refers to roses that generally have only one flowering period, usually in the latter part of early summer and into mid-summer and lasting for several weeks. Occasionally a few flowers appear later, but not sufficient to create a spectacular display. However, there are some ramblers and shrub roses which flower in late spring, early summer or late summer.

Repeat-flowering is also known as "recurrent and "remontant;" these roses have two or more flushes of flowers a year. Where a variety produces flowers between the main flushes, these are known as "perpetual" and "continuous" flowering, but these terms can create a false impression about the flowering period, which is neither perpetual nor continuous, though it still gives good value.

ABOVE: "Fru Dagmar Hastrup" has single shell-pink flowers, is very fragrant and repeat-flowering. Often grown as a hedge, it has large red hips in the fall.

Miniature standard
8–12in (stem)

Patio rose 15in

Dwarf bush
18–24in

Bush rose 24in
(or more)

Half-standard
30in (stem)

Full-standard 39in stem

Weeping standard
51in (stem)

RIGHT: the creamy-white semi-double blooms of "Nevada" smother the whole bush, hiding the leaves and thornless red stems. It needs plenty of space.

See also: Garden trees pages 127–129

RIGHT: not truly blue, the variety "Blue Moon" is more a shade of lilac. The full double flower of many petals is very fragrant and the blooms look their best indoors in a vase.

Pillar rose 7–8ft

LEFT: "Pascali" has a good reputation for being more resistant to rain than most white roses and the blooms hold their shape. The stems are long and straight and good for cutting.

Miniature climber
4–6ft

Climber
7–30ft (or more)

RIGHT: "National Trust" is an outstanding crimson Hybrid Tea rose, excellent for the front of the bed or border. The blooms are held upright and their color does not fade. The foliage is coppery red when young.

Rambler 7–30ft (or more)

See also: Climbing and screening plants pages 138–139

ABOVE: the lovely "Albertine" is an old favorite, a climber with fragrance.

FAVORITE CLIMBING ROSES (z4–9)

"Albertine" (pinkish-white; scented)

"Mme Alfred Carrière" (creamy-white; highly scented)

"Mme Grégoire Staechelin" (clear pink shaded carmine)

"New Dawn" (pearl-pink; fragrant)

"Parkdirektor Riggers" (deep crimson; fragrant)

HIGHLY SCENTED ROSES (z4–9)

"Fantin-Latour" (pink climber)

"Gloire de Dijon" (buff-colored climber)

"Mme Hardy" (white climber or shrub)

"Mme Isaac Pereire" (pink climber or shrub)

"Zéphirine Drouhin" (pink climber)

ABOVE: "Ruby Wedding," a deep red rose for the small garden or the front of the border, popular as a celebration gift.

BELOW: an unusual British-bred modern shrub rose, the striking, deep yellow "Graham Thomas."

TOP SHRUB ROSES (z4–9)

"Blanc Double de Coubert" (pure white; hightly scented)

"Fritz Nobis" (pale salmon pink; scented)

"Frühlingsgold" (creamy yellow; fragrant)

"Graham Thomas" (yellow; fragrant)

POPULAR HYBRID TEA ROSES (z4–9)

"Grandpa Dickson" (light yellow; fragrant)

"Peace" (pinkish-yellow; fragrant)

"Ruby Wedding" (red)

"Silver Jubilee" (soft salmon pink; fragrant)

"Whisky Mac" (amber-colored; fragrant)

LEFT: "Peace," the world's best-loved rose, always vigorous and attractive from first bud to full-blown bloom.

See also: Colorful perennials pages 142–145

ABOVE: yellow climbing roses such as "Golden Showers" have great appeal for their deep golden color and their long flowering period.

ABOVE: Bold and bright "Stars 'n' Stripes" is universally recognized for its strawberry red stripes against white.

BEST OLD-FASHIONED ROSES

"Charles de Mills" (crimson-maroon; fragrant) (z4–9)

"Ispahan" (clear pink) (z4–9)

"Mousseline" (blush-pink) (z4–9)

moschata (clear pink) (z6–9)

gallica "Versicolor" (pale pink with crimson stripes; fragrant) (z5–9)

LEFT: one of the best of the old-fashioned roses, "Ispahan," a clear pink.

ABOVE: the blooms of "Silver Jubilee" are shapely with long, coppery pink petals, shaded with peach.

CONTAINERS

LEFT: container gardening is an effective way of bringing the brilliance of blooms to every porch, patio and balcony.

USING CONTAINERS

Growing plants in containers adds a new dimension to gardening, revitalizing dull areas and introducing instant color and interest.

THERE ARE pots, urns, planters, troughs, tubs and window-boxes to choose from, made of terracotta, plastic, wood and stone. So you will always be able to find something suitable to include in your garden.

Containers bring the garden on to patios, terraces and balconies and, when secured to walls or window sills, they introduce a vertical element. Free-standing containers, such as urns and tubs, can be used to flank flights of steps with color, to make focal points in lawns or to add height. Pairs of containers at either side of entrances add importance and convey a welcoming message to visitors.

The greatest advantage of container gardening is that the containers can be moved around the garden at will to create a series of different effects. Furthermore, you can replace the plants in them when they have passed their best, or even if you decide that you want a change of color scheme, thus you are assured of a continuous display of flowers to suit.

Large containers can be used in many ways. To make an expanse of paving more interesting, place a large container in the middle as a focal point. This device is tremendously successful, provided the

LEFT: an urn can be used to make a colorful focal point on a lawn.
BELOW: flowers and foliage spill out in abundance from a trough, window-box and urns.

ABOVE: window-boxes are the most common form of container, and are equally at home in both city and country, brightening windows throughout the year.

See also: Colorful perennials pages 142–145

RIGHT: carefully positioned hanging baskets can transform any house. They are generally hung close to a front door or above a patio, but are also effective suspended from trellises, arbors and porches. They are useful for improving features such as carports or for decorating long stretches of bare wall. The choice of plants is truly enormous—geraniums, fuchsias, lobelia, petunias, either singly or mixed together, are all superb. Baskets can also be planted with tomatoes or strawberries.

container is big enough and the plants bold enough to make a statement. To make an area of paving appear smaller, place large, plant-filled containers in each corner. This is also a good ploy if you have an irregularly shaped terrace, as the large pots in all the corners will create a sense of unity and detract from the irregularity. Large containers are also good for flanking doorways and marking steps, creating focal points and marking out areas of the garden.

In many respects, small containers are more difficult to place. Several small containers scattered about do not necessarily make a bold impact and can look fussy. Furthermore, a group of small containers can also be more difficult to maintain. However, they do come into their own when placed around the edges of larger containers to soften their outlines.

The distinctive and dramatic shape of urns makes them look best alone. Rather than clustering them like pots, position them singly or in pairs to highlight any special features, mark a focal point or to lead the eye toward a distant point of interest. They can be placed at ground level, but are often used to enhance architecture and look good positioned at the top and bottom of a flight of steps.

Try to create different levels when you group containers and arrange them in a tiered manner. Not only is this visually more exciting than a uniform row of pots, but each planting will be displayed to best effect and create a terrace-like cascade of foliage. Do not mix too many different types of containers in one group. Either choose containers of a similar style, or stick to one type of material, such as terracotta.

WHERE TO HANG YOUR BASKET

• Position matching hanging baskets on either side of a front door, so that cascading plants slightly cut across the uprights of the frame. This will make the door area appear larger and more distinguished. Ensure, however, that the baskets cannot be knocked and that water does not drip on other plants or make a pathway slippery.

• Windows can be treated in the same way as the front door, with foliage and flowers dissecting the framework on the outer edges. If the window also has a window-box, ensure that water from the hanging basket does not drip on to it.

• Where a large expanse of bare wall stretches between two windows, brighten the area by securing a hanging basket halfway along it. Where a house has three equally spaced windows, use two hanging baskets of flowers for symmetry.

• Porches can often be swathed in climbers, but they also look superb with hanging baskets suspended from above. As part or all of the basket is under cover, regular watering is essential, but take care to prevent drips.

• Large areas of wall benefit from a few well-placed baskets. Take the color of the wall into account when selecting flower colors.

• Carports are stark and functional and in need of plants to brighten them. Position a couple of hanging baskets on either side of the front. Include white flowers and silver-leaved plants, as they show up well at night.

• Roof gardens especially benefit from a little color at head height, but always ensure that the hanging basket is not positioned in a particularly blustery and windswept position.

• Balconies also benefit from hanging baskets, but ensure that strong wind cannot damage the plants and that water does not drip on them or people below. Use plastic baskets with drip-trays built into their base.

See also: Annuals and biennials pages 146–147

LEFT: all sorts of items can be used as containers, such as this old wheelbarrow.

RANGE OF CONTAINERS

The range of containers for growing plants is huge. It includes not only purpose-made, ornamental ones such as hanging baskets, wall baskets, window-boxes, troughs, tubs and urns, but also more unexpected items such as sinks, old wheelbarrows, tires and grow-bags. Almost anything can be called into service.

THE SCOPE for originality and novelty is endless; if a container can hold sufficient suitable compost to support plants, it becomes a candidate for creating anything from a splash of color as a focal point on a lawn or patio to a garden in microcosm.

Some of the larger containers, like tubs and window-boxes, can be used for plants throughout the year. Hanging baskets are best reserved for summer performances, although these need not be confined to conventional ornamentals: you can plant them with low-growing, cascading roses or with attractive and succulent strawberries and tomatoes. Small urns are best used for spring and summer flowering displays.

TYPES OF CONTAINER

Many different types of container are available in clay, plastic and fiberglass. Stone urns can become special features, while wooden tubs can liven up a dull patio. Hanging containers can be made from plastic, terracotta and different metals. As a general rule, pots with a diameter smaller than 9in should not be used for hot, dry situations. Some vases and urns, though attractive, have relatively small planting areas. Always check that they will give sufficient depth of soil or compost to accommodate plant root systems both in the center and at the edges—4in is only just sufficient for small edging plants.

See also: Bedding plants pages 148–149

Choosing containers

THE PRECISE choice of container is always very much a matter of personal taste, but the right scale and shape are of the utmost importance for creating a pleasing effect.

• *Size* A container with a sizeable volume of growing medium will dry out less rapidly than a smaller container; it will also be capable of sustaining larger, more vigorous plants.

• *Stability* Always look for containers with large or heavy bases to give stability, especially where there is to be regular traffic of people.

• *Weight* Some containers, especially stone ones, can be very heavy to lift and move, although this is a bonus for stability. Such containers are not easily brought home in a car: special delivery may have to be arranged. Some vases are made in sections, but even their individual parts can be weighty and awkward to transport.

• *Drainage* For drainage, there should always be one large hole or several smaller holes in the base of the container.

• *Materials* Containers made in natural materials will usually look best, but will be more expensive to acquire, especially if they have been hand-crafted or sculptured.

Tubs, pots, urns and planters

THESE CONTAINERS vary widely in shape and size and the types of plant that suit them. Large tubs are ideal for shrubs as well as summer-flowering bedding plants and spring-flowering bulbs. Urns are smaller and hold less compost. They are usually more decorative in character and so are perhaps best devoted to summer-flowering plants and displays of bulbs in spring.

Clay pots and planters are informal and functional by nature. Plastic and fiberglass alternatives are available, however, and these can be used in place of the traditional stone types. They are less costly, lighter and have considerable potential, especially displayed at some distance, filled with cascading plants to mask their synthetic origins.

Stone urns tend to be rather formal in appearance, while wooden tubs are less formal and are more suitable for a patio or small back yard.

Window-boxes and troughs

WINDOW-BOXES can transform windows throughout the year and troughs can be given the same yearly cycle of plants as window-boxes.

Wood is the most common material used for window-boxes and troughs. It can be painted, stained or left untreated for a rustic, natural look. Terracotta is also popular because its texture and color harmonize naturally with plants. Because of their weight, position these containers either on strong, cement or brick window sills, or use at ground level as a trough.

Reconstituted stone is also heavy and therefore best positioned at ground level. Its surface has a natural, stone-like appearance and soon mellows. Cement troughs are suitable only for use at ground level. Fiberglass and plastic are ideal: both are durable, light and rot-proof.

Hanging baskets and wall baskets

HANGING BASKETS, suspended from overhead structures such as beams or projecting roofs or by means of brackets, can introduce decoration to vertical surfaces. Wall baskets are like large hanging baskets cut in half vertically and secured to a wall. Mangers are similar, but usually larger; formed of flat strips of metal, they also tend to look rather more robust.

Hanging baskets and wall baskets are usually made of plastic-coated wire which is light and durable. Much less weather-resistant are the wicker types, perhaps best suited to indoor use. Wooden hanging baskets are rustic and informal in character, while, at the other end of the spectrum, wrought-iron types tend to have a formal appearance. Some of the most efficient types are made of plastic with attached "drip" saucers to catch spare water. There are also terracotta and metals which, while ornamental, can be rather heavy. Terracotta also absorbs water readily, meaning the baskets are quick to dry out.

See also: Bulbs pages 152–153

CHOOSING PLANTS

Urns, tubs and planters stand on flat surfaces such as walls and patios, while window-boxes, wall baskets and hanging baskets adorn vertical surfaces. It is therefore essential to choose appropriate plants for each type, both to show off the plants to perfection and to suit the container.

RECTANGULAR-SHAPED containers present planting challenges similar to those offered by window-boxes. The difference in siting affects the angle at which they are viewed: some stand at ground level, some are raised on legs and others are set on or against walls.

Containers raised on walls or legs offer an opportunity to use trailing plants, which are best seen from the sides. Conversely, where containers are mainly seen from above, choose plants with bright faces that peer upward. For those at ground level, low-growing herbaceous perennials create attractive features.

Most containers have a face side from which they are mainly viewed, but those on the tops of low walls may be viewed from both sides. Always ensure that the most noticeable sides are well-clothed with plants; if bare—especially during mid-summer, when plants should be drenching troughs in color—they look unattractive and give an air of neglect.

Grouping plants

THE WAY plants are grouped in containers is just as important as the grouping of the containers themselves. Much is a matter of individual taste, but there are certain points it is helpful to bear in mind.

Free-standing containers

ONE WELL-CHOSEN plant can often look better than a mixed planting, but if you do mix plants, aim at having one main plant in the middle surrounded by smaller plants. Always aim for as bold an effect as possible and make sure the planting is in scale with the containers themselves. For example, low, flat-growing plants will look lost if planted alone in a wide-topped vase or urn, whereas if they are dominated by a tall central plant, the whole design comes into proportion.

Medium-sized, main-feature plants can be grown with stronger-growing trailing plants to keep the display well in scale.

Trailing plants will help to soften harsh outlines, but remember to leave sufficiently exposed any container with a pleasing shape, especially if it has prominent decoration.

Window-boxes

TO COUNTERACT the long narrow shape of a window-box, you should make every attempt to avoid planting in straight rows. More informality can be given to the display by varying the heights of the main plants and by softening the effect with filler plants. One way to make an attractive planting is to group main-feature plants first and then put fillers in between.

A succession of seasonal displays is a worthwhile approach. Separate units can be made up in advance and inserted as the plants come into flower. However, most gardeners will find it more convenient to rely on two main displays in spring and summer, planted the previous fall and spring.

It is important to remember when selecting plants for window-boxes that they need to look attractive when seen from both indoors and out. To achieve this, a series of low, bushy plants that will make mounds of color along the top of the container is the first requirement. Intersperse these with plants that have sprawling or trailing flower stems which can be directed toward the front and sides of the box. This will help to soften its outline.

RIGHT: careful plant selection can achieve effects where the container disappears under a blanket of blooms.

QUICK TIPS FOR PLANT COMBINATIONS

- As well as considering color, mix plants with contrasting flower shapes.

- Mix low-growing plants such as forget-me-nots with taller ones such as tulips or daffodils.

- Aim for a variety of habits: combine trailing or hanging plants with upright ones for variety.

- Cover the container with bushy and trailing plants that create dominant patches of color.

- Avoid using too many different plants or your container will lack definition and form.

See also: Location pages 110–111

Hanging baskets

WHEN GROUPING plants in a hanging basket, it is useful to have one larger central plant surrounded by smaller-growing kinds, but planting several of a single kind can be equally effective. The side plants in a basket will usually be trailing types, with taller, bushier plants set in the top so that the finished planting creates a ball of color.

Considering backgrounds

FOR CONTAINERS displayed against a white background, choose contrasting flowers such as blue forget-me-nots, golden or red wallflowers, pink daisies, yellow *Crocus chrysanthus*, blue or red hyacinths, and yellow daffodils. To subdue the contrast slightly and link the planting with its backdrop, intersperse a few white flowers. To create displays that shine out against dark backgrounds, select plants such as white, cream or yellow hyacinths, yellow *Crocus chrysanthus*, yellow-variegated ivies, vivid yellow polyanthus, white tulips, and bright yellow daffodils.

When planting against red-brick walls, choose light-blue forget-me-nots, white hyacinths, bronze and cream wallflowers, blue grape hyacinths, yellow-variegated ivies, yellow polyanthus and white tulips. For rich contrast with gray stone walls, go for vibrant colored blooms such as red wallflowers, deep-blue forget-me-nots, pink tulips and pink or blue hyacinths.

COMPOSITION

A tall, thin container looks better if planted with trailing subjects.

Flat, low-growing plants are acceptable if the container is below eye-level.

Adding a tall main plant to low-growing plants lends proportion.

Often one well-chosen plant looks better than a fussy planting.

See also: The role of plants pages 112–113

SEASONAL DISPLAYS

The simplest and easiest way to use containers is to plan a series of plantings, one for each season. Either opt for a single-color theme, such as white and silver, or create a splash of color using a mixture of plants.

TOP RIGHT: effective single-color theme, using French marigolds (*Tagetes patula*).
ABOVE: variegated foliage and ivies set off mixed flowering plants.

SUMMER IMPACT

• = recommended for hanging baskets

•*Ageratum houstonianum* (floss flower)
Fluffy heads of blue, pinkish-blue or white flowers with coarse green leaves. Good filler.
•*Begonia*
Glossy leaves and double or single heads of brightly colored flowers from pink, red and orange to yellow and white. Very colorful; some have ornamental leaves. Use both fibrous and tuberous varieties. Good all-rounder for single as well as mixed plantings.

Chrysanthemum frutescens (marguerite)
Daisy-like flower with white, yellow or pink flowers; the white form is the most commonly seen. Good base planting.
•*Fuchsia*
Bushy or pendulous shrubs with dainty hanging flowers in a range of colors and color combinations involving variations on the themes of white, purple, pink and crimson. Good main feature plant for displays.
•*Impatiens walleriana* (busy Lizzie)
Continuously flowering plant with cup-shaped or

flat blossoms in shades of red, pink, lilac and white.
•*Pelargonium* and *Geranium*
Red, pink, magenta or white flowers with plain green or multi-colored leaves. Good for color. Many varieties available.
•*Petunia* x *hybrida*
Small plants with trumpet-shaped flowers, some of which have a white stripe down them. Colors include pink, purple, yellow and white.
Salvia splendens
A vigorous plant producing narrow spikes of violet-blue or white flowers. Good main-feature plant.

SUMMER MIXING AND MATCHING

Here are two superb combinations of plants for planting in summer window-boxes:

• Marguerites (*Chrysanthemum frutescens*), trailing petunias cascading over the front and edges of the container, floss flower (*Ageratum houstonianum*), dwarf marigolds and ivy-leaved pelargoniums.

• Swiss Balcon or Continental geraniums, godetias, trailing and compact impatiens, ivy-leaved pelargoniums, and *Kochia scoparia* "Childsii" to add some height to the display. The graceful, ferny *Grevillea* can also be planted to give·height.

Tagetes (marigold)
Tall or short bushy plants with single or double flowers ranging from yellow to orange. Good filler.

See also: Plant associations pages 114–120

LEFT: a subtle display of greenery in a terracotta trough with *Juniperus* "Blue Star," *Juniperus communis* "Compacta," *Erica* "Sir John Carrington," *Euonymous* "Emerald and Gold," *Hebe pageii* and small-leaved ivies.

SCENTED SUMMER DISPLAYS

Few window-boxes are as captivating as those packed with fragrant plants:

• Plant sweet alyssum (*Lobularia maritima*, earlier known as *Alyssum maritimum*) with its fragrance of new-mown hay at one corner, and cool, sweetly scented pansies at the other. Between them use short varieties of the fragrant flowering tobacco plant (*Nicotiana alata*) and deep-purple heliotrope (*Heliotropium* x *hybridum*), which is said to smell of cherry pie.

Foliage for year-round interest

FOLIAGE PLANTS are an important part of any planting, but particularly so container plantings, which tend to have short periods of interest created by seasonal plants. Foliage, however, provides a permanent background structure against which flowers can come and go.

Gray-leaved plants such as *Helichrysum petiolare* and *Senecio bicolor*, syn. *cineraria bicolor*, play a useful part in different color schemes. When reds and blues are combined with white, gray will "cool" the impact of the strong hues. Its neutral tones make the visual leap to pure white less dazzling. A subdued background of gray foliage will bring out the best in pastel pinks, mauves and misty blues, and will delicately harmonize container color schemes.

Golden foliage tones have affinities with yellow flowers and mid-green leaves. Their presence intensifies the richness of deep blues and violets. Variegated foliage such as *Hebe* x *andersonii* "Variegata" and *H.* x *franciscana* "Variegata" and variegated ivy is decorative in its own right but, mixed with flowering plants, it adds interest and texture.

Summer and fall

MOST SUMMER interest is created by brightly colored annuals in a variety of colors. Red, pink and purple are popular summer colors; when mixed with interesting foliage plants, the result is lively and eye-catching. Many summer displays will last well into the fall and can then be replaced with winter plants. But, to tide you over, there are several plants such as fuchsias and sedums that will provide falltime color and interest.

When composing your planting scheme, choose plants with contrasting flower shapes. Masses of tiny blooms, such as sweet alyssum and trailing lobelia, create a hazy effect softening the edges and hiding the container. They contrast well with the larger plants that form the main focus of the container.

LEFT: nasturtiums, ranging in color from yellow to red, are ideal for planting at the edge of tubs and window-boxes.

FALL EFFECTS

• = recommended for hanging baskets

•*Fuchsia*
See page 182.
Heliotrope x *hybridum*
Large heads of tiny, dark purple, sweetly scented flowers. Good base planting.
•*Nicotiana alata*
Tall or short plants with stems of white, green, pink or red deliciously scented flowers.
•*Pelargonium*
See page 182.
Sedum spectabile
(stonecrop)
Large, flat, pink heads of flowers spread above fleshy stems and grayish-green leaves. Excellent for color.

See also: Fuchsias pages 150–151

Winter and spring

FOLIAGE COMES into its own in winter, along with shrubby plants that produce berries. These can be supplemented with winter-flowering bulbs in mild climates. Spring interest is mainly created by bulbs and biennials which burst into color from early to late spring, and sometimes into early summer. Yellow is a favorite spring color, either on its own with some fresh foliage or combined with white, cream and, perhaps, a hint of blue. For more of an impact, add a splash of yellow to a vibrant mixed planting of reds, blues and whites.

When planting containers for winter, concentrate on shape and form to create bold, striking outlines using a variety of foliage plants. Fill in the gaps with bulbs.

SCENTED WINTER DISPLAYS

The foliage of some miniature conifers has an intriguing aromatic quality when bruised. Interplant these conifers with small bulbs such as the honey-scented *Iris danfordiae* or violet-scented *I. reticulata* for a wonderful winter display that both looks and smells delightful.

- *Chamaecyparis lawsoniana* "Ellwoodii" (resin and parsley).

- *Chamaecyparis pisifera* "Boulevard" (resinous bouquet).

- *Juniperus communis* "Compressa" (apple-scented).

RIGHT: *Narcissus* "Tête à Tête" and polyanthus make an appealing display.

WINTER HIGHLIGHTS

Miniature and slow-growing conifers are particularly useful for providing winter interest. *Chamaecyparis lawsoniana* "Ellwoodii" Slow-growing and forms a dark-green columnar shape. For a golden color choose "Ellwood's Pillar."

Chamaecyparis pisifera "Boulevard" Slow-growing and forms a cone shape with intense silver-blue foliage.

Juniperus communis "Compressa" Dwarf and compact, with dark-green, silver-backed, needle-like leaves. This is a miniature form of the Irish juniper and is widely grown in containers of all kinds. *Thuja orientalis* "Aurea Nana" is compact and fan-shaped, with golden foliage. Berries are another way of introducing color into winter containers.

- *Cotoneaster microphyllus thymifolius* A creeping nature, with small, narrow leaves and white flowers in early summer. In the fall and early winter these are followed by bright scarlet berries.

- *Gaultheria procumbens* (partridge berry/ winter green) Evergreen, with creeping stems and bright red berries in winter.

RIGHT: a display for all seasons—a wooden trough with silver-blue and gray-green conifers, golden euonymus and ivies.

See also: Patios pages 68–71

COLOR THEMES FOR SPRING

• For simple impact, pack the window-box with bright yellow narcissi, which are ideal for this container.

• Underplant red *Tulipa fosteriana* or *T. greigii* with a sea of blue forget-me-nots. Include a few grape hyacinths for darker accents and texture. Edge the box with double daisies.

• For an alternative version of the ubiquitous red-white-and-blue theme, try combining a range of hyacinths with the daisies and forget-me-nots.

• Mix wallflowers in tapestry colors, or choose reds and yellows to accompany tulips and daffodils.

• For sheer brightness intersperse multi-colored polyanthus with low-growing trumpet daffodils.

• For simple two-color contrast, plant yellow polyanthus in a sea of blue grape hyacinths.

SPRING COLOR

• = especially recommended for hanging baskets

• *Bellis perennis* (daisy)
Small tufts of green leaves from which grow crimson, pink or white daisy flowers. Good container filler.

• *Crocus*
A bulb with small, goblet-shaped flowers in colors ranging from purple and lilac to orange, yellow, and white. Good for color and shape.

• *Erysimum* (wallflower)
Spikes of scented flowers in shades of red, orange, and yellow. Good base planting.

• *Hyacinthus orientalis* (hyacinth)
Pink, blue, white, yellow, orange, or red "drumsticks" of heavily scented flowers. Good for their color, shape and perfume.

• *Iris reticulata*
Miniature iris with a pretty single purple flower.

• *Muscari armeniacum* (grape hyacinth)
Vibrant blue flowers produced on a fleshy green spike. Excellent container plant for color and shape.

• *Myosotis sylvatica* (forget-me-not)
A cloudy haze of mid-blue flowers produced in great profusion. A very good filler.

Narcissus (daffodil)
A varied group of bulbs with yellow, orange, and white flowers. Excellent for color and good for the main feature.

• *Primula* (polyanthus)
Soft, velvety flowers in a range of different colors.

• *Tulipa* (tulip)
Spikes of bright, cup-shaped blooms. Their colors include yellow, white, and purple.

ABOVE LEFT: a rustic trough with wallflowers, tulips and daisies.

ABOVE RIGHT: a spring display of grape hyacinths and polyanthus.

ABOVE: a scented spring window-box of *Juniperus* "Blue Star," *Iris reticulata*, white and striped crocus, *Chamaecyparis minima* and a mixture of ivies.

See also: Outdoor living pages 104–105

HANGING BASKETS

Use the following plant recommendations, arranged by color, to put together your own basket according to your desired color scheme. For a mixed planting, choose a few plants from each section or stick to one color scheme and integrate some foliage.

TRAILING FOLIAGE

Hedera helix The small-leaved forms are best.
Helichrysum petiolare (liquorice plant). *H. p.* "Aureum" or "Limelight" has soft golden leaves, and there is also a gray-leaved form *H. microphyllum.*
Vinca minor "Variegata" (lesser periwinkle) has green and creamy-white variegated leaves. There are several other forms to choose from.

PLANTS WITH WHITE FLOWERS

Begonia semperflorens "Viva" has pure white flowers amid rich bottle-green leaves.
Brachyscome iberidifolia (Swan River daisy) "White Splendor" bears a wealth of white flowers throughout summer.
Campanula carpatica (tussock campanula) "Bellissimo" has a trailing nature ideal for hanging baskets and comes in either blue or white.

Convolvulus tricolor (dwarf morning glory) "White Ensign" has white flowers, each with a pretty yellow throat.
Impatiens walleriana (busy Lizzie) There are a number of named varieties; the hybrid "Tempo Series" has a white form.
Lobelia erinus Look out for white forms of this very popular plant.
Lobularia maritima (sweet alyssum) is available in a variety of colors, including white.
Nemophila atomaria "Snowstorm" has white

flowers peppered with small black spots.
Nierembergia "Mont Blanc" creates masses of cup-shaped white flowers with small, yellow eyes.
Petunia x *hybrida* "Super Cascade Improved Mixed" has a cascading habit. Make sure you select the white-flowered form.

ABOVE: begonias, here with vibrant orange flowers, put on a brilliant display of flowers throughout the summer months. The foliage, which is a rich bottle-green color, is also pleasingly attractive.

ABOVE LEFT: geraniums and busy Lizzies, both very popular hanging basket plants.
BELOW: prolific and vigorous, nasturtiums make a brilliant impact.

See also: Arches and arbors pages 102–103

PLANTS WITH YELLOW FLOWERS

Antirrhinum (snapdragon) "Sweetheart" is a low-growing variety, while "Yellow Monarch" is taller.

Tagetes tenuifolia pumila (marigold) has slender stems, sweet-smelling leaves and yellow flowers.

Viola x *wittrockiana* (pansy) "Rhine Gold" has yellow flowers blotched black and "Flame Princess" has rich, clear-yellow to cream flowers blotched scarlet to mahogany.

PLANTS WITH RED OR PINK FLOWERS

Lobularia maritima (sweet alyssum) "Trailing Rosy-red" has cerise-pink flowers.

Begonia x *tuberhybrida* "Show Angels" comes in a range of colors including rose-pink. "Clips Mixed" has double flowers available in both mixed and separate colors, including pink and bright scarlet.

Impatiens walleriana (busy Lizzie) comes in many colors, including shades of blush, rose and scarlet.

Lobelia erinus "Cascade Mixed" includes lilac and crimson forms.

Tropaeolum majus (nasturtium) Some varieties of this have deep-red and scarlet flowers.

Pelargonium peltatum (ivy-leaved geranium) The red or pink flowers are held amid shapely trailing foliage.

Petunia x *hybrida* "Super Cascade Improved Mixed" variety has several forms, including pale, delicate pinks, vibrant cerise, rich crimson and warm red.

LEFT: an attractive mixed-theme hanging basket containing an impressive mass of flowering plants, including begonias, *Lysimachia*, petunias, lobelia, busy Lizzies, and fuchsias.

See also: Location pages 110–111

PLANTS WITH BLUE FLOWERS

Anagallis linifolia "Gentian Blue" has masses of glowing deep-blue flowers with golden stamens.

Brachyscome iberidifolia "Blue Star" produces a veritable mass of light-blue, daisy-like flowers. "Purple Splendor" is a more violet-toned variety.

Campanula carpatica "Bellissimo" has both white- and blue-flowered forms.

Campanula isophylla has star-shaped blue flowers.

Convolvulus tricolor "Blue Ensign" is a bright vivid blue-flowered form of morning glory.

Lobelia erinus "Blue Cascade" is a pastel blue that is more companionable than strong, dominating blues when it is mixed with other plants.

Petunia x *hybrida* "Super Cascade Improved Mixed" is available in mixed and individual colors, including a range of blues. Most have slightly warmish tones, tending toward lavender when pale and toward violet when dark.

ABOVE: a globe of pinks and purples, as displayed here, can transform an otherwise dull area. The plants need regular care, watering and trimming.

RIGHT: *Pelargonium* "Parasol" has attractive trailing foilage.

Foliage

Gray-leaved plants can be used to good effect in hanging baskets. Their neutral tones tend to cool down vibrant colors such as reds and blues, while they will generally show off to advantage pale shades of pink, blue and mauve.

Plants such as *Helichrysum petiolare* are therefore useful for setting off different color schemes.

Plants with yellow variegation and golden foliage, by contrast, harmonize with deep blue and violet colors and have affinities with both yellow flowers and mid-green leaves.

See also: Fuchsias pages 150–151

ABOVE: glowing purple-blue petunias are effective on their own.
LEFT: this basket is hidden by an abundance of tumbling pink-themed blooms.
BELOW: a display of *Fuchsia* "Swingtime," red and white and graceful.

FUCHSIAS FOR HANGING BASKETS

Fuchsias always capture attention and to many eyes are the aristocrats of container planting. Some have single flowers with just four petals, while semi-double types have five, six or seven. Double types have eight or more petals. Fuchsias especially suited to hanging baskets include:

"Cascade": Single flowers with white sepals flushed carmine and deep red petals.

"Falling Stars": Single flowers, with pale scarlet sepals and turkey-red petals with slight orange tints.

"Lena": Semi-double flowers with rose-magenta petals flushed pink.

"Marinka": Single flowers with rich red sepals and dark red petals.

"Swingtime": Double flowers with shiny red sepals and milky-white petals.

PLANT CARE AND CULTIVATION

For healthy plants and prolific flowering, make sure your containers get the very best start and use the right type of compost. Keep this well-watered and regularly cut off the dead flowers and weed the containers. Summer-flowering plants will need feeding regularly.

Growing mediums

WELL-DRAINED yet moisture-retentive compost is essential for all plants in containers. The planting medium must also be fertile for summer-flowering bedding plants, which need to develop rapidly and sustain growth throughout the summer. Spring bulbs, planted in late summer or the fall, do not need high fertility.

For a suitable compost, use a mixture of equal parts loam-based and peat-based compost. The peat part retains moisture, while the loam-based part provides nutrients, especially the minor ones. The addition of perlite or vermiculite further assists in the retention of moisture. Proprietary composts especially designed for use in hanging baskets are available and make it easier to get the mixture right.

ABOVE: *Ageratum* "Adriatic" is a fine container plant with clusters of fluffy flowers lasting all season.

Drainage

IT IS ESSENTIAL that containers have adequate drainage otherwise the planting medium will get waterlogged and the plant roots rot. Make sure the containers have at least one large central drainage hole if not more, and place a layer of crocks (broken pieces of clay flowerpot) on the bottom of the container before filling it with compost. Containers should also be raised from the ground on bricks or flat stones so any excess water can drain out.

A layer of well-washed pea gravel can be used instead of crocks for more permanent displays, such as those involving shrubs or small trees.

Planting

WHEN PLANTING containers, it is a good idea to place the plants, still in their pots, on top of the soil so you can experiment with different arrangements before you plant them. Once you have decided on the best composition, press each pot lightly into the soil and remove it, thus leaving an indentation so you can see where to make the hole.

The planting holes should be big enough to accommodate the roots with a little room to spare. Carefully remove the plants from their pots: place your hand flat over the surface of the pot with the stem of the plant between your two fingers. Carefully ease off the pot. If the root ball is particularly solid, very gently tease it apart to loosen it slightly before planting it. Once planted, firm the compost around the plant and water well.

See also: The role of plants pages 112–113

Planting a hanging basket

START PLANTING a hanging basket in mid- to late spring in warm areas, but wait until early summer in cold regions. Planting can be earlier if a greenhouse or conservatory is available to give the plants protection during cold nights in spring, when frost is forecast. They need a reasonably sunny position.

1 Rest the basket on top of a large bucket to hold it firm and line it with a sheet of black plastic or moss.

2 Fill the bottom half with compost and lightly firm it with your fingers. Trim off excess plastic.

3 If preferred, make some planting holes in the side of the basket and insert a variety of plants.

4 Arrange the plants in the basket and pack in compost to just below the rim.

5 Firm the compost around all the plants and then water them through.

6 Hang your planted basket in your chosen position for maximum effect.

ABOVE: hyacinths are at their best in containers, an indispensable part of spring displays with their trim shape, pastel colors and sweet fragrance.

OPPOSITE: a brilliant mixture of *Begonia semperflorens* with the glowing red *B. x tuberhybrida*, set off to advantage in a handsome terracotta pot. Try different compositions before planting a container.

PLANTING BULBS

Bulbs can be used on their own for a spectacular seasonal display or they can be interspersed with other plants, so creating a splash of temporary color before the other plants come into their own. For a spectacular display of flowers, plant your bulbs in two layers, one on top of the other.

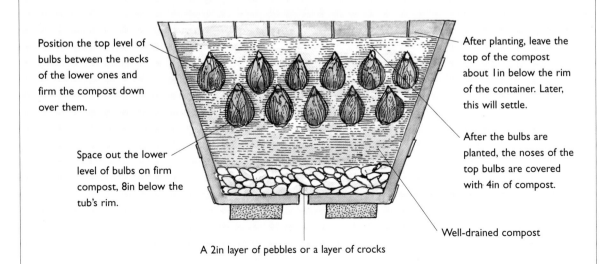

Position the top level of bulbs between the necks of the lower ones and firm the compost down over them.

After planting, leave the top of the compost about 1in below the rim of the container. Later, this will settle.

After the bulbs are planted, the noses of the top bulbs are covered with 4in of compost.

Space out the lower level of bulbs on firm compost, 8in below the tub's rim.

Well-drained compost

A 2in layer of pebbles or a layer of crocks

See also: Plant associations pages 114–120

Regularly removing dead flowers—or "deadheading"—encourages the development of further buds and prolongs the display. Blooms left on plants decay and encourage the onset of diseases. Where plants have long flower-stalks, cut these back to the base. Where flowers are borne in tight clusters close to the main stem, use scissors to cut them off. Pick up all the dead flowers and place them on a compost pile. Left among the plants, they encourage diseases.

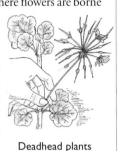

Deadhead plants regularly.

Watering

THE RELATIVELY small volume of compost and large number of plants in containers and hanging baskets make it essential to water the compost regularly during summer and to keep it evenly moist at other times of the year. At all times avoid waterlogging as this can encourage the plants to rot.

Hanging baskets tend to dry out quicker than containers since more of their surface is exposed to the air. If the plants appear to wilt during early afternoon on exceptionally hot days, yet the compost is moist, this is because they cannot absorb moisture quickly enough. The plants usually recover by the evening. If you discover a neglected hanging basket, cut back any severely wilted stems and immerse the compost in a bowl of water. Remove and place in a cool position until the plants recover.

Spray plants regularly with insecticide.

Place small sticks of insect killer in the compost.

Feeding

SUMMER-FLOWERING bedding plants need feeding regularly from early to late summer, at about three-week intervals. Spring-flowering displays formed of bulbs and biennials like wallflowers and daisies do not need to be fed, but do use fresh and fertile compost. Only feed winter-flowering displays in late spring and mid-summer.

A liquid fertilizer is the most widely used and convenient way of feeding plants. In this form, it is readily available for absorption by the plants. Sticks and pills of concentrated plant fertilizer are popular and provide nutrients over a long period. They are clean and quick to use, but the chemicals are not so readily available to plants as those applied in water. They are suitable only for summer-flowering plants.

Granular and powdered fertilizers are more widely used in gardens, where they can be dusted on the soil's surface, lightly hoed in and then watered. Dissolve them thoroughly in clean water first.

Pest control

WHENEVER PLANTS are massed together it encourages the presence of pests. Aphids are the main pests and must be controlled before they reach plague proportions by spraying the plants several times throughout summer with a systemic insecticide.

Spraying plants with an insecticide from an environmentally friendly aerosol or through a hand-held spray are popular methods of using chemicals. An alternative way is to insert small sticks impregnated with insect-killing chemicals into the compost, so that roots absorb the chemicals and make plants toxic to insects. These are best used in long-term plants grown in lobbies, porches or indoors.

Encouraging bushiness

TALL, LANKY plants can be encouraged to put out more side shoots if you nip out their growing points while young. Fuchsias, for example, benefit from having their shoots snapped sideways or the tips pinched off after three sets of leaves have formed. Try to position the break just above a leaf so that you do not leave a short stem, as this will die back and decay.

LEFT: a novel arrangement using a series of containers to form a pillar.

See also: Hardiness zones pages 108–109

GARDEN TECHNIQUES

Every successful gardener needs to develop a repertoire of different techniques to suit all occasions and needs. The pages that follow will help you do just that and will provide you with all the information you need. Keep them to hand for ease of reference in the future.

THE ANSWER, they say, lies in the soil—and no truer word about gardening was ever said. Good soil means good plants. Probably the most important thing you can do before you do anything else in the garden is therefore to get to know your soil. Then, if it needs it—and most soils do—you should find out how you can improve it.

No gardener can hope to make the most of his or her garden without at least the minimum of basic tools. What are these tools, and which pieces of equipment are essential as opposed to just desirable?

But it's the gritty essentials of plant cultivation that is probably dearest to every gardener's heart. The gardener who can do this by instinct is lucky indeed—nowadays most of us need to learn a few whys and wherefores first. Find out how to control weeds, how to have the most beautifully manicured lawn and how to propagate plants —by sowing seed, taking cuttings, and division. Learn, too, about pruning—when and how in each case—for roses, shrubs, climbers, hedges and trees. Not many of us are fortunate enough to have a greenhouse, the one place in the world where the gardener has total control—over soil, water, temperature and light. Find out how to get the best use out of your relationship with your greenhouse.

LEFT: there are many useful techniques that will help make light work of your garden.

KNOW YOUR SOIL

Soil is the result of organic forces working on the inorganic rock. In a ceaseless process, the nature of the parent rock decides much of the character of the resulting soil.

PLANT NUTRIENTS

A good soil will contain all the nutrient elements necessary for the well-being of plants. The main nutrients present, in relatively large quantities, are nitrogen, potassium and phosphorus plus lesser amounts of magnesium, calcium, sulphur, carbon, hydrogen and oxygen. The minor, or trace, elements are iron, manganese, boron, molybdenum, zinc and copper. A plant lacking any of these elements may suffer.

ABOVE: *if your garden has acid soil choose plants such as rhododendrons and ericas.* BELOW: *rock plants need well-drained soil.*

TYPES OF SOIL

From the gardener's point of view, soils are classified according to the amount of sand or clay particles they contain. They are also described according to their acidity or alkalinity.

CLAY

Clay soils are difficult to cultivate because they are slow-draining and have little air penetration. They are sticky when wet, hard when dry, slow to warm up in spring and described as heavy. They are usually rich in nutrients. To test a soil for clay, squeeze a moist sample between finger and thumb. If the particles slide readily and the soil looks shiny, it has a high clay content. A squeezed handful will readily bind together.

The addition of organic matter greatly improves clay soils, allowing water and air to pass through them. Added lime causes particles to bind together, forming larger air spaces.

SAND

Sandy soils drain rapidly and there is ample air for plant roots. They are easy to cultivate and quick to warm up in spring, but they dry out very easily and, because of their rapid drainage, nutrients are quickly washed away. To test a soil for sand, squeeze the particles between finger and thumb. If the sand content is high the particles will both look and feel rough. A squeezed handful of soil will not bind together well. Improve sandy soils by the addition of organic matter such as garden compost.

SILT

Silty soils have particles intermediate in size between

See also: Compost-making pages 198–199

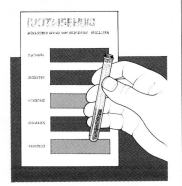

sand and clay. They are sticky and fairly heavy, and can be difficult to cultivate because they are not flocculated and liming is of little help. Improve the texture of silt soils by applying large amounts of humus-producing material.

LOAM

This is the ideal soil, containing a mixture of clay, sand and silt, plus organic matter and plant nutrients. It is easy to cultivate, retains moisture and nutrients, yet is well drained. Loam varies and may be classified as light, medium or heavy, depending on the clay-to-sand ratio.

ABOVE LEFT, FROM TOP:
add organic matter to improve clay soil;
sandy soils also benefit from organic matter;
choose lime-loving plants for chalk soils;
lime benefits peat soils.

SOIL PROFILE

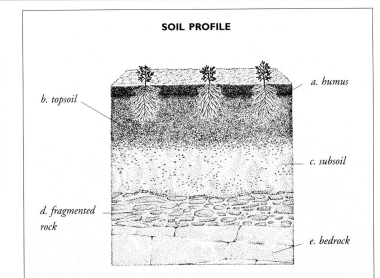

a. humus
b. topsoil
c. subsoil
d. fragmented rock
e. bedrock

In most temperate climates, a cross-section of the soil (known as a soil profile) will show five separate layers or "horizons." The topmost layer (a) will consist of humus unless the ground has recently been cultivated, in which case this layer will have been incorporated in the topsoil. The most important layer as far as the gardener is concerned is the topsoil (b). Ideally this should be 2–3ft deep. It should contain adequate supplies of plant nutrients and organic matter, and should be well-drained and aerated. Below the topsoil is the subsoil layer (c), consisting of partially broken-down rock. It is infertile but can contain useful nutrients. A layer of fragmented rock (d) may occur between the subsoil and the solid parent rock or bedrock (e).

PEATMOSS

Made up of partially decomposed organic matter, peaty soils are inclined to be acid and poorly drained. The addition of lime, nutrients, coarse sand, grit or weathered ashes and the construction of artificial drainage systems improves their quality.

HUMUS

The dark brown crumbly organic matter within the soil is humus. It consists of plant and animal remains in various stages of decay and ensures the continued survival of bacteria, which are essential if a soil is to be fertile. Humus also retains moisture, keeps the soil well aerated and is a source of plant nutrients. On cultivated

ground humus breaks down more quickly than it would if it were left undisturbed. Therefore, it is very important that the soil is amply and regularly replenished with well-rotted manure, compost, leafmold or other humus-forming material whenever possible.

DRAINAGE

Both water and air are necessary in the soil if plants and soil organisms are to thrive. In poorly drained soils, the roots of plants are restricted to the top few inches of ground where they cannot anchor the plant firmly or search very far for nutrients. Lack of air inhibits the plant's uptake of minerals from the soil.

ACIDITY AND ALKALINITY

The amount of lime a soil contains governs its acidity. A soil rich in lime or chalk is said to be alkaline. One which lacks lime is described as acid or sour. The degree of acidity or alkalinity is measured on the pH scale which runs from 0 to 14. A soil with a pH above 7.0 is called alkaline, and one with a pH of below 6.5 is called acid. Soils with pH readings above 8.5 and below 4.5 are rare. Most plants prefer a soil with a pH in the range 6.5 to 7.0.

See also: Improving the soil pages 196–7

IMPROVING THE SOIL

As soon as a piece of land is dug, the process of humus breakdown is speeded up. This means the soil structure and the organic and chemical content may have to be altered. There are many materials, bulky or granular, organic or inorganic, that can be used to improve soil and turn it into the best possible growing medium for a wide range of plants.

INORGANIC SOIL CONDITIONERS

On heavy soils, inorganic soil conditioners—such as weathered wood and fuel ashes, coarse sand, grit, sawdust, wood shavings and pine needles—help make cultivation easier. They open up the soil, allowing in air, but they are best applied in combination with organic matter.

MODIFYING pH

Some plants need acid soil, while others prefer chalky alkaline soil. While it is best to try to grow plants suited to your prevailing soil conditions, it is possible to adjust the pH value of your soil. To raise the pH value (in other words to increase the alkaline balance of the soil), add hydrated lime, ordinary ground limestone or chalk (calcium carbonate) as directed on the packet.

It is much more difficult to lower the pH of your soil to make it more acidic. Start by enriching the soil with a

BELOW: *different plants like acid or alkaline soils—you can adjust the pH of your soil to suit those you wish to grow.*

See also: Acidity and alkalinity page 195

peatmoss substitute and other acidic organic matter. Then apply flowers of sulphur at the rate of 4oz per 3ft^2 on sandy soils and 8oz per 3ft^2 on heavy soils. Test the soil every month. An effective drainage system will also help leach some of the chalk out of the soil.

FERTILIZER

There are two basic kinds of fertilizer, organic and inorganic, and both are equally valuable in the garden.

All organic fertilizers contain carbon and have been derived from living organisms. Before organic fertilizers can be absorbed by the plant they must be broken down in the soil by bacteria and fungi into inorganic chemicals, so organic fertilizers encourage soil bacteria and thus increase fertility. They are released for plant use relatively slowly.

APPLYING FERTILIZERS

• *Apply to the ground before sowing or planting or as a top-dressing while plants are growing.*

• *Apply base dressings to the soil a few days before sowing or at the time of planting, working it into the top few inches.*

• *Dust fertilizers around plants while the soil is moist and hoe lightly into the top few inches.*

• *Soluble powder or liquid form can be watered on to the soil or sprayed over plant foliage.*

• *These foliar feeds are generally quick-acting and should be applied when the soil is moist and in dull weather.*

Inorganic fertilizers do not contain carbon. They cannot improve soil texture and do not add any humus, but they are often very quick-acting and richer in nutrients.

All fertilizers are labeled to show their nutrient content in terms of nitrogen (N), phosphoric acid (P_2O_5) and potash (K_2O). Some fertilizers are described as "straight," meaning that they supply just one of these nutrients; others are called "compound" and supply varying quantities of all three nutrients.

ORGANIC ENRICHMENT

Bulky organic manures improve soil texture and structure. They are often rich in trace elements which may be lacking in fertilizers, and they release their nutrients relatively slowly. Most plants thrive in soil that has been dressed with well-rotted manure or compost in the fall before planting. Fresh manure should not be added to the soil before it has had a chance to decay, because in its fresh state it gives off harmful ammonia. Also, until bacteria decay occurs, nitrogen in the soil is not available to plants.

ABOVE: *apply well-rotted manure or compost to the soil in the fall before planting.*

THE VALUE OF ORGANIC MATERIAL IN THE GARDEN

SOIL STRUCTURE
Enriches the soil composition by making the nutrients in the soil more accessible, which improves its fertility and makes it easier for the plant roots to grow down through the soil.

SOIL HEALTH
Helps reduce both diseases and soil pests.

OTHER USES
Bulky matter can be used as a mulch to ensure that the soil remains moist, to control weed growth, and to act as a component in growing media.

PLANT FOODS
Some plant foods contain crucial nutrients; these include phosphate, potash and nitrogen and minor, or trace, elements.

CHOOSING ORGANIC MATERIALS

COIR (COCONUT FIBER)
Coir can be used as an element in growing media. It is only appropriate for acid-loving plants (pH 5.5–6.3) and is available from garden depots.

GARDEN COMPOST
Garden compost is a valuable alternative to animal manures. It may consist of a wide variety of garden and kitchen waste which has been rotted down over a period of several months. It is relatively rich in nutrients and a good soil conditioner. It may be applied as a mulch or dug into the soil.

SEAWEED
Seaweed contains plant nutrients, particularly potash, and it decomposes quickly. It may be dug straight into the ground while wet, or else composted with garden waste and applied when partially broken down. Dried seaweed meal can be bought from garden suppliers.

Grass cuttings

SPENT MUSHROOM COMPOST
Although they vary in their nutrient value, the spent composts sold off by mushroom growers are well worth using to boost the organic content of soils. They usually contain animal manure, loam and chalk in varying quantities and can be used in all soils except for those that are being used to grow lime-hating plants.

Weeds

Fall leaves

WORM COMPOST
This is very beneficial as a plant food, a soil conditioner, and for potting compost. It can be applied wherever feeding is needed, and is ideal for adding to hanging baskets and planters and for top-dressing pots. Scatter the compost thinly on to the soil and mix it into the first few inches. It can be home-made or bought at a garden depot.

Hedge clippings

See also: Compost-making pages 198–199

COMPOST-MAKING

A compost pile will cheaply and quickly turn backyard and kitchen waste into valuable soil-enriching material.

PRINCIPLES OF COMPOST-MAKING

• To make good, crumbly compost the pile must be properly constructed so that the organic material can decompose rapidly and not just turn into a pile of stagnant vegetation.
• Air, moisture and nitrogen are all necessary if bacteria and fungi are to break down the raw material efficiently. Air is allowed in through the base and sides of the pile. Water should be applied with a can or hose if the pile shows signs of drying out, and moisture can be kept in by covering the pile with sacking, old carpet or polyethylene sheeting. Nitrogen must be provided in the form of grass mowings, young nettles or manure, or by adding a compost activator.
• Site the pile in a sheltered and shady place but not under

ABOVE: *a well-made compost pile produces organic matter, to feed plants such as dianthus and penstemons* (below).

trees or where tree roots may move into the compost. It must be protected from the drying sun and wind. Allow ample time for decomposition.

COMPOST CAGE

Either buy a compost cage or make your own.
• Put up a square cage of wire netting, supported by four stout posts driven into the ground. Make the front removable to allow the rotted compost to be easily extracted.
• For large cages, make a false floor by placing a layer of twiggy branches or brushwood in the base, or support a few short planks on bricks to permeate the compost.
• Sacking or polyethylene can be weighted down with bricks on the top of the pile to keep the moisture in.

COMPOSTABLE MATERIALS

Garden and kitchen waste in great variety can be turned into good compost if properly mixed. One of the secrets of ensuring rapid decomposition is not to allow large quantities of

See also: Basic tools pages 200–201

GREEN MANURE

The practice of sowing certain crops and then digging the resulting plants into the ground to enrich the soil, to provide a source of nitrogen and to improve texture is known as green manuring. Rape, annual lupins, vetches, mustard and perennial rye grass may all be used. Broadcast the seed quite thickly over the ground in spring or early summer and then rake it in. The plants will grow quickly; dig them in just before they flower.

one particular material to build up in the pile. All the following materials may be composted if properly mixed together: animal manure and urine, annual weeds, crushed egg-shells, dead flower heads, lawn mowings (unless the lawn has been treated with hormone weedkillers), pea pods, potato peelings, soft hedge clippings, tea leaves, tree and shrub leaves, vegetable leaves and stems. Do not use woody material or any vegetation that has been sprayed with herbicides or is affected by diseases and pests.

CONSTRUCTING THE PILE

Layer the material and lightly firm it down with the head of a rake or the back of a fork. Add the activator if necessary. Continue until the cage is full. Keep a cover over the top of the pile, and if the compost becomes dry, remove the cover and water it to encourage the rotting process.

MAKING COMPOST

1 *Chop garden material into small pieces with a sharp spade. This will aid decomposition.*

2 *Tease out dense lumps of garden material in order to allow air in.*

3 *Turn the contents of the compost pile from time to time in order to speed up the process.*

When the cage is full a 2in layer of soil may be spread over the top instead of sacking or polyethylene. Leave the cage and if possible start to construct a second cage.

USING THE COMPOST

The compost should be brown and crumbly, though some of the material may still be recognizable. Unrotted material may be left behind as the basis of the new pile.

Use only very well-rotted compost as a mulch, as partially decomposed material may contain weed seeds that will soon germinate and become a nuisance. Alternatively, dig in the compost during soil cultivation during the fall and winter at the rate of 10lb per 3ft².

LEAFMOLD

The leaves of deciduous trees and shrubs may be rotted down on their own to make soil-enriching leafmold. A wire cage (similar to that made for compost) makes a suitable container. A fast space-saving alternative is to pack the layers

RIGHT: *you can make a compost cage very simply or buy one ready-made. Air must be able to enter through the sides and base of the heap, and water should be applied if the pile gets dry, plus nitrogen from green clippings or a compost activator. All three elements are essential to break down the materials.*

of leaves and fertilizer in black polyethylene sacks that have been perforated to allow in air. Filled, tied at the top and stood in an out-of-the-way corner of the garden, the sacks of leaves

will form good leafmold which can be used in the spring following a fall collection. Leaves that are kept in outdoor cages may take rather too long to decay.

MAKING LEAFMOLD

Leafmould from the leaves of deciduous trees is rich in plant foods, especially nitrogen. The collected leaves can be packed into an open-air pile or you can make a simple container out of wire stretched between four posts that have been driven into the ground.

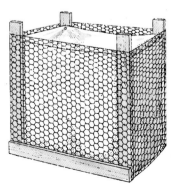

BASIC TOOLS

Good basic tools are indispensable for any work in the garden. Choose them with care, selecting the right size and type for your particular needs. With proper maintenance they can last a lifetime.

LEFT: *a popular garden rake is a spring-toothed rake which is useful for collecting up leaves and grass.*

ALTHOUGH A good spade or fork is not cheap, with care it will probably have as long a life as its owner.

It is also essential to find a tool that is of the right size and model to suit your particular needs. The tool must perform the task that it is meant for efficiently, and it is also wise to take into account how frequently it is likely to be used, as this could determine the amount it is necessary to spend.

To preserve your tools it is vital to clean off any gardening dirt with an oily cloth; cutting and pruning tools should be sharpened frequently and tools that are not needed during the winter should be very well oiled and kept in a dry place.

SPADES

Spades are available with shafts of different lengths and blades of different sizes. The standard spade blade measures 11½ x 7½in; that of the ladies' spade 10 x 6½in; and that of the border spade 9 x 5½in. Choose whichever is most comfortable to use and bear in mind that heavy digging will probably be easier with the middle size. Choose a shaft length to suit your height.

The shaft of the spade should have a gentle crank to allow maximum leverage, and the strapped or tubular socket should be securely attached to the shaft. Metal treads welded to the upper edge of the blade make digging heavy soil less painful to the foot.

Spades that have stainless steel blades are far more expensive than those equipped with blades of forged steel, but they are exceptionally long-lasting and penetrate the soil much more easily than ordinary steel spades.

USES

An essential tool for digging and trenching, the spade is also efficient for skimming weed growth off the soil before cultivation begins.

Always hold the spade upright when cutting into the soil prior to lifting it, so that the ground is cultivated to the full depth of the blade. The spade is also useful when you are planting trees and shrubs, and for mixing compost.

FORKS

The fork is just as useful as the spade and is similarly manufactured. The four tines may be square in cross-section, as in the general purpose or digging fork, or flat as in the potato fork which is designed to avoid tuber damage at harvesting time. The head of the digging fork measures 12 x 7½in, and that of the smaller border fork 9 x 5½in. Both stainless and forged steel types are available.

USES

A fork is easier to use than a spade for digging heavy soil, though it cannot be used to skim off weeds. It is essential for breaking down rough-dug soil and for lightly cultivating well-worked ground before seed-sowing and planting. The smaller border fork can be used to cultivate the soil among herbaceous plants and shrubs, and the larger fork is useful for moving compost and manure. Both can be used to aerate lawns.

HAND FORKS

Of the same size as a trowel, the three- or four-pronged hand fork is similarly made.

USES

For transplanting seedlings, for working among tightly packed plants such as alpines in the rock garden, and for intricate planting and weeding, the hand fork is unsurpassed.

RAKES

The most popular type of garden rake has a steel head 12in wide which is fitted with teeth 2in long. The shaft should be approximately 5ft long and smooth to allow a

See also: Cultivation techniques pages 202–203

SHAFTS AND HANDLES

The shafts of tools can be made from several different materials, including wood, metal, and plastic. Wood is traditional and long-lasting. Make sure that the wood of the shaft is close-grained and that the grain runs down the length of the shaft. Check that it is smooth and not likely to splinter.

Shafts made from polypropylene are light-weight yet strong, and lighter tools such as hoes and rakes are often equipped with tubular aluminum alloy shafts which are coated with plastic. All three materials will offer a good service if they are not ill-treated.

Spades and forks are fitted with handles in three shapes: "T," "D," and "YD." Try all three and find the most comfortable.

good backward and forward motion. Larger wooden rakes are useful for raking up leaves, grass and debris, which clog in steel rake teeth. However, wooden rakes wear out faster.

USES
The main use of the rake should be to level soil that has been previously broken down to a reasonable tilth with a fork. Although the rake will make the soil texture even finer, it should not be over-used or the soil will be inclined

to pan. Move the rake backward and forward over the soil in a sweeping motion, first in one direction and then at right angles to ensure an even finish.

HOES

There are many different types of hoe but the two most important are the Dutch hoe and the draw hoe. Both are equipped with 5ft handles and forged or stainless steel blades. The head of the Dutch hoe consists of a horseshoe-shaped piece of metal, across the open end of which is attached a flat 4–5in blade designed to cut almost horizontally through the soil. The rectangular or semi-circular head of the draw hoe is of a similar width but is attached at right angles to the handle and is used with a chopping or scraping motion.

USES
The Dutch hoe is perhaps the best tool for general weeding, as the gardener skims it backward and forward just below the surface of the soil while walking backward. In this way the cultivated ground is not walked over and the weeds (severed from their roots) are left to dry out in the loose soil. The Dutch hoe is also used for breaking up surface pans.

With the draw hoe the gardener must move forward, chopping the soil and pulling it toward him or her slightly, or scraping the weeds off the surface. The draw hoe (despite its disadvantage of forcing the gardener to walk over the cultivated soil) is safer to use among closely spaced plants than a Dutch hoe. Both types of hoe can be used to draw seed drills against a taut garden line, and the draw hoe

ABOVE: *the gardener's constant companions: the hand fork is ideal for working among tightly spaced plants, while the trowel is good for planting out small bedding and vegetable plants.*
RIGHT: *when buying a spade or fork, take care to choose the correct blade size and shaft length to suit your own height.*

is used to earth up vegetables such as potatoes, leeks and celery.

TROWELS

An invaluable planting tool, the trowel usually has a wooden or polypropylene handle, 4–6in long. Longer-handled versions are available but may be less comfortable to use. If possible try to buy a trowel with a stainless-steel blade rather than one made from forged steel, for you will find this much easier to use, less likely to bend and it will not rust.

USES
The trowel may be used like a shovel or flour scoop and also as if it were a digging claw. Either method may be used depending on the preference of the gardener. Scoop the soil out of the hole. Insert the plant in the hole and refirm the soil around the roots with the hands. Use the trowel for planting bedding and herbaceous plants, vegetables and bulbs.

WHEELBARROWS

In larger backyards and on the vegetable plot a wheelbarrow can save a lot of time and energy. Always check the weight distribution of a barrow before buying it—as much of the load as possible should be placed over the wheel so that the barrow, and not the operator, takes most of the weight. Barrows are available with large, inflated, ball-shaped wheels, and these are especially useful if the land to be traversed is soft. Small, two-wheeled barrows can be easier to load, unload and push than single-wheeled types. Solid-tyre models are adequate where sinkage will not be a problem. Make sure that the chosen barrow is large enough without being too heavy.

USES
Compost, manure, soil, sacks of fertilizer, and all manner of equipment can be moved around the garden with the aid of a barrow. Stand the barrow upright against a wall or under cover when it is not in use.

See also: Weed control pages 210–211

CULTIVATION TECHNIQUES

For the best results, always choose the right cultivation technique for the job in hand.

LEFT AND BELOW: *digging and raking are two of the essential techniques for the good preparation of a vegetable garden.*

DIGGING SENSIBLY

• *Remember to keep the spade vertical; a slanting cut achieves less depth.*

• *Drive the spade in at right angles to free the clod of earth and allow it to be lifted cleanly.*

• *Lift up small spadefuls of soil that are light and easy to handle.*

• *Dig a little ground at a time on a regular basis. Cultivate a 3¼ft strip every day rather than attempting to dig the entire plot at once.*

IT IS NECESSARY to cultivate the ground for several reasons:
• to control weeds.
• to incorporate manures, composts and fertilizers.
• to relieve compaction and improve soil texture.
• to allow in air.

CULTIVATION

It is best to dig heavy soils in the fall and winter so that frost, wind, snow and rain can gradually break down the clods of earth. Never work on any soil when it is frozen or very wet as it is all too easy to damage its structure.

Light soils can be cultivated at any time during winter and early spring, provided they are allowed to settle for two or three weeks before the crop is sown or planted.

Forking Use a fork on very stony or heavy ground and for cultivating the bottom of trenches during double digging and trenching. The disadvantages of using the fork for the entire digging operation are that it is unable to slice cleanly through surface weed growth, and that light soils may fall through its tines.

Raking The main reason for raking is to level a piece of ground, either for seed-sowing, planting or laying paving materials. They can also be used to cover seeds after sowing, to replace the soil in drills and to collect leaves and other garden debris. Use long, steady movements of the arms, drawing the rake to and fro and supporting it so that its teeth sweep over the surface and do not dig in.

Hoeing Hoeing serves two useful purposes: it keeps down weeds and so reduces

competition for light and nutrients; and it relieves compaction and allows vital air into the soil. It is also claimed that a layer of fine soil on the surface of the ground acts like a mulch and prevents excessive water loss.

The Dutch hoe is the most versatile and can be used for weeding between plants and making drills. When weeding,

See also: Basic tools pages 200–201; Plant care and cultivation pages 204–209

hold the hoe with the blade parallel to the ground and pull it along the ground to uproot the weeds. For making a drill, hold the hoe at an angle with the corner pointing downward and drag it along, so leaving a small drill.

Single digging This is adequate for most ordinary soils of reasonable depth which do not overlay an intractable subsoil. The soil is cultivated to the depth of one spade blade or "spit."

If the plot is very wide, divide it in two lengthways and

NO-DIG GARDENING

Some gardeners believe that digging is harmful to the soil as it disturbs the activity of bacteria and earthworms and so upsets the natural balance. Non-diggers prefer to apply thick mulches of well-rotted compost, manure or peat to the surface of the soil and let earthworms and other organisms incorporate this enrichment. Seeds are sown in the compost and subsequent mulches are applied while the plants are growing.

DOUBLE DIGGING

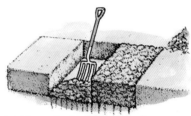

1 *Take out a trench 2ft wide and one spit deep at one end of the plot. Position the soil alongside the spot to be occupied by the final trench. Divide the plot in two if it is very large.*

2 *When all the soil has been removed from the first trench, fork over the base to the full depth of the fork's tines. Fork compost or manure into the lower layer of soil.*

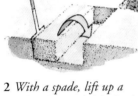

3 *Next, start to dig and throw forward the soil adjacent to it following the same procedure as for single digging. Make sure that the soil is turned over, and remove perennial weeds as you go.*

4 *When 2ft of soil has been thrown into the first trench, the second trench will have been created and the base forked over. Continue until the entire plot of soil has been dug to a depth of about 20in.*

SINGLE DIGGING

1 *Take out a trench one spit deep and 12–20in wide across one end of the plot. Pile the soil at the opposite end of the plot (it will eventually be used to fill the final trench). If the soil is to be manured as it is dug, throw the organic matter into the bottom of the trench at this point and mix it in well.*

2 *With a spade, lift up a comfortable spadeful of soil and throw it forward into the trench, turning it upside-down as you go. Watch out for any perennial weeds and remove any that you come across as you go.*

3 *Work along the first trench, throwing the soil over and forward with your spade until another trench has eventually been created.*

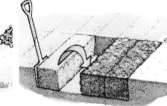

4 *More manure may then be added and the operation repeated. When the end of the plot is reached, the soil from the first trench is used to fill the last.*

---

take out the first trench on one half of the plot, depositing the soil at the same end of the other half. Now work down the first strip of land and back up the second, throwing the soil from the first trench into the last one.

Double digging With double digging the soil is cultivated to a depth of two spits. This is especially useful on land which has not been cultivated before or where a hard subsoil layer is impeding drainage and the penetration of plant roots.

MULCHING

Mulching means coating the ground with a layer of material. There are two types: biodegradable (leafmold, bark and compost; newspaper and old carpet) and non-degradable (plastic or polythene sheeting). Both help to discourage weeds, particularly non-degradable sheet materials. Before you apply a mulch, water the soil and make sure the surface is warm. This is

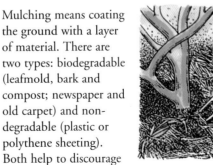

because the mulch will prevent water percolating into the soil and act as an insulator, so preventing the soil from warming up quickly.

Mulches have several other important uses.

• *They help to keep the soil moist.*

• *They help to keep the soil warm in winter and cool in summer.*

• *They protect the topsoil from heavy rain.*

• *Organic matter also improves the structure of the soil, as well as supplying plant nutrients.*

See also: Weed control pages 210–211

PLANT CARE AND CULTIVATION

Plants are available in several different forms, each of which demands a different treatment in terms of planting and aftercare.

ABOVE: *antirrhinums in a multi-colored display are examples of plants that can be grown from seed under glass, although they are usually bought as plants.*

BUYING PLANTS

Plants are sold as "bare-rooted," "balled," or "container grown."

BARE-ROOTED PLANTS
This is the cheapest way of buying most plants. Bare-rooted plants are lifted from a nursery bed and most of the soil is shaken from around their roots. Bare-rooted plants should be transplanted only in the fall and winter when they are dormant (or nearly).

BALLED PLANTS
These are lifted with as much soil as is practicable, held around the plant with some type of sacking or polythene. Balled plants are more expensive than bare-rooted ones, but if the work of balling and replanting is well done, they have a better chance of survival. The planting season is a little more extended, balled evergreens often being moved in early spring or early fall.

See also: The role of plants pages 112–113

CONTAINER-GROWN PLANTS

Container-grown plants are those that are really well established in pots, polyethylene bags or anything else which will ensure that all the roots and the soil around them can be transported and planted with the minimum of disturbance. Although more expensive than bare-rooted or balled plants, container-grown plants can be put in at any time of the year when the soil is in good working condition. Most of the shrubs and climbers offered for sale in garden depots are container grown.

TRAYS OF PLANTS

Trays of plants vary in quality enormously. Seedlings may be dried out and dying, they may be thin and spindly, they may have yellowing leaves, or they may be so far advanced that the roots are actually growing out through the base of the tray. Pick sturdy, compact plants that are growing evenly. Always select a full tray or a section of a tray, rather than loosely wrapped plants.

SEEDS

The great value of buying seeds is that you can get a far greater range of annuals and biennials than if you are depending on the purchase of pregrown bedding plants. Read the instructions on the packet thoroughly and make sure that the plant is for you. Many people believe that plants will flower from seeds in a short time. This is not necessarily true, many of the more beautiful plants that you can grow from seeds need a whole year, in which they must be transferred from their initial growing place into containers, before being planted out in their flowering positions the following year.

CUTTINGS

The cheapest plants of all are those that you propagate yourself from cuttings. Shrubs grow surprisingly fast from cuttings and many are very easy to root.

A clear plastic bag and a window ledge will suffice for small numbers of cuttings, but results are quicker and better

ABOVE: *the splendid shrub Pieris, with its glowing red leaves which appear in spring, is usually bought as a container-grown plant.*

with an electrically heated propagator. A cold frame is not essential when it comes to acclimatizing the young plants to outside conditions but it helps. Alternatively, you can stand the pots outside for an increasing amount of time during the warmest part of the day; eventually you should be able to leave them outside over a mild night—but do not rush the process.

PLANTING

CONTAINER-GROWN AND BALLED PLANTS

Dig a hole just a little larger than the container and slip the plant into this with as little root disturbance as possible. Fill any remaining space with a mixture of peat and broken-down soil.

Pot-grown plants can usually be tapped out quite safely by turning them upside down and rapping the rim of the pot sharply on something firm, such as the handle of a spade thrust well into the soil. Carefully hold the plant while doing this so that it does not fall to the ground or snap off. In the case of balled plants and those grown in polythene bags, cut and strip off the covering material with the plant on the edge of, or actually in, the hole it is to occupy.

BARE-ROOTED PLANTS

Dig a hole large enough to ensure that there is space for all the roots to lie naturally, with room at the top for a covering of 1 or 2in of soil over the uppermost roots.

Another way to determine depth is to look for the dark soil mark on the stem or stems, indicating where the soil came to in the nursery bed, and to replant so that this is just beneath the surface.

With bare-rooted plants it is also necessary to work soil around and between the roots and to make this easy it often pays to prepare in advance a planting mixture composed of well-broken soil mixed with about a third its bulk of peat and containing a light sprinkling of bonemeal.

Whatever type of plant is being used, once the soil has been returned around and over the roots it should be made thoroughly firm by pressing all round with the foot, after which a little loose soil or peat can be scattered over the soil to leave everything tidy.

ROOT SYSTEMS

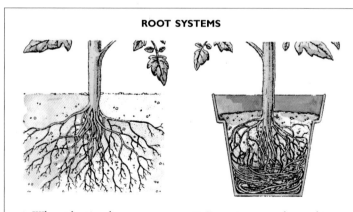

1 *When planting bare-rooted plants, dig a hole that is big enough for the roots to lie completely naturally. Allow 1–2in above the plant's roots for a covering of soil.*

2 *For pot-grown plants, dig a hole a little larger than the container. Turn the plant upside down and tap the rim, then slip it into the hole, taking care not to disturb the roots.*

See also: Plant associations pages 114–120; Shrubs for year-round interest pages 132–135; Plant propagation pages 216–225

WATERING AND FEEDING

If plants are to grow healthily without check, they must have access to a constant supply of water or they will wilt and growth is temporarily halted. If water is not made available to them soon after wilting, their leaves will turn crisp and brown and they will eventually die. It is particularly important to keep vegetables and fruit well-watered. Sandy soils will dry out more quickly than clay soils, and will have to be watered sooner in a drought.

WHEN TO WATER

You are most likely to need to water growing plants—particularly herbaceous and bedding plants—in spring and summer, rather than in the fall and winter. But this is also the prime planting season for deciduous trees and shrubs, and it is a good idea to water them in well unless the ground is extremely moist at planting time. This is not necessary so much to keep the plant growing as to settle the soil particles around the roots in readiness for growth the following spring.

WATERING CANS

The simplest method is to use a watering can. Choose a can with a long spout, good balance when full and a long reach. Galvanized steel cans are durable but expensive. Plastic is cheaper but not so long lived.

Both will split if water is allowed to freeze in them in winter. Spray heads or "roses" are supplied with most cans and these vary from fine to coarse. Use a fine rose on seeds and seedlings.

When using a can fitted with a rose to water trays of seedlings, begin pouring to one side of the plants then pass the can over them, maintaining a

ABOVE: lawns can be kept watered using rotating or oscillating sprinklers as a permanent fixture, or the sprinklers can be attached to hoses.
LEFT: the simple watering can with a long spout and varying spray heads works best.

steady flow. Move the can away from the plants before stopping the flow of water. This technique avoids any sudden surges of water which can both damage tender plants and displace compost.

WATERING HOSES

If you have a tap nearby, a hose is quick and easy to use. It may be left running on a patch of

See also: Containers pages 174–192

LEFT: *shallow-rooted summer bedding plants in flower borders need regular watering.*

SUSCEPTIBLE SITES

• *Beds and borders against walls are particularly prone to drying out and need regular watering.*

• *Plants in tubs, pots, and particularly hanging baskets will need regular applications of water through the summer because they can dry out very quickly. When filling the container with compost, leave a gap between the surface of the soil and the rim of the container to allow a sufficient amount of water to be applied. Water when the top 1in of the container compost dries out; aim to keep it always damp but not sodden.*

PLANTING

After planting trees and shrubs, water them in well to settle the soil around the roots.

When you are planting in containers, leave a gap between the compost and the rim of the pot to allow for watering. When watering, carefully fill this space.

soil and moved around at intervals, or it may be held over a particular plant or group of plants. Take care not to allow strong flows of water to wash away soil and expose the roots of plants. Buy a strong hose which will not kink when bent and which will retain its suppleness over the years. Cheap hoses will crack and leak, especially if used in cold weather. Hoses reinforced with nylon thread are especially strong. A wide range of clip-on connectors and nozzles is available.

SPRINKLERS

There are two main types of sprinkler, both of which can be attached to a hose. The oscillating type consists of a perforated tube which rocks backward and forward, distributing its water over a square or rectangular area. The rotating sprinkler ejects water from one or more nozzles which are forced around by the water pressure. This type of sprinkler covers a circular area. Both sprinklers may be controlled to a certain extent by the water pressure—the higher the pressure the larger the area they will cover.

Sprinklers may be less effective on ornamental plants than on vegetables, especially in summer. The foliage of some ornamentals will deflect much of the spray, and heavy blooms and foliage can be weighed down and damaged by the water. Sprinklers are best used on ornamentals not in bloom.

MULCHING

A 2–3in thick layer of organic matter spread around plants growing in beds and borders will slowly decompose and help to enrich the soil. Mulching will also suppress weed growth as well as helping to conserve soil moisture. Mulches are best laid in spring on top of moist soil and any remaining material can be forked into the soil in the fall.

FEEDING

Plants that are grown both in open ground and in containers must always be kept supplied with nutrients. This will help to ensure a healthy rate of vigorous growth.

Outdoors, the rain—topped up with regular watering when necessary—will leach plant foods from the soil. In addition, the nutrients in container compost are quickly used up by the developing plant and it will need a further supply of nutrients as it grows.

See also: Garden trees pages 127–129; Shrubs for year-round interest pages 132–135

STAKING A TREE

*1 Secure the tree to the stake
with two tree ties, placed 2in
from the top and 12in above
soil level.*

PROTECTING PLANTS

STAKING AND SUPPORTING

Newly planted trees will need
staking until they have grown
enough roots to support
themselves. Other garden
plants produce large heavy
blooms and therefore need
constant support.

Trees Dig the planting hole
and check that it is large
enough for the tree's roots.
Then knock a stake into the
soil until one-third of its length
is buried. The stake should be
either a length of 2 × 2in
wood, treated with a
preservative other than
creosote, or a larch pole
similarly protected. Position the
stake to windward of the tree.
The top should be just below
the lowest branch.

With the stake firmly in
place, plant the tree. Then fix
one tree tie 2in from the top
of the stake and another 12in
above soil level. Check the ties
regularly and loosen them as
necessary.

SUPPORTING FLOWERS

*1 Support top-heavy
flowering plants with
bamboo poles. Tie the
stems of the plants to
the poles with soft
twine or raffia.*

*2 Support herbaceous
plants by inserting
bushy twigs among
them. The plants will
grow through the
branches.*

*3 Special wire plant
supports on legs can
also be used to
support herbaceous
plants. They come in
several different sizes.*

ABOVE: *a wigwam of canes
supporting climbing or top-
heavy flowering plants can add
dramatic height to a border.*

Flowers Support plants with
top-heavy stems either with
stout bamboo poles or 1in
wooden stakes pushed into the
ground alongside them. Fasten
the stems to the supports with
soft twine or raffia. Make sure
that the support does not
touch the flower or damage
may result.

Support bushy herbaceous
plants by pushing twiggy
branches among them while
they are small. As the plants
grow they mask the branches
but are held steady by them.
More permanent herbaceous

See also: Garden trees pages 127–129; Climbing and screening plants pages 138–141 plant supports include wire hoops on legs. These are available in various sizes and can be adjusted as the plants grow taller.

WIND PROTECTION

Wind can cause great damage in the garden, particularly to newly planted trees and shrubs. The plants may be blown over and they may become desiccated, which causes their foliage to wilt and turn brown. Screens may be used to shelter trees or shrubs.

FROST PROTECTION

The crowns of tender perennial garden plants are susceptible to frost. Protect them by laying a piece of wire netting over each crown. Cover this with dry straw or bracken and fasten another layer of netting over the top to make a warm blanket. You can protect larger plants and shrubs by surrounding them with a cylinder of wire netting filled with straw or bracken.

OVERWINTERING

During winter the care of hardy perennials that remain in their flower beds and herbaceous borders is relatively straightforward as they need little tending. Toward the end of summer, when the foliage has begun to die, cut them back down to the ground so that a maximum of 2in of stem shows above ground. Remove any dead foliage from the soil nearby to prevent any possible rotting from the waste material left around the plant and to discourage insects.

Tubers such as corms, rhizomes or bulbs may need to be removed entirely from the soil and placed in a dry, airy, frost-free place during the winter months.

See also: Colorful perennials pages 142–145

MOVING TREES AND SHRUBS

1 *Cut a vertical slit in the soil around the plant with a spade. Make the slit 12–24in away from the stem, depending on size.*

2 *Take out a trench 12in wide and one spit deep, starting from the slit. Sever any roots that protrude into the trench.*

3 *Thrust the spade under the rootball at a 45° angle cutting the roots. When it will move, ease the rootball on to a sheet.*

4 *Dig a new hole 12in wider all round than the rootball. Add leafmold or peatmoss substitute and two handfuls of bonemeal.*

MOVING TREES AND SHRUBS

The operation is best carried out between early winter and late spring. Considerable amounts of water may be lost by evergreen shrubs and conifers during the move, and an anti-desiccant spray may be applied to the foliage immediately before transplanting to reduce transpiration.

STORING PLANTS

Small plants can be easily stored in a temporary trench dug in a spare corner of the garden. This technique, called heeling in, should also be used for bare-root shrubs and container-grown plants which are not to be planted immediately. Thrust a spade vertically into the ground to a spit depth and pull it back, while still in the earth, to form a trench. Lay the plants against the upright side of the trench and replace the soil loosely.

PINCHING

Pinch out the growing tip of plants such as fuchsias in order to encourage the growth of side-shoots and a bushy habit.

ABOVE: *the rural-garden favorite* Lathyrus odoratus *or sweet pea can be supported on canes, trellis, wire or netting.*

DEADHEADING

Deadheading is the removal, of flower heads as soon as they have died. Perennials and biennials will flower at least once a season if you deadhead them as soon as the first flowers have died.

WEED CONTROL

A weed is a plant growing where it is not wanted. Weeds compete with crops for light, water and nutrients. They also create a micro-environment around plants in which diseases and pests, such as aphids and whitefly, flourish. All in all, weeds should be removed.

ANNUAL WEEDS

Annuals are plants that complete their life-cycle within a single growing season, and they are often able to undergo more than one life-cycle in a season. Annuals are also characterized by the production of large numbers of seeds so that the weed seed population in the soil is constantly replenished and the weeds keep reappearing.

When winter digging, skim off annual weeds and dig them into the bottom of each trench, along with organic manure or garden compost. Subsequent cultivations should kill the young weed seedlings that emerge.

BELOW: *the battle against weeds is constant. Regular hoeing and mulching will keep them at bay, contact weedkillers being the ultimate deterrent.*

PERENNIAL WEEDS

Perennial plants live from year to year and usually have underground organs—stems or roots—which enable them to survive through the winter.

Weed control begins with winter digging prior to growing the first crops. Cut down any woody perennials and dig out all the roots. Double-dig the whole of the garden in the first instance and remove all perennial weed roots and rhizomes. Burn or dispose of them all and never use them for compost-making.

HOEING AGAINST WEEDS

When hoeing, make sure the blade is always sharp so that the weeds are severed from their roots rather than pulled up with them.

Choose a warm, drying day so that the weeds wilt and die quickly after hoeing. Take care when hoeing closely around crop plants because any damage caused is quickly colonized by disease organisms. Keep the hoe in the upper, surface layers of the soil so as not to bring up more weed seeds to germinate and cause further problems. The dry soil produced by surface hoeing acts as a mulch which in itself inhibits weed growth.

RIGHT: use the Dutch hoe to slice weeds from their roots. This has the distinct advantage that it is used while you are walking backward, with the result that cultivated soil is not disturbed.

MULCHING AGAINST WEEDS

Weeds can also be controlled by using mulches. Use non-biodegradable sheet mulches such as black polyethylene. Black polyethylene forms a complete physical barrier to weed growth; it also warms up the soil and conserves moisture. It is usually necessary to bury the edges of the polyethylene to prevent it blowing away and holes must be cut in it through which to plant. A black polyethylene mulch can bring crops forward and hasten their maturity by as much as three weeks but, unfortunately, pests can thrive in the moist conditions produced. Organic mulches perform similar functions but have the advantage that they can be dug into the soil at the end of the season, thus improving both its structure and its fertility.

USING CHEMICALS AGAINST WEEDS

Weedkillers will kill most, if not all, weed growth, both above and below ground, leaving the site free of weeds and ready for cultivation and planting. It is possible to use non-persistent contact weedkiller against annual weeds but it must be applied at a low level with a dribble bar when there is no wind and no danger of drift. It is inactivated rapidly on contact with the soil but kills any green tissues with which it comes into contact so it must be handled with care.

More toxic and persistent weedkillers should not be used where you are growing fruit or vegetables. Whenever you are using chemicals of any sort, it is very important that you always follow the manufacturer's instructions carefully.

NEGLECTED BACKYARDS

The problems confronting any gardener who is faced with the task of taking over a neglected backyard differ enormously. They vary according to the nature of the site and the length of time it has been neglected.

For sites that are to be used for permanent features, such as lawns or shrubberies, it is best to dig the site and, in doing so, to bury any established annual weeds. Remove small patches of perennials by forking out. For sites that are to be cultivated and cropped regularly, devote a season to removing all the weed seeds before cropping begins.

Where backyards have been neglected for several years, strong-growing perennial weeds are likely to dominate. In borders or beds many smaller plants may already have succumbed to perennial grasses, and areas of sod may have been reduced to coarse grass, weeds and moss.

Reclamation can be particularly difficult after any extended period of neglect. In beds and borders, for example, few garden plants other than bulbs remain in sufficiently good condition to merit careful removal before dealing with weeds.

If there is only a small area of infested ground, forking out the roots or rhizomes of perennial weeds is possible. Over larger areas this method is usually much too arduous except perhaps for the dedicated gardener. The only effective approach is to use weedkillers.

METHODS OF WEED CONTROL

1 *In closely planted flower borders, hand weeding is often the only practicable method of properly controlling weeds.*

2 *In front of shrub borders, tap-rooted weeds such as dandelions are best removed with a small hand fork.*

3 *Carefully hoe annual weeds, keeping the blade level with the surface layers of the soil as you work.*

4 *During winter digging, remove all perennial roots and rhizomes and get rid of them for good by burning them.*

5 *Use sheets of black polyethylene or organic mulches as a barrier to weed growth, to conserve moisture and warm the soil.*

6 *Use a dribble bar to apply contact weedkiller at ground level just on top of each weed. Do not use on windy days.*

LAWNS

A beautiful, well-maintained lawn is a valuable feature of a great many gardens, and does a lot to enhance their intrinsic beauty.

PREPARING THE SITE

Ideally, the best site is open to the sky with no large trees nearby but, failing this, it should not be shaded for more than half the day in summer. The soil should be reasonably well drained; waterlogged land must be drained first. If sowing grass seed by hand, mark out the lawn in 3¼ft wide strips with string and stakes. If the soil is very fertile and has been weeded once or twice beforehand, allow ½ oz of seed per 3ft². If the soil is less rich and has not been weeded before sowing, double this quantity. Nothing need be done until the seedlings are well grown if the soil is moist. If the surface dries out before germination, use a fine spray or lawn sprinkler.

LAYING SOD

Sod is lawn grass that has been seeded, cut loose from the soil and rolled or stacked. About ¾in of soil is attached. It achieves an instant lawn and prevents erosion on slopes.

Prepare the site as for seed; early fall and spring are the best times for laying. Apply a lawn fertilizer before laying and rake it in.

SOWING GRASS SEED

1 *Divide the seed into two halves and, if sowing by hand, broadcast one batch walking lengthways across the site and the other batch walking crossways.*

2 *After sowing the seed, lightly rake over the entire seedbed, taking great care not to bury the seed too deeply, otherwise it may not be able to germinate.*

ABOVE: *achieving a perfect lawn takes a lot of time and work, but there is no finer setting for flower-filled borders. Choose an open, well-drained site for a new lawn, which can be made from seed or by laying sod.*

See also: Mowing pages 214–215

FERTILIZERS

Lawns must be fed in order to maintain a healthy condition. Toward the end of spring apply about 4oz per 3ft^2 of lawn fertilizer evenly over the grass, taking care not to exceed the specified amount. In the summer apply the lawn fertilizer again, but using about 2oz per 3ft^2. During the fall lay a special lawn dressing appropriate for the season with a low percentage of nitrogen in relation to phosphoric acid and potash. While you are doing this, also lay a fine top-dressing of peat over the lawn at a rate of about 4oz per 3ft^2 and then brush this into the ground.

WATERING

Watering the grass in dry weather is essential to avoid the lawn turning yellow and then brown. If the lawn is closely mown it will also need to be watered more frequently as the soil is more exposed to the hot sun.

Apply water gradually in sufficient amounts to soak about 1in into the soil; if it is applied too quickly the water merely cakes the surface and runs off it. Fine sprinklers are better than harsh jets as they give an even distribution.

SCARIFYING

Scarifying—to scratch or make small cuts in the lawn with a rake—is important as it eliminates debris and moss, scatters wormcasts and works fertilizers and peatmoss top-dressings into the ground. Gather the moss as you go so you do not scatter it from one area to another.

Using a spring-toothed rake, first rake in one direction and then at right-angles so that all the area is covered. This should be done about once every two weeks from spring through to late summer. Thoroughly rake again before applying fertilizer during the fall.

AERATING

Aerating the lawn will promote healthy growth. The easiest way to aerate it is to spike it with an ordinary

garden fork, pushing the tines about 3in into the ground and levering backward on the handle so that the sod is raised slightly; repeat this every 6in over the lawn.

EDGING

• Trim the grass growing horizontally over the edge of the lawn, using a mechanical edge trimmer or a pair of long-handled shears.

• Cut the edge of the lawn with a special edging tool or a sharp spade.

• When planting close to a lawn, it is useful to lay a line of flagstones between the flower borders and the lawn; leave a channel about 2in wide and 3in deep so that the verges of the lawn can be trimmed easily.

• Lay paths abutting lawns about ½in below the level of the lawn so that the lawnmower can be used over the edge. Leave a channel between the lawn and path.

LEFT: *use a spring-toothed rake to remove dead grass, moss, leaves and wormcasts. Cover the whole lawn, raking first in one direction, then at right angles.*

Aeration is usually done in the early fall, although it can be performed whenever needed.

WEEDING

Eradicate weeds using special weedkillers in spring and early summer, a few days after the application of fertilizer. For persistent coarse weeds, you should repeat applications every two to three weeks.

LAYING SOD

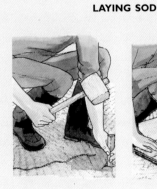

1 *Before you start laying sod, you should apply a dressing of fertilizer to the ground a few days beforehand, unless the soil is already rich.*

2 *If you've applied a dressing of fertilizer, you should rake this in and incorporate it really well into the soil. This will encourage the sod to knit together.*

3 *Mark out the exact shape of your lawn by hammering in pegs at interavls and stretching a length of string or twine between them.*

4 *Lay the sod in straight lines, ensuring that each length is as close as possible to the preceding one. Allow a 1–2in overlap at the edge.*

5 *Stagger rows of sod by laying half pieces. Do not walk on newly laid sod but lay down planks as pathways. These will help to spread out the weight.*

6 *When you have finished laying the sod, trim back the edges. Use an edging tool to do this and you will be left with a neat, sharply defined edge.*

MOWING

Mowing a lawn keeps the grass short enough to be neat and attractive without hindering growth. Mowing too close weakens the grass and allows moss and lawn weeds to become established but, on the other hand, where lawns are allowed to grow too long, coarser grasses become increasingly dominant and finer grasses deteriorate. The best approach is to mow regularly but not too closely.

FREQUENCY OF MOWING

Increase or decrease the frequency of mowing according to the rate of growth, which varies from season to season, and may be influenced by bad weather, feeding, irrigation, the varieties of grass being grown and the general health of the turf itself.

Different types of lawn require a different frequency of mowing. Fine lawns, for example, should be mown every two to three days,

average lawns at least every seven days and preferably at intervals of three to five days and, for other sod lawns, mow at least once a week.

REMOVING THE MOWINGS

If your lawnmower has a grass box it will automatically collect the mowings. Otherwise, use a spring-tined rake.

Only leave the mowings on the lawn if the weather is particularly hot and dry. In this case, it is good to leave them in place because they will act as a mulch and will help to preserve the moisture.

ABOVE: *mow fine lawns frequently, every two or three days, and average lawns such as this one* (left) *at least once a week or, preferably, at intervals of three to five days.*

See also: Lawns pages 212–213

HEIGHT AND FREQUENCY OF CUT

This chart indicates the height and frequency to which different quality lawns should be cut for the period late spring to the early fall. The figures given are only a rough guide, and should be varied according to the weather and the state of the sod. Outside this period the height of cut should be increased by ¼in.

TYPE OF LAWN

ORNAMENTAL   AVERAGE   UTILITY   MEADOW

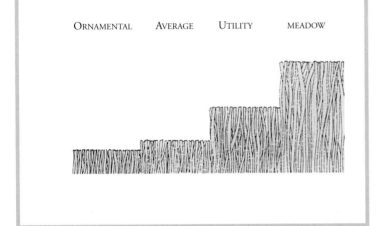

MOWING TIPS

• *Always plan the direction of mowing to minimize overlapping, reversing and abrupt changes of direction.*

• *Mow when dry as wet mowings clog the machine and grass box and lengthen the mowing time.*

• *Scatter wormcasts before mowing.*

• *During the colder months, do not mow when cold winds are blowing as the leaftips may be wind-scorched.*

• *Rake before mowing if the grass contains weeds.*

• *Repeated backward and forward movements result in an uneven cut.*

• *Always mow at right-angles to the line of the previous mow as this helps to control weed grasses.*

PERFECT FINISH

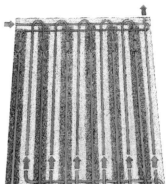

ABOVE: *a neat, branded finish of contrasting light and dark strips can be obtained by using a mower with a rear-mounted roller. Work across the lawn and mow each succeeding parallel strip in the opposite direction to the previous one.*

NEGLECTED LAWNS

First mow the lawn (set the lawn mover blade as high as the grass necessitates; a rotary mower is best, or for long, thick grass use an auto-scythe). Next, work it over with a wire-tined rake to remove the dead grass thatch and moss. Add a proprietary lawn fertilizer in late winter and water if needed. If there are any wide-leaved weeds dig them out and apply a lawn weedkiller immediately after raking. Some bare patches may appear after you have weeded and used weedkiller; if this is the case, loosen any compacted soil, rake it smooth and either insert turf or sow some seeds. Once an abandoned lawn has been carefully tended, it should be back to a healthy, normal state after one growing season.

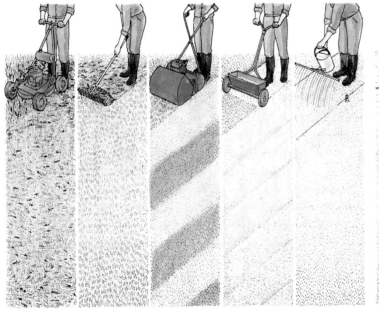

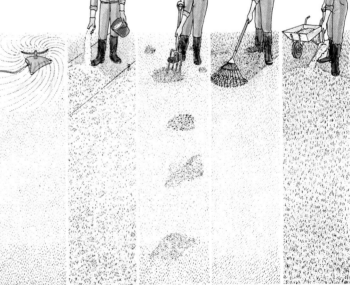

See also: Basic tools pages 200–201; Cultivation techniques pages 202–203

PLANT PROPAGATION

Propagating plants is not a particularly difficult procedure, but to propagate plants successfully, it is necessary—as always—to be well prepared. You will need a clean and tidy working area, you must use efficient and effective tools and kit, and you should follow a standardized procedure, which is outlined here.

TOOLS AND EQUIPMENT

Most important of the gardener's special tools and equipment for efficient and successful plant propagation are a sharp knife, a pair of pruners, a dibbler, suitable compost and a selection of pots and seed trays.

The use of the right tools is essential. It gives the plant material the very best start in life. If the plant material is damaged, it will die and become a prime site for possible rots which will infect the cutting.

For the best results, it is important not just to push a cutting into the compost. Always make a hole in the compost first, using a dibbler of a suitable size, and then plant the prepared cutting in that hole. A dibbler should be approximately the same diameter as the cutting that is to be planted.

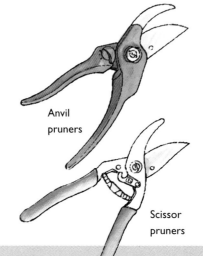

Anvil pruners

Scissor pruners

PRUNERS

Anvil pruners have one cutting blade and a flat metal surface. Scissor pruners also have one sharpened blade, but normally only the internal surface is ground flat. This blade cuts by rotating past the anvil blade as in a conventional pair of scissors. It is advisable to use scissor-type pruners for propagation because they make a cleaner cut and cause less crushing and bruising in the region of the cut.

See also: Basic tools pages 200–201; Plant care and cultivation pages 204–205

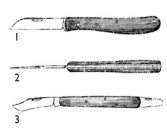

KNIVES

A knife is without doubt the most important piece of equipment needed for propagation. For most tasks, a medium-weight knife with a sharp carbon-steel blade is best. For grafting, select a fairly heavy knife. Use a knife with its blade set well back into the handle (2). A budding knife has a spatula end for prizing open flaps of bark (3). It is a useful luxury—an ordinary propagation knife is really quite adequate.

Most gardeners use a knife with a straight cutting blade, which is easy to sharpen (1), but some prefer a slightly curved blade. For cuttings, a scalpel or craft knife with replacement blades will give the cleanest cut.

ROOTING HORMONES

Certain chemicals will promote or regulate growth responses in plants when used in minute dosages, and they are used by gardeners for plant propagation. The majority of rooting hormones are powders. In many cases fungicidal chemicals are also incorporated into the powders, so helping against any rots that may develop in the cuttings.

HOW TO APPLY ROOTING HORMONES

Dip the base of a stem cutting into water, then push the base of the cutting on to the hormone powder so the powder sticks to the wet base.

OPPOSITE AND LEFT: the right tools for the job are an essential requirement for successful propagation. The compost in which the cuttings will be grown is just as important—it must be water-retaining and well-aerated. Good peat substitutes are now widely available.

PEATMOSS

It is possible to buy composts where peatmoss has been replaced by other materials such as coir (coconut fiber) or bark. These peatmoss substitutes are more environmentally sound than peatmoss itself.

POTTING COMPOSTS

A compost is a soil substitute for propagating and establishing plants. The medium must be well aerated, it must be able to retain water and hold nutrients and to conduct warmth. In the following recipes, all the ingredients are measured in parts by volume.

CUTTINGS COMPOST

A compost for rooting cuttings really requires only two considerations: the retention of sufficient moisture and the provision of an aerating agent.

Equal parts peat (sieved) and sand (1⁄16–1⁄8in grade)

COMPOST FOR GERMINATING SEEDLINGS This does not differ greatly from that produced for rooting cuttings, except that the nutrient value has to be a little higher.

Per 35 cu ft of compost:
2 parts peatmoss (sieved)
2 parts sand (1⁄16–1⁄8in grade)
1 part loam (sterilized)
1½oz ground limestone
¾oz superphosphate

POTTING COMPOSTS FOR YOUNG PLANTS

For the establishment and growing on of young plants, the compost must contain enough water and nutrients, have the correct pH value and be moisture-retentive. Loam has a steadying and controlling influence on both water and nutrients that peat does not provide, and so peat-based (that is, loamless) composts require a higher degree of management and maintenance.

LOAMLESS POTTING COMPOST
Per 35 cu ft of compost:
3 parts peat (sieved)
1 part sand (1⁄16–1⁄8in grade)
4oz any fertilizer base
4oz ground limestone

POTTING COMPOST WITH LOAM
Per 35 cu ft) of compost:
7 parts peat (sieved)
2 parts sand (1⁄16–1⁄8in grade)
1 part loam (sterilized)
4oz any fertilizer base
4oz ground limestone

HOW TO MIX COMPOSTS

The important aspect of mixing compost is to obtain an even and uniform end product so it is essential that you mix all the ingredients thoroughly.

Evenly layer up all the ingredients into a pile on a clean concrete floor. The lime and fertilizers should be sprinkled into each sand layer. The whole lot should then be mixed well with a clean shovel.

See also: Compost-making pages 198–199

SOWING SEED

When sowing seed in containers, use a "sowing" or "seed" compost and choose a container large enough to allow the seedlings space to develop to the required size.

ABOVE AND LEFT: *to achieve spectacular results like this, seeds must be given tender loving care. Moisture, warmth and protection from sunlight are the prime requirements.*

The seeds should be sown evenly over the compost either by placing large seeds by hand or by gently shaking small seeds from the packet. Cover them by sieving on compost. Fine seeds need a light dusting, larger seeds need proportionately more. Label the pot and water it in by standing the container in a shallow bath of water. Make sure the water does not overflow. After watering stand out to drain. Alternatively water from above, using a watering can with a fine rose.

To keep seeds moist and warm, cover with a sheet of glass so that water condenses on the glass and falls back into the compost. To minimize temperature fluctuations, cover the glass with a sheet of paper. Place in a warm, dark place.

THE DEVELOPING SEED

Monitor regularly and, as soon as the seedlings emerge, both paper and glass should be removed. The container should then be placed in a well-lit area, out of direct sunlight to avoid any risk of scorching.

If the seedlings are to be kept in their container for some time they should be given a liquid feed diluted according to the manufacturer's instructions. This is because many seed composts contain only a phosphate fertilizer.

TRANSPLANTING

As soon as the seedlings can be handled, transplant them into a more suitable compost, leaving enough space for the unrestricted development of the young plants.

There should be about 24–40 seedlings per tray. Fill a container with a good quality commercial compost, and firm to the base with the tips of the fingers. Strike off the compost level with the rim. Lightly firm with a presser board so that the compost is ¼–⅜in below the rim of the container.

See also: Annuals and biennuals pages 146–147; Bedding plants pages 148–149

SOWING SEEDS

1 *Soak large seeds in water for 12–24 hours before sowing in compost.*

2 *Firm the compost into the corners and base using the tips of the fingers.*

3 *Remove excess compost until level with the rim, and lightly firm the surface.*

4 *Sow half the seed across the container, keeping your hand low to prevent bouncing.*

5 *Turn the container through 90°. Sow the remaining seeds.*

6 *Lightly cover the seeds by sieving on compost, keeping the sieve low over the seeds.*

7 *Label the seeds with their full name and date of sowing.*

8 *Water in the seeds from above the compost, using a can with a fine rose.*

9 *Cover the container with a pane of glass to keep the seeds moist and warm.*

10 *Place a sheet of paper over the glass until seedlings emerge. Monitor regularly.*

HARDENING OFF

After the seedlings have been transplanted, they have to be gradually weaned to a stage at which they can be planted out and survive cool temperatures, fluctuating water conditions and the effects of wind without their growth rate being affected. Once the transplanted seedlings have reestablished, move them to a cooler environment. For this purpose there is no real substitute for a cold frame, which should be kept firmly closed. Over the course of a few weeks increasingly air the frame during the day by raising the lid, until the frame is continually aired during the day and night: indeed the lid may be completely removed during the day if it is warm. Eventually the lid can be discarded altogether.

WATERING AND FEEDING

Regularly check the seedlings in the frame to ensure that they are not drying out excessively. Do not give them too much water. Err on the side of dryness rather than risk waterlogging. Another aspect of seedling management is feeding. Feed seedlings regularly using a proprietary liquid fertilizer at intervals stated by the manufacturer. Avoid excessive feeding as this produces over-vigorous plants which will check growth on transplanting.

TRANSPLANTING SEEDLINGS

1 *Lift one seedling free of compost by holding its leaves and gently pulling.*

2 *Hold the seedling in one hand. Make a hole with the dibbler in a new container.*

3 *Water in seedlings and place in a warm place, at about 70°F (21°C).*

HARDENING OFF

1 *Raise the cold frame lid in order to give the young seedlings the opportunity to harden off.*

2 *Water, using a fine rose, to ensure the seedlings do not dry out. Add a fungicide and liquid feed regularly.*

See also: Potting composts page 217

CUTTINGS

It is possible to propagate some plants by taking cuttings. This involves cutting off a piece of stem, root or leaf and growing it on in a separate pot.

ABOVE AND RIGHT: *examples of spring and fall cuttings. Hardwood cuttings from cotoneaster are taken in the fall and softwood cuttings from fuchsia in spring.*

MAKING A STEM CUTTING

There are several kinds of stem cutting, the most popular being softwood, semi-ripe or hardwood cuttings. These are characterized by the woodiness of their stems.

SOFTWOOD CUTTINGS

These are taken in spring, just as the new shoots are beginning to harden but growth is still soft. Use the soft side shoots (a tip cutting) of shrubs and alpines; shrub cuttings should be about 3in long and alpines about 1–1½in long. But for perennials take a new, young basal shoot (a basal stem cutting) about 2in long. This means taking a cutting that has a piece of the woody stem attached to it.

Hardy plants, including a wide range of shrubs, climbers, perennials and alpines, can be propagated by softwood cuttings. This also applies to many greenhouse plants including fuchsias.

SEMI-RIPE CUTTINGS

These are taken in summer when the stem tissue is firmer and woodier. Take a main shoot and cut off the side shoots

for propagation. Each cutting should be about 4–6in long. For some species with large leaves, you can also take a cutting just above and below a leaf bud (a leaf-bud cutting).

HARDWOOD CUTTINGS

These are taken from the fall through spring, when the wood is at its hardest. There are two types: broad-leaved evergreen cuttings and leafless deciduous cuttings. The cuttings should be 6–9in long; cut just beneath a bud at the base of the plant and just above a top bud if the tip is soft.

PREPARING AND PLANTING

Cut across the stem just beneath a leaf joint, or node. Make the cuttings with a razor blade, knife or pruners, depending on the hardness of the stem.

To help the cuttings root (or strike), you can wound the flesh by taking out a sliver of bark from the lowest 1in of the cutting.

Fill a pot with cuttings compost and make a hole with a dibbler. Plant the cutting with its bud about level with the compost surface. Firm sufficiently to prevent rocking. Label and water in. Place hardy cuttings in a cold frame and less hardy cuttings in a well-lit, more protected environment, such as a mist unit or closed case.

Plant hardwood cuttings straight into the ground.

HEEL CUTTINGS

Heel cuttings are often used for stem cuttings that take some time to develop roots, for example, those that are planted in the fall and have to survive through the winter before rooting, or those

WHERE TO CUT A STEM

Hardwood cuttings should be 6–9in long, cut just below a bud at the base of the plant.

Semi-ripe cuttings are taken in summer, cutting between buds; cuttings should be 4–6in long.

ROOTING HORMONES

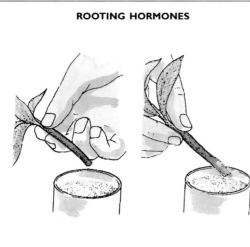

1 *Apply the hormone powder by dipping the base of the stem of the cutting into the powder.*

2 *Make sure none of the hormone powder sticks to the outside of the stem. Scrape off any excess.*

LEAF-BUD CUTTINGS

1 *Select a new stem with an undamaged mature leaf and a viable bud in its axil.*

2 *Using a pair of secateurs, make an angled cut just above the bud.*

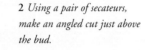

3 *Make a straight cut with the secateurs about 1–1½ in below the top cut.*

4 *Plant in a pot with the bud level with the surface of the compost. Firm well. Water in.*

hardwood cuttings that are planted in a cold frame. Heel cuttings are also made from softwood and greenwood stems that are left to develop in a partially controlled environment such as a propagator.

Heel cuttings can be taken at any time of year. A young side shoot is stripped away from its parent stem so that a heel—which is a thin sliver of bark and wood from the old stem—also comes away at the base of the cutting.

The reason for taking a stem cutting with a heel is to give the cutting a firm base so that it is well protected against possible rots. The other reason for a stem cutting is that it exposes the swollen base of the current season's growth, which has a very high capacity to produce roots.

HEEL CUTTINGS

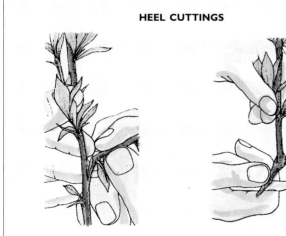

1 *Hold the bottom of a side shoot between the thumb and forefinger. Pull down sharply.*

2 *Neaten the long tail on the heel and any leaves. Dip the basal cut in a rooting hormone. Make a hole in the compost and plant the cutting. Water in.*

RIGHT: Pieris forrestii *is among the most popular varieties of this attractive hardy evergreen shrub. Softwood cuttings are taken in spring.*

See also: Colorful perennials pages 142–145; Rock-garden plants page 154

TAKING A ROOT CUTTING

WHEN TO TAKE ROOT CUTTINGS

Root cuttings are taken in the dormant season from young, vigorous roots. They are about a pencil thick.

The size of a root cutting depends upon the temperature of the environment it is left to grow in. Generally speaking, the warmer the environment, the quicker the cutting will grow and the smaller it can be. No cutting should, however, be less than 1in.

An open-ground cutting should be at least 4in long as it will need to survive for some 16 weeks. A cold frame/cold greenhouse provides a warmer environment, and reformation will occur in about eight weeks; the cuttings need be only just over 2in long. In a warm (65–75°/F18–24°C) greenhouse or propagator, regeneration time is reduced to four weeks, so root cuttings need be only about 1in long.

PREPARING THE PLANT

Before propagating from root cuttings, prepare the parent plant itself so that it will develop roots that will have a high capacity to regenerate stem buds and so produce new plants.

ABOVE: *the passion flower is propagated by root cutting.*

TAKING THE CUTTING

1 *Cut off any fibrous lateral roots that you see on undamaged young roots.*

2 *Make a right-angled cut on a root where it was severed from its parent.*

3 *Cut away the thin root end at the appropriate length, using a sloping cut.*

PREPARING THE PARENT PLANT

1 *Lift a healthy, vigorous plant from the ground during the dormant season.*

2 *Wash the roots in a bucket of water or hose them clean.*

3 *Then cut off the roots close to the crown, using a sharp knife.*

4 *Return the plant to its position in the ground and leave it to reestablish itself during the growing season.*

ABOVE: *poppies provide a blaze of dazzling color in summer gardens, at their best in the full sun. The scarlet Oriental poppy is probably the most favored of the available varieties. These plants may be propagated by root cutting—the cuttings are removed during the plant's dormant season from healthy, vigorous growth.*

PLANTS PROPAGATED BY ROOT CUTTING INCLUDE
Alpines: *Anemone, Geranium, Primula denticulata* and *Verbascum*
Herbaceous plants: *Acanthus, Eryngium, Papaver* and *Phlox*
Shrubs: *Chaenomeles, Daphne, Prunus, Rhus* and *Rhubus*

See also: Plant propagation pages 216–217

LEFT: *also propagated by root cutting is the shrub* Chaenomeles *(Japanese quince). Pictured here is the bright "Cardinalis" but there are many other varieties.*

LAYERING

This is a method of propagation in which a stem is encouraged to produce roots so that a new plant is formed while still attached to and nourished by the parent plant. Some shrubs layer themselves naturally: simply lift them from the soil, cut them from the parent plant and replant. The simplest way of propagating by layering is to select vigorous young shoots and to peg them down around the parent plant. First dig the soil around the main plant and prepare the shoot by cutting a notch halfway through at a leaf joint about 12in from its tip. After first treating the cut surfaces with a rooting powder, peg the shoot down.

AIR LAYERING

This method can be used with stems that cannot easily be bent down to the ground. Cut the stem of the plant as for ordinary layering and treat with rooting hormone. Making sure that the wound is open, wrap the whole area in moist sphagnum moss and cover it with a sheet of plastic. Within about eight weeks, roots will have formed and this part of the plant can be cut and potted up separately.

OFFSETS

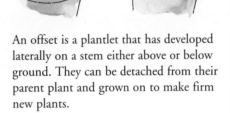

An offset is a plantlet that has developed laterally on a stem either above or below ground. They can be detached from their parent plant and grown on to make firm new plants.

PLANTING THE CUTTING

1 *Fill a pot with compost. Make a hole with a dibbler. Plant the cutting vertically in the compost. Plant the remaining root cuttings 1–1½ in apart.*

2 *Cover the pot with grit. Strike off the grit until it is level with the rim. Label, and leave the cuttings to develop. Do not water until the roots have appeared, then apply a liquid feed.*

RUNNERS

A runner is a more or less horizontal stem that arises from a crown bud and creeps overground. The leaves are normally scale-like, and rooting may occur at the nodes. The lateral buds develop as new plants, and eventually the stem of the runner deteriorates, leaving a new isolated plant.

DIVISION

Dividing a plant is a common way of propagating many herbaceous perennials, and it is also used to rejuvenate favorite plants and keep them in a vigorous condition.

HERBACEOUS PLANTS WITH FIBROUS CROWNS

Herbaceous perennials with fibrous roots and a relatively loose crown are propagated by division. Normally, the central part of the crown becomes woody over the course of two or three years. As this woody area does not produce many shoots and generally loses vigor, it is discarded and the remainder of the clump is divided into suitable-sized portions for planting out and reestablishing a new crown.

WHEN TO PROPAGATE

The only variable feature of this form of propagation is timing. As a general rule, the best time is directly after flowering, as this is when the new vegetative shoots are being produced and the new root system is developing. In very late-flowering subjects, spring propagation is advised.

ABOVE RIGHT: *lilies are propagated by scaling, taking scale leaves from the bulb and then planting the tiny bulblets.*

ABOVE: *hosta, one of many herbaceous plants propagated by division.*

DIVIDING HERBACEOUS PLANTS WITH FIBROUS CROWNS

1 *Lift the plant that is to be divided directly after it has flowered.*

2 *Shake off as much soil as possible. Wash the crown and its roots in a bucket.*

3 *Shorten all tall stems above the ground to minimize water loss.*

4 *Break off a piece with at least one good "eye" from the edge of the crown.*

5 *Divide any intractable pieces with an old carving knife or similar blade.*

6 *Make a hole and plant the new clump. Firm soil and label the plant. Water thoroughly, using a watering can with a spray attachment.*

See also: Colorful perennials pages 142–145
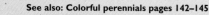

HERBACEOUS PLANTS WITH FLESHY CROWNS

Many herbaceous plants develop a compact, fleshy crown that is not easy to pull apart. The best way to propagate these plants is by division. The size of divisions will depend on preference, but must include at least one developed shoot. Avoid latent buds, which do not always develop satisfactorily.

WHEN TO PROPAGATE

Propagate herbaceous plants with fleshy crowns toward the end of their dormant season.

SEMI-WOODY HERBACEOUS PLANTS

Some perennials that have upright, sword-like leaves increase in size by producing a sort of offset. This develops into a large crown of individual shoots, each with its own individual root system.

In spring, lift them and shake out the soil, if necessary hosing or washing the crown clean. Pull the various pieces apart. Cut the clump with a spade or hatchet if it is hard and woody in the middle, and replant the divisions fairly quickly in order to avoid the roots drying out.

DIVIDING PLANTS

The following herbaceous plants are propagated by division:

Alchillea • Alchemilla
Alyssum • Aster • Astilbe
Aubrieta • Campanula
Chrysanthemum
Delphinium • Erigeron
Geranium • Hemerocallis
Hosta • Lupin • Mimulus
Rudbeckia • Scabious
Veronica

BULBOUS PLANTS

• *Bulblets are tiny bulbs that develop below ground on some bulbs. Remove the flower stem and bury it until bulblets develop in the leaf axils.*

• *Bulbils are tiny bulblets that grow on a stem above ground. These can be picked off and grown on.*

• *Bulbs like lilies are propagated by scaling: take several scale leaves from the bulb, dust them with fungicide and place them in a plastic bag of damp peat and grit. Blow into the bag and seal it, and place it in an airtight closet. When bulblets appear on the scales, plant each scale leaf and collect the bulblets when the leaf dies.*

• *To propagate by scooping, remove the basal plate of a bulb using a coffeespoon. Dust the cut surfaces with fungicide and set upside down on a tray. Store in a warm closet until bulblets appear on the cut surfaces, and then plant the bulb upside down with the bulblets just below the compost surface. Lift and separate the bulblets at the end of the season and plant at once.*

• *Scoring is similar: make two scores at right angles to each other on the basal plate of the bulb. Place in a warm, dry area until the bulb case opens out. Dust with fungicide. Place the bulb on a tray and store in a warm closet until the bulblets develop.*

• *Divide corms like crocuses and gladioli by cutting them in pieces, each one with a bud. Dust these in fungicide, leave them in a dry place and plant them when they have developed a tough outer coat.*

• *Crown rhizomes can be divided into clumps and the rootstock of creeping rhizomes trimmed and replanted.*

DIVIDING HERBACEOUS PLANTS WITH FLESHY CROWNS

1 Lift the plant to be divided toward the end of its dormant season.

2 Wash the crown well. Cut off a piece with at least one developed bud.

3 Dust the cut surfaces with a fungicidal powder. Then replant immediately.

NATURALLY DIVIDING ALPINES

Alpines such as Aubrieta Gentiana (Autumn gentian), Campanula and Primula (European species) lend themselves to propagation by division because their crowns separate naturally into individual new plantlets each season.

After flowering, or in the spring if the plant flowers in the fall, lift the plant and tease the divisions apart. Replant as soon as possible.

RIGHT: *the tall bearded iris "Ranger" is an excellent sight in summer gardens. This variety can be increased by division at planting time. Bulbous varieties are propagated from bulblets, which are removed when the bulbs are lifted.*

See also: Bulbs pages 152–153

PRUNING AND TRAINING

There are many plants in the garden that will benefit from judicious and regular pruning. This will encourage healthy growth the following year.

PLANTS THAT NEED PRUNING

Woody plants are the prime candidates for pruning and these come in the form of ornamental shrubs (including conifers), climbers, hedges and topiary and trees, as well as fruit trees, bushes and canes. Roses are deciduous flowering shrubs which need regular pruning to keep them healthy and capable of creating a radiant display each year.

PRUNING TOOLS

Pruning tools should be functional as well as comfortable to use. They must be kept sharp if they are to function easily and successfully. Wash and wipe them after use and, if they are not to be used for a few weeks, coat metal parts lightly with oil.

ABOVE: *careful pruning produces rewards like this magnificent arch of rambling roses.*

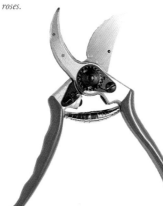

PRUNERS

Pruners are available in two basic forms—scissor and anvil. The scissor-like type cuts when one blade passes the other, while the anvil type has a sharp blade that cuts when in contact with a firm, flat, metal surface known as an anvil.

ABOVE: *cross-over loppers.*
LEFT: *scissor-type pruners.*

BRANCH OR TREE LOPPERS

Use these for cutting shoots high on fruit trees or climbing plants. They cut shoots up to 1in thick and from branches 10ft high.

LOPPERS

These have long handles and enable thick shoots to be removed without having to use a saw. There are two types of cutting action—cross-over and anvil. Loppers are easy to use, but are soon strained if used continuously to cut excessively thick and tough shoots.

SAWS

Folding saws are ideal for carrying in a pocket. Most straight-bladed, fixed-handled saws cut branches 5in thick. Saws with curved blades cut on the pull stroke. Because the blade is tapered and pointed, the saw is usable in narrow spaces.

KNIVES

Pruning knives are mainly reserved for paring cut surfaces smooth before applying fungicidal wound paint. However, they are essential when bark-ringing trunks or notching and nicking buds. Knives are available in many sizes, with blades that fold into the handle.

HAND SHEARS

These are ideal for trimming hedges and heathers. Most models will cut stems up to the thickness of a pencil.

POWER HEDGE CLIPPERS

These are essential for extensive hedging. Gasoline-powered generators that power electrical hedge clippers are ideal in areas far away from power supplies. Also, there are cordless types which can cut about 900 sq ft of hedging before needing to be recharged from a mains electricity supply. However, most types are powered by mains electricity.

See also: Basic tools pages 200–201

MAKING THE RIGHT CUT

Part of the technique of pruning roses is to make clean cuts slightly above outward-pointing buds. Use sharp secateurs that are large enough to tackle the work. Cuts more than ½in wide should be painted with a fungicidal wound paint to prevent the entry of diseases, and to give protection from dampness and frost.

ABOVE: *a fine example of a hybrid Tea Rose, "Vital Spark." After planting, Hybrid Teas are hard pruned to three or four buds about 5–6in above the plant's base to encourage strong shoots.*

PRUNING ROSES

In order to encourage an annual feast of flowers, it is essential that roses are regularly and carefully pruned.

PREPARATORY PRUNING

1 *Cut out dead wood directly at the shrub's base. Also remove shoots that have been damaged by wind, and cut out those infected by diseases. If the cut surface is brown, the stem is infected and a lower cut is needed where the wood is white.*

2 *Cut out thin, weak and spindly shoots, right to their bases. Ensure that the center of the shrub is open and that air can circulate throughout the bush. This helps shoots to ripen and enables them to resist the entry of disease spores.*

3 *The shoots that remain should be strong, healthy and well spaced out. The next stage is to prune them either "hard," "moderately," or "lightly" (see Ways of pruning, below left).*

MAKING THE WRONG CUT

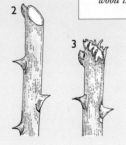

Do not cut too far above the bud otherwise the shoot may die (1). Do not cut too close to the bud, leaving it partly unsupported (2). Do not use blunt pruners which will not give a clean cut (3).

The quality and size of flowers can also be influenced by the severity with which plants are pruned: Hybrid Tea roses (now known as Large-flowered roses) need a quite different pruning regime from that required by a rambler rose, for example, or those used to form hedges.

BUSH ROSES

PREPARATORY PRUNING
Whether pruning Hybrid Tea or Floribunda bush roses, the initial task is the same.

HARD PRUNING OR LOW PRUNING
• For newly planted Hybrid Teas and Floribundas to encourage strong shoots.
• For weak-growing Hybrid Teas.

• To rejuvenate Hybrid Teas, but not established Floribundas.
• Cut the stems back to three or four buds above the plant's base, leaving short stems 5–6in high.

MODERATE PRUNING OR MEDIUM PRUNING
• For most Hybrid Tea and Floribunda roses, especially those in ordinary soil.
• Cut the stems back by about half their length; if there are any weak ones, they will need more severe treatment.

LIGHT PRUNING OR HIGH OR LONG PRUNING
• For vigorous Hybrid Tea roses as it checks growth
• For all bush roses growing in sandy soils
• Remove the top third of all shoots

WAYS OF PRUNING BUSH ROSES

Hard pruning, leaving three or four buds 5–6in above the base, encourages growth.

Some varieties benefit from moderate pruning, where stems are cut back to about half their length.

In light pruning, all shoots are cut back to about two-thirds of their length.

See also: Ways with roses pages 168–173

SPECIES AND SHRUB ROSES

These are non-climbing roses. Some of them grow into arching shrubs, some form attractive spreading mounds, while others are more upright.

PRUNING GROUPS

It is possible to simplify the pruning of these roses by categorizing them into three groups—although there are many types that do not fit into this classification.

GROUP ONE

• Species roses (but not climbers) and their close hybrids
• Japanese or Ramanas rose, (*R. rugosa*) and hybrids
• Burnet rose (*R. spinosissima*) and hybrids
• The French rose (*R. gallica*)
• Hybrid Musks

INITIAL PRUNING

Before planting, cut off coarse and weak roots. Also shorten damaged and unripe shoots. During the first and second years, cut out a few old shoots in winter.

RIGHT: *deep-pink blooms of the hybrid perpetual rose, "Ferdinand Pichard."*

PRUNING GROUP ONE SPECIES AND SHRUB ROSES

1 *During late winter or early spring of the second year, completely cut off badly positioned shoots that have developed from the plant's base. Also cut back the tips of any vigorous shoots.*

2 *During the subsequent summer, the plant will produce flowers on shoots that are borne on old wood. At the same time, strong, new shoots will develop directly from the shrub's base.*

3 *In the early fall of the same year, after the flowers have faded, cut out thin and weak growths, as well as those that may be damaged or diseased. Also cut back the tip of each shoot.*

4 *During the third and subsequent years, regular pruning is essential. During late winter or early spring, cut back lateral shoots. Also cut out one or two old shoots at the base.*

5 *In mid- and late summer of the same year the shrub will bear flowers on lateral shoots that have developed on the old shoots. During the same summer, fresh shoots will grow from the shrub's base.*

6 *During the early fall, cut back the tips of shoots to encourage the development of laterals that will bear flowers during the following year. Cut out weak shoots, and totally remove old ones.*

GROUP TWO

This comprises roses that flower chiefly on short lateral shoots as well as sub-laterals originating from two-year-old, or older, wood, including:

• *R.* x *alba* types
• Provence rose (*R. centifolia*) and its types
• Moss roses
• Most Damasks
• Modern shrub roses which have one main flush of bloom in mid-summer

RIGHT: *the modern shrub rose "Red Max Graf" is highly recommended for growing over walls.*

LEFT: Rosa conina *"Andersonii,"* an exceptionally hardy plant, suitable for heavy soils.

PRUNING GROUP TWO SPECIES AND SHRUB ROSES

1 *In late winter or early spring of the second year, cut back by about a third all those shoots that earlier developed from the base of the shrub. Also, cut back to two or three eyes all laterals that have developed on flowered shoots.*

2 *From mid- to late summer of the second year, flowers will be borne on lateral shoots that were cut back earlier. During this period, new shoots will be growing from the shrub's base. Cut off the flowers as they fade.*

3 *Slightly later, from early to late fall of the second year, cut back shoots that are extra long. By doing this, the risk of the shrub being damaged or roots loosened by strong winds during the late fall and winter is reduced.*

4 *In late winter and early spring of the third and subsequent years, cut back by a third new shoots that have developed from ground level. Also cut back laterals on flowered shoots to two or three eyes. Then cut out a few old shoots at the base.*

5 *In summer of the same year, the bush will bear flowers on lateral shoots that were cut back earlier. The cycle of fresh shoots growing each year and later developing side shoots which will bear flowers will be repeated the following season.*

6 *Later in the season, from early to late fall, cut off the ends of stems that are extra long. This reduces the area of stems and helps to prevent the shrub's roots being disturbed when shoots are blown by strong winds during late fall and winter.*

INITIAL PRUNING
Before planting, cut off damaged and weak roots and lightly cut back the tips of diseased and thin shoots.

GROUP THREE
Species and shrub roses in this group include most China and Bourbon roses and many modern shrub types. Although they have a similar nature to those detailed in Group Two, they differ in that they flower recurrently throughout summer and into the fall both on the current season's shoots and on laterals and sub-laterals that develop from both two-year and older shoots.

PRUNING GROUP THREE
Because many of the flowers are borne on laterals on old wood these plants soon become congested if pruning is neglected, so regularly remove dead flowers and thin out twiggy clusters during summer. Encourage the development of fresh shoots from ground level by cutting out old ones during winter and cut out all diseased shoots at the same time.

See also: Ways with roses pages 168–173

CLIMBERS AND RAMBLERS

Many of these roses flourish despite neglect, although many others respond well to regular pruning. Indeed, in many cases this is the only way to control their growth. All of these can be pruned as for Group Three.

CLIMBING ROSES

There are several types of climber:
• Noisette roses: an old group, with small, rosette-type flowers. They need a warm, frost-free position.
• Climbing Tea roses: these are similar to the Noisettes, but with more of a Hybrid Tea appearance.
• Climbing Hybrid Teas: these have a Hybrid Tea nature and are usually sports (natural mutations) of Hybrid Teas.
• Climbing Bourbons: these are characterized by their old rose-type flowers. Like most other climbers, they flower repeatedly.
• Modern climbers: this is a relatively new grouping. They are repeat-flowering, with flowers resembling those of Hybrid Teas.

PRUNING GROUP ONE CLIMBERS AND RAMBLERS

1 When you buy a rambler in the late fall to early spring, cut back coarse, unevenly long roots. It will probably have three or four stems, each up to 4ft long. Cut these back to 9–15in long. Then plant in firmly in good, well-drained soil.

2 During spring, young shoots will develop from buds at the top of each stem. These will form the initial flowering stems and framework, although the aim must eventually be to encourage fresh shoots to develop from the plant's base every year.

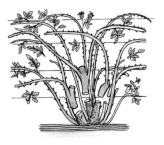 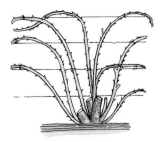

3 In late summer or fall of the following year (as well as all subsequent ones), cut out flowered shoots to their bases, leaving, tying in and spacing out on supports all strong shoots that developed earlier that season. Do not damage these shoots by tying them too tightly.

4 At the same time, cut back all shoots that are growing from these main ones to within two or three eyes of their base. Rejuvenate neglected ramblers by cutting all shoots back. Although this means losing the following season's flowers, it is the best way to restore regular flowering.

LEFT: *a modern repeat-flowering climber, "Sympathie." Pruning and maintenance are easier on climbers than on ramblers.*

PRUNING GROUP TWO CLIMBERS AND RAMBLERS

The pruning of these plants is the same during their first year as for Group One, which they closely resemble, though they develop fewer shoots from their bases. Prune them immediately after the flowers fade, completely cutting out old shoots and training in new ones. If no basal shoots are present, cut the old stems to within 15in of their bases. Cut back old shoots to vigorous sideshoots, and cut short lateral shoots back to two or three eyes above their point of origin.

BELOW: *delightful effects can be obtained from a miniature climbing rose like "Bush Baby."*

PRUNING GROUP THREE CLIMBERS AND RAMBLERS

 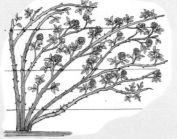  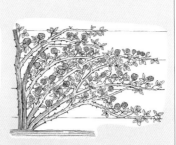

1 During the plant's dormant season, when a young climber is received from the nursery, cut back any coarse and uneven roots. In addition, you should cut out any weak shoots at their bases and lightly cut back the tips of unripe and damaged shoots. Once you have done all that, you should then plant the rose firmly, spacing out and loosely tying in the stems in order to create a permanent framework.

2 During mid- and late summer of the following season, continue to tie in new shoots that develop from the existing framework, as well as those that grow from ground level. The formation of this framework distinguishes climbers from ramblers, which each season replace stems that are cut out with fresh shoots from ground level. In the case of climbers, a permanent framework is created. A few flowers will appear at the ends of new shoots. As soon as the flowers fade, cut them off. Do not be disappointed if only a few flowers appear; it is more important to build up the plant's framework.

3 From between mid-fall of the same year and early spring of the following one, cut back all lateral shoots that have borne flowers to within three or four eyes of their points of origin. Additionally, cut out weak and diseased shoots and tie in leading shoots to the framework. Thin and weak shoots arising from the climber's base should also be cut out. If pruning is left until early spring, also cut out frost-damaged shoots, especially from slightly tender varieties which have been given a too cold or wind exposed position. Loose shoots that repeatedly flap against supports may also be damaged: check all loose shoots and cut them out as necessary.

4 During the following mid- and later summer, flowers are borne on the tips of new growths as well as on lateral shoots. When the flowers fade, cut them off. Also tie in new shoots as they grow. Later in the same season, from mid-fall to early spring, cut back all lateral shoots that have borne flowers to three or four eyes of their point of origin. At the same time, cut out weak and diseased shoots and tie in to a supporting framework of leading shoots.

• All the pruning and training activities detailed here should be repeated each year: completely cut out old and exhausted stems to within a few inches of the climber's base to encourage fresh, strong growths to develop.

RAMBLING ROSES

There are three main types of rambling rose. These are described below:

• Multiflora Hybrids: large bunches of small flowers, with stiff growth. Their pruning is detailed here in Group Two.

• Sempervirens Hybrids: graceful ramblers, with long, strong growth and sprays of small flowers. Their pruning is described in Group One.

• Wichuraiana Hybrids: these have graceful growth and quite large flowers borne in elegant sprays. They develop long, flexible shoots from their bases. Their pruning is described in Group One, although some rose experts suggest they can be left with little pruning. In such cases, however, they eventually form thickets.

See also: Ways with roses pages 168–173

STANDARD ROSES

These have a single stem which supports an upright head of branches. A weeping standard consists of a single stem from which hangs an umbrella of weeping branches.

PILLAR ROSES

These are upright climbers rarely growing higher that 10ft. They are sometimes trained against supports and their branch stumps left long enough to make tying-in easier.

WEEPING STANDARDS

These are a popular form of standard rose and have a cascading, weeping appearance. They are mainly produced by budding rambler varieties on 4–6ft tall stems of *Rosa rugosa*. Pruning is quite simple; during late summer or the early fall, completely cut out two-year-old shoots that have flowers. This will leave young shoots that developed earlier during summer to produce flowers in the following year. If there are insufficient young stems to replace the old ones that are cut out, leave a few of these

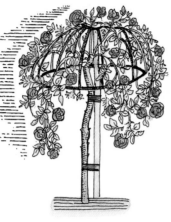

older ones and cut back any lateral shoots on them to two or three eyes. Ensure the main stem is secured to a stake.

PRUNING STANDARD ROSES

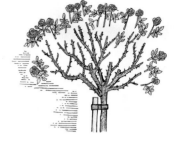

1 *During late winter or early spring after being planted, cut back strong stems on Hybrid Tea varieties to three or four eyes of their bases. With Floribunda varieties, cut stems to six to eight eyes.*

2 *In the following fall or early winter, cut off the flower heads and completely remove soft, unripe and thin shoots. This reduces the risk of wind damaging the standard's heads during early winter.*

3 *During late winter and early spring of the following year, the first thing to do is to cut out any dead, weak and diseased shoots. Also cut out any crossing shoots that cross the plant's center.*

4 *Cut new shoots on Hybrid Teas to three to five eyes, and laterals to two to four. With Floribundas, cut new shoots to six to eight eyes, and laterals to three to six eyes.*

PRUNING PILLAR ROSES

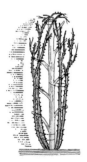

1 *Pillar roses are usually easy to prune, as all the shoots are easy to reach. During the first summer after being planted, pillar roses develop long stems. Train these in an upright manner and secure them to a rustic pole, preferably one where a few short branches have been left to create support for stems.*

2 *In the following summer, the plant bears flowers on small, lateral shoots which have grown on the long stems that develop during the previous year. Additionally, during summer, fresh, long shoots develop from the plant's base. Cut off all flower trusses as they fade to keep the plant neat and tidy.*

3 *During late fall or early winter of the same year, cut back all lateral shoots that developed flowers. Prune back some of the young shoots produced during the year, attempting to retain a symmetrical outline. Ensure they are spread evenly around the plant and not all clustered on the sunny side.*

4 *Also in late fall or early winter of the same year, cut out weak shoots that have developed from the plant's base. Also remove diseased and dead wood, and totally cut out a few of the very old shoots. The same cycle of cutting out old stems and training in all the new ones must be repeated each year.*

5 *During subsequent years, lateral shoots on the previous year's growth will bear flowers in summer. Cut these off as they fade (above left). In late fall or early winter, cut out all laterals that produced flowers. Totally sever old wood and completely remove a few of the old stems (above right).*

PRUNING SHRUBS

Shrubs are among the most popular garden plants. When they are correctly pruned, they will produce colorful flowers each year that will last for several weeks. Some of them create their display in spring or summer, others in winter when there is otherwise a lack of color.

PRUNING DECIDUOUS SHRUBS

Deciduous shrubs shed their leaves in the fall and develop fresh ones in spring. Not all deciduous shrubs need annual pruning, but those that do can be divided into three types according to their flowering time: "winter," "spring to mid-summer" and "late summer."

BELOW: *late summer-flowering shrubs such as Ceanothus are pruned in late spring of the following year.*

THE RIGHT CUT

The position of a cut in relation to a bud is important and influences subsequent growth. The above illustration shows the correct position of a cut: slightly sloping, with the upper point just above a bud. If the cut slopes downward and toward the bud (A), there is a danger that it might be damaged. If the cut is too high (B), the stub will die back and allow diseases to enter. Cuts that are positioned extremely close to the bud (C) may leave it unsupported and damaged.

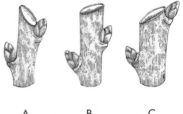

A   B   C

See also: Shrubs for year-round interest pages 132–135

See also: Location pages 110-111

CLIMATE VARIATIONS

To suit the climate in temperate regions, flowering deciduous shrubs are arranged in three groups. These groupings are based on the expectation that from late spring or early summer the weather will be free from frost. In reality, however, there are considerable differences in the severity of weather and the date of the last frost in spring or early summer. The local climate must therefore be taken into consideration; freezing temperatures might damage freshly developed young shoots.

In areas that rarely experience frost, pruning can be performed safely in late winter. If in any doubt about the severity and timing of frosts in your area you could consult the meteorological office. Alternatively, local horticultural clubs or gardening associations often have a good idea of the micro-climates.

ABOVE: *weigelas flower on shoots produced during the previous season. Flowered shoots are cut out as soon as their flowers fade.*

WINTER-FLOWERING DECIDUOUS SHRUBS

These need little pruning other than shaping when young and the removal of branches that cross the plant's center, creating congestion and reducing the maturing and ripening influence of the sun. Always cut out pest- and disease-damaged shoots; if left, they encourage the decay to infect and damage other parts.

Prune winter-flowering deciduous shrubs as soon as their display is over. This gives shrubs the maximum amount of time in which to produce new shoots and for them to ripen before the onset of cold weather in the following fall or early winter. It is easier to control the size of winter-flowering shrubs than any other type.

EARLY-FLOWERING DECIDUOUS SHRUBS

These flower between late spring and mid-summer, and should be pruned as soon as their flowers fade.

First cut out thin and weak shoots, and those that cross a shrub's center. Then cut out to within a couple of buds of their base all shoots that have borne flowers. The removal of flowered shoots leaves young ones that will bear flowers during the following year. If shrubs have been neglected for several seasons, many can be rejuvenated by cutting back the complete shrub. However, this usually means foregoing flowers for one season.

LATE SUMMER-FLOWERING DECIDUOUS SHRUBS

These are pruned during late spring of the following year. If pruned immediately after their flowers fade, the young shoots that subsequently develop would be damaged by frosts during winter. By leaving pruning until the following year, the fresh young shoots will not be exposed to frost.

First, cut out dead and diseased shoots, then those that cross the center of the shrub. At the same time, cut out thin and weak shoots. Next cut to just above a bud all those shoots that produced flowers during the previous year. Pruning varies slightly according to the individual shrubs.

PRUNING HYDRANGEAS

Mop-head hydrangeas (*Hydrangea macrophylla*) are superb garden shrubs which flower from mid-summer to fall. Leave the flower stems and old flower heads in place until late winter or early spring, then cut out all shoots that produced flowers during the previous year. This radically thins out the shrub, allows light and air to enter and encourages the development of fresh shoots which will bear flowers later in the year.

ABOVE: *leave old flower heads and stems on hydrangeas until the following year.*

BELOW: *pink, mauve or white hydrangeas are a marvellous sight in late summer.*

WINTER COLOR

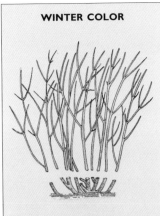

Many shrubs are grown
for their attractive stems
which provide color in
winter months. These
shrubs include the
common dogwood
(*Cornus alba*) and golden-
twig dogwood (*C.
stolonifera* "Flaviramea").
In spring, cut down all
stems to within 3in of
the ground. This
encourages the
development of fresh
stems that will create a
bright feature during the
winter months.

REJUVENATING SHRUBS

Large, overgrown evergreen shrubs
such as the spotted laurel or
gold-dust tree (*Aucuba japonica*
"Variegata") can be rejuvenated
by cutting back all stems to within
12in of the ground in spring.
If the shrub is exceptionally large
and old, cut the stems 2–3ft
high. Heavy-duty, double-action
loppers are usually needed, or a
curved saw.

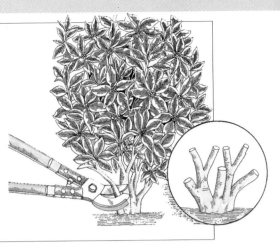

BELOW: *pink or
crimson weigelas has
graceful, arching
stems and should be
pruned annually.*

ABOVE: *use loppers or strong
secateurs to cut tough woody
stems. Dogwoods, for example,
should be cut to about 3in
above their base.*

PRUNING EVERGREEN SHRUBS

Evergreen shrubs are clothed
in leaves throughout the year,
with old leaves continually
falling off and new ones being
formed. Once established,
these shrubs need no more
pruning than cutting out weak,
diseased and straggly shoots in
spring. Never prune evergreen
shrubs in winter, as any young
shoots that subsequently
develop could be blackened
and damaged. This could mean
that pruning has to be
performed again
in spring, to cut out
these newly
developed and
blackened shoots.
In exceptionally

cold areas, it is better to defer
pruning until early summer.

If an evergreen shrub is
grown for its spring or early-
summer flowers, such as
Darwin's berberis (*Berberis
darwinii*), which blooms during
late spring and early summer,
delay pruning until after the
display has faded.

PRUNING LAVENDER

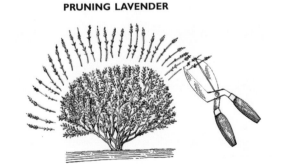

Lavender flowers from mid-
to late summer and is
pruned by lightly trimming
over the plants in late
summer, using a pair of
sharp hand shears. Do not
cut into young shoots; just
trim off the old flowers.

If a plant has become
particularly straggly, cut the
stems hard back in late
spring. This encourages the
development of new young
shoots from the plant's base.
Lavender hedges are clipped
to shape in spring.

See also Shrubs for year-round interest pages 132–135

PRUNING CLIMBERS

*Certain climbers need regular pruning to encourage
flower production, to ensure the plant remains vigorous
and to keep them nicely shaped. Many, however, do not
need pruning, except to remove dead wood as necessary.
For deciduous climbers that flower in spring or early
summer, prune back the growths produced the previous
year immediately after flowering. Deciduous climbers that
flower in summer and the fall on growths formed in the
current season should be pruned in early spring.*

ABOVE: *a sunny combination
—"Harrison's Yellow" rose and
yellow honeysuckle.*
BELOW: *climbing roses require
only light pruning.*

PRUNING AN OLD CLIMBER

Eventually—especially if
neglected over several years
—many climbers develop
a tangled web of old
wood. Slowly, the
climber's ability to flower
is diminished and it
becomes full of congested,
old, unflowering shoots.
Cut back in spring.

1 *Cut out as
much of the
old, congested
growth as
possible. Usually
it is a matter of repeatedly
snipping out small pieces
of entangled shoots.*

2 *Use sharp
pruners
to cut old,
dead, twiggy
shoots to a healthy stem.*

3 *At the
same time,
cut back
diseased shoots to strong and
healthy shoots. If left,
they will spread infection
and disease.*

4 *Some
climbers
continually develop new
stems from their bases; the
old ones eventually become
thick, unproductive and
congested. Use strong loppers
to cut off these shoots at
their base.*

RENOVATING HONEYSUCKLE

Even the name honeysuckle evokes thoughts of canopies and arbors drenched in fragrant flowers. Unfortunately, in many ways some honeysuckles—including the Japanese honeysuckle (*Lonicera japonica*), early Dutch honeysuckle (*L. periclymenum* "Belgica") and late Dutch honeysuckle (*L. p.* "Serotina")—are too undemanding for their own good, and will continue to flower for many years without having to be pruned. In time, however, the weight of their leaves and stems can often break their supports. If a honeysuckle does become a mass of old stems, in spring cut back the complete plant to within 15–20in of the ground.

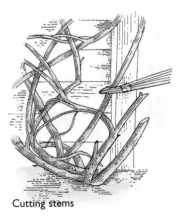

Cutting stems

Where it is just a mass of thin, tangled shoots, cut back the dead shoots from the base and use hand shears to trim thin shoots back to new growths.

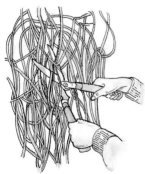

Cutting shoots

See also: Arches and arbors pages 102–103

RIGHT: *wisteria is a vigorous plant but can soon become overgrown if it is not given regular pruning.*

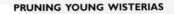

PRUNING YOUNG WISTERIAS

1 *Young wisterias need careful pruning and training to ensure that a strong framework is created. During late winter or early spring in the year after being planted, cut back the strongest shoot to about 2½ft above the ground. At the same time, completely cut off all the other shoots.*

2 *During mid-winter of the second year, cut back the central leading shoot to within 2½–3ft of the topmost lateral shoot. At the same time, lower the laterals so that they are horizontal and cut them back by a third. Sever these lateral stems just beyond a bud on the upper side. Tie them to the wires.*

3 *During winter of the third year, cut back the central leading shoot to within 2½–3ft of the uppermost horizontal stem. Then lower the topmost horizontal shoots and cut them back by about a third. The lower horizontal shoots will also have grown by this time; cut off about a third of their new growth.*

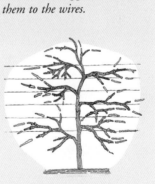

4 *In subsequent winters, continue forming new tiers of horizontal shoots, as well as encouraging the growth of the leader shoot. When the desired height has been reached, cut it off fractionally above the uppermost horizontal shoot. At the same time, cut back the sideshoots to within about 3–4in of their base.*

PRUNING ESTABLISHED WISTERIAS

Once a framework has been formed, the most important objective is to keep the climber in check—lateral shoots may grow up to 12ft in a single year and unless this over-exuberant growth is pruned, the plant can soon become a jungle of stems and may grow too large for its allotted area. Severely pruning a wisteria during winter will only encourage even more rapid growth. However, by cutting it in summer it is possible to restrain the plant without encouraging massive growth.

In late or early winter, cut back all shoots to within two or three buds of the point where they started growing in the previous season. Where a plant becomes too large, also prune it in mid-summer, cutting the current season's young shoots back to within five or six buds of the plant's base.

PRUNING CLEMATIS

Gardeners often dread pruning clematis, fearing that it is complicated and confusing. Any pruning should be made according to the three categories which are based on the age of the growth on which the flowers are produced.

1 *During late winter after planting, cut back the main shoot to the lowest pair of strong buds. Rigorously cutting back the plant in this way encourages the development of fresh shoots. During the following summer, healthy young shoots develop and must be trained and secured against a wire or wooden framework. Pruning in this way encourages the development of strong shoots from ground level.*

2 *In late winter of the second year, cut back each shoot to its lowest pair of strong buds. This also includes shoots that developed from ground level during the previous year and are starting to form a bushy plant. During the following summer, vigorous shoots must be spaced out and secured to a supporting framework. From mid- to late summer flowers will appear on shoots produced earlier in the same season.*

Different varieties of clematis need different types of pruning —those that flower in late summer or fall, such as C. jackmanii (left) and C. viticella (above), need much harder pruning.

3 *During late winter of each subsequent year, cut all growths back to leave a pair of strong buds at their base. In the same way as in previous years, shoots grow from these buds and bear flowers from mid-summer to the fall. Tie shoots to a framework. On a neglected plant, cut half of the stems back into older wood to encourage the development of shoots from ground level; cut the others back to buds. The following year, cut back the other half.*

TYPES OF CLEMATIS

The first group contains species and hybrids that flower in summer and fall on shoots produced during the same season. This group begins new growth in spring by developing fresh young shoots from the ends of old shoots. The second group is formed of vigorous spring- and early summer-flowering types that bear flowers on short shoots which arise from growths that have developed in the course of the previous year.

The third group encompasses the hybrids that bear flowers from late spring to mid-summer on shoots produced during the previous year. This means that during any one year, as well as flowering on the previous year's growths, the plant is also producing shoots that will bear flowers later in the same year, creating a second flush of color in late summer and early fall.

GROUP ONE INCLUDES:

Clematis jackmanii hybrids, such as "Comtesse de Bouchaud,"

"Hagley Hybrid" and "Mrs Cholmondeley," *C. orientalis; C. tangutica; C. texensis* hybrids, including "Etoile Rose," and "Gravetye Beauty;" *C. viticella* hybrids, including "Earnest Markham," "Lady Betty Balfour," and "Ville de Lyon."

See also: Clematis pages 140–141

PRUNING GROUP TWO

1 *During late winter of the first year after being planted, prune plants by cutting the stem to slightly above the lowest pair of healthy, strong buds. This severe pruning encourages the development of strong shoots that will help to form the climber's framework. During the summer, space out and secure these stems to a permanent framework of wires or a wooden trellis. The initial training of shoots is important to ensure that light and air can reach the shoots.*

2 *In the late winter of the second year, cut back by half the lengths of the main shoots that developed during the previous year and were secured to a supporting framework. Ensure each shoot is cut back to slightly above a pair of strong, healthy buds. If shoots low down on the climber develop flowers early in the year, cut them back to one pair of buds from their base. During the summer months, fresh shoots will grow; space them out and secure to the supporting framework.*

3 *During the early summer of the following and subsequent years, use pruners to cut back all growths that produced flowers earlier in the year to one or two buds from their point of origin. Within this group, the mountain clematis (*C. montana *and* C. chrysocoma*) are very vigorous and are sometimes left unpruned. This eventually creates a tangled plant; rejuvenate by cutting to near ground level in later winter. Where plants are allowed to scale trees, leave them unpruned.*

GROUP TWO INCLUDES:
C. alpina, including "Frances Rivis;" *C. armandii,* including "Apple Blossom" and "Snowdrift;" *C. chrysocoma,* including "Markham's Pink;" *C. montana,* and its many forms such as "Alexander', Elizabeth," "Rubens," and "Tetrarose."

GROUP THREE INCLUDES:
Lanuginosa types, including "Beauty of Worcester," "Nelly Moser," "W. E. Gladstone," and "William Kennett;" Patens types, including "Barbara Dibley," "Lazurstern," "Marcel Moser," "Marie Boisselot," "The President," and "Vyvyan Pennell."

PRUNING GROUP THREE

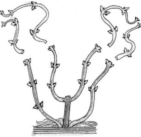

1 *During late winter after being planted, cut back the stem to the lowest pair of strong, healthy buds. During late spring and early summer, young shoots will grow rapidly and need to be trained and secured to a framework of wires or a wooden trellis. Shoots will also develop from ground level and these, too, should be trained to the framework. Occasionally, a few flowers are produced during the first year.*

2 *In late winter of the second year, cut back by half all the main shoots which were produced during the previous year. Sever them just above a pair of strong, healthy buds. During the following summer, train the new shoots and space them out on the supporting framework. In this second season, plants usually develop a few flowers on new growth, often into the fall. Creating a strong framework of shoots is absolutely essential.*

3 *During early and mid-summer of the third and subsequent years, immediately after the first flush of flowers has faded, cut out a quarter to a third of mature shoots to within 12in of the plant's base. When plants are grown against a wall, the shoots can be readily reached and the method of pruning indicated above is ideal. However, when plants are grown on an arbor, stems cannot be untangled and plants are therefore best left unpruned.*

ABOVE: Clematis montana *is a small-flowered spring variety, which quickly covers trellises, arches, walls and trees and should be pruned after flowering. Usually white, there is also a pink form, "Rubens," which has bronzy leaves.*

See also: The role of plants pages 112–113; Climbing and screening plants pages 138–139

PRUNING HEDGES

Some hedges need pruning to create attractive shapes, while others are pruned to promote regular flowering. Pruning deciduous hedges helps to produce a mass of shoots from their base; hedges with thin bases are always an eyesore. In areas where there is a risk of high snowfall, the top of the hedge should be sloped so that snow falls quickly and easily off the top.

PRUNING FORMAL HEDGES

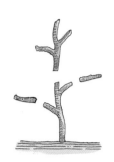  

1 *Deciduous hedging must be cut down by about half (side-shoots too) immediately after planting. Bare-rooted plants are planted from late fall to early spring; container-grown plants at any time.*

2 *During the following year, from late fall to early spring, severely cut back the leading shoot and side shoots, by about a half. Unless pruning is severe, the base of the hedge will be unsightly and bare in summer.*

3 *In the third winter, cut back all new shoots by a third. During the following season, shoots will be bushy and start to form a solid screen. Water young hedges regularly and feed them in spring and mid-summer.*

CONIFEROUS HEDGES

When the leading shoots of conifers reach 6–12in above the desired height, cut off their tops about 6in below this point. This leaves sufficient space for the hedge's top to create a bushy nature at the desired height of the hedge.

EVERGREEN HEDGES

When they are planted, these must be treated in the same way as the deciduous hedges.

Large-leaved evergreen shrubs, which invariably create informal hedges, need little initial pruning other than cutting back long shoots to just above a leaf-joint. However, cutting back the tips to a point slightly above the leaves encourages the development of stronger shoots. At the same time, you should cut out any diseased or damaged shoots.

If, during the second season, large-leaved shrubs are not creating a sufficiently bushy outline, cut a few shoots back to encourage the development of new sideshoots.

BELOW: *the trim lines of a well-maintained yew hedge. Taxus baccata is seen at its best in large, formal settings.*

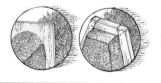

SHAPING A HEDGE

To establish uniform height, stretch a taut string between stout poles for a short distance. For longer hedges, however, it is easier to use a template known as a batter.

BELOW: *use string or a batter (shown above) to maintain a level height when shaping a hedge.*

See also: Hedges pages 130–131

PRUNING TREES

Trees require less regular pruning than shrubs, although during their formative years it is essential that crossing branches are removed.

REMOVING A LARGE BRANCH

1 *When cutting off a large bough, remove it in several stages. Never cut it off close to the trunk in a single stage as the tree may be damaged. Cutting off a branch in several parts also makes it more manageable to move.*

2 *First of all, cut back a large branch to about 18in from the trunk. Then use a saw to cut two-thirds of the way through the branch from below. Position the cut as close as you can to the trunk, but not so close to it that it scrapes the bark. Making the first cut underneath the bough ensures that bark below the branch does not subsequently become damaged.*

3 *Cut through the remaining part of the branch from above. Position the saw so that the two cuts align and do not create a step. If they do not quite meet, use a coarse file to level them. If the two cuts are a long way out of alignment, it may be necessary to make a further cut to create a flat surface. Use a sharp saw—it makes the job easier.*

4 *Use a sharp knife to smooth the edges of the cut. If the edges are left rough, the cut both looks unattractive and extends the time the wound takes to heal. When smooth, coat the surface with a fungicidal wound-paint to prevent diseases entering the tree and eventually causing extensive damage to the trunk.*

TYPES OF TREE

Most deciduous trees are pruned in winter when dormant. Flowering cherries and other members of the prunus family, however, must be pruned in spring or early summer, when their sap is rising, to prevent diseases.

With conifers it is essential that they are checked every year to ensure they have only one leader shoot. If two are allowed to grow, the conifer develops a forked top, which is unsightly and may split.

ABOVE: *the deciduous* Acer palmatum *"Seiryu" is prized for its beautiful foliage. Acers or maples do not need pruning, but dead or diseased wood should be cut out in spring.*

Occasionally, an established tree needs to be pruned because it has become too large and it is intruding on other plants, or into a neighbor's territory. When choosing a tree, it is useful to find out what its size will be after 15 or 20 years' steady growth.

POLLARDING

Trees in towns and cities often become too large for the area in which they were planted. Also, where roads are widened, overhanging branches may obstruct traffic. If this happens, branches are often cut back to the trunk, encouraging the growth of long stems that cluster around the top of the trunk. The need for pollarding can be avoided by selecting trees that will not intrude on neighboring buildings, roads or gardens. Always select a species and variety to suit the position.

RETAINING SYMMETRY

Evergreen conifers that have a symmetrical outline require little attention once they are established. During their early years, however, when they are still establishing their shape, it is important to make sure that only one central shoot is allowed to develop.

Use a sharp pair of pruners to cut out one of the forked shoots. If the conifer is still very young, it is a good idea at this stage to tie the leading shoot temporarily to a cane in order to support it.

See also: Garden trees pages 127–129

IN THE GREENHOUSE

A greenhouse is the perfect all-weather place to cultivate plants. Not only does it extend the range of plants you can grow, but it provides the right atmosphere to propagate and overwinter less hardy plants, or grow tender ones. As well as the extra heat, factors such as the quality of light and length of day all play a part in helping plant growth.

TYPES OF GREENHOUSE

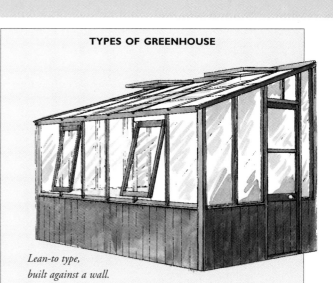

Lean-to type, built against a wall.

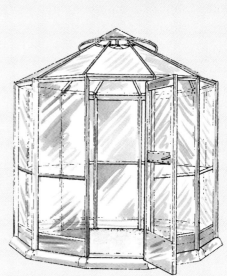

A circular model gives the plants maximum light from all sides.

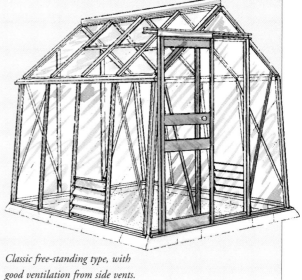

Classic free-standing type, with good ventilation from side vents.

TYPES

There are many types of greenhouse to choose from, including free-standing and lean-to models. They may be built of wood, metal or PVC. Wood tends to look more attractive than metal and it is marginally warmer, easier to repair and better for fitting shelves. However, it is heavy to construct, while steel and aluminum are light and easy to handle. Metal frames are also larger than wooden ones so can be fitted with larger panes of glass, which result in better light penetration.

ABOVE: *the main point about a greenhouse is that it should provide plenty of light—with good ventilation to keep the temperature down. Protection from draughts and quality of construction are also important.*

See also: The role of plants pages 112–113; Plant associations pages 114–120

Avoid overhanging trees and nearby buildings, which may cast shadows, and windy, exposed sites that will cause a loss of heat. Your greenhouse should also be near some sort of water and electricity supply and it must be easily accessible.

If you want your greenhouse to have one shady side and one sunny side, you should position it so that it faces sunrise. However, if you want both sides to receive direct sunlight, rotate the structure by 90°.

HEATING

For most of the year the sun should keep your greenhouse warm enough. However, during winter you may need to generate some additional heat, in which case it is best to install some kind of heater, which will increase the humidity. If you plan to raise plants in spring, use an electric propagator to provide heat for the seed trays and plant pots.

HUMIDITY

In periods of particularly hot weather, you may also need to increase the humidity of your greenhouse. To do this, stand the pots on moist ground or capillary matting. Pour water or stand trays of water on the floor.

SHADING

In periods of very hot weather it may be necessary to shade your greenhouse. Either put up blinds or paint the inside with a special shading paint, which is available from garden depots.

VENTILATION

Proper ventilation is required to prevent high temperatures and stagnant air. Only close the vents when the weather is particularly inclement.

HYGIENE

It is very important to keep your greenhouse clean as this helps prevent pests and diseases spreading. Regularly remove dead leaves and debris from the greenhouse and do a really thorough clean at least once a month.

ROUTINE MAINTENANCE

- Keep the glass clean using water only. A hose and long-handled brush is the best way of doing this. If the dirt is really ingrained, use a solution of descaler.
- Replace any broken panes of glass.
- Check that all gutters and downpipes are in working order.
- Check metal frames for signs of rust and, if necessary, treat these with a rust remover.
- Check wooden frames are in good condition and replace any rotting wood.

WATERING

Make sure your plants receive the correct amount of water, bearing in mind that the heated environment will increase moisture loss. Also, certain types of potting mixture retain moisture better than others. In cold, cloudy weather your plants will need less water than in hot, sunny weather; keep a regular check on whether or not they need more water by feeling the potting mixture.

When you are watering plants, make sure you do not splash the foliage or leave puddles of the water on the floor or benches as this will encourage fungal diseases.

COLD FRAMES AND COVERS

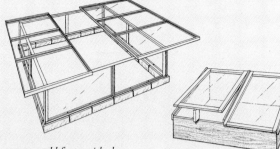

ABOVE: *cold frame with glass sides and a glass top, which slides open when plants are being hardened off.*

ABOVE: *the hinged-top type can be wedged open.*

Cold frames and clear covers are most useful for hardening off plants in spring before they are transplanted, and for protecting plants. Being portable, covers are mostly used in the vegetable garden to protect plants already growing, while cold frames are used mainly to overwinter uprooted plants and to protect young seedlings.

The most popular cold frames are metal with glass sides and glass tops. You can also get those with wooden sides and glass tops, and there are also ones with brick sides. Some of the tops are hinged so you can wedge them open when hardening off plants, while others are sliding. The hinged types are best since they protect the plants from rain, but they do have a tendency to blow shut in windy weather.

There are many different types of cover, such as round, tunnel-shaped and, tent-shaped, in both glass and plastic. Choose one to suit the plants you want to protect. Glass is better for more permanent covers, while plastic is perfectly good for the temporary covering of crops.

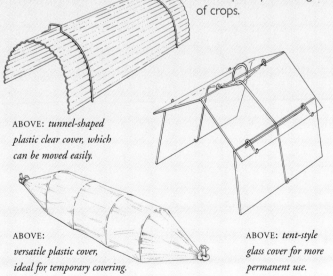

ABOVE: *tunnel-shaped plastic clear cover, which can be moved easily.*

ABOVE: *versatile plastic cover, ideal for temporary covering.*

ABOVE: *tent-style glass cover for more permanent use.*

See also: Location pages 110–111; Plant care and cultivation pages 204–205

TROUBLESHOOTING

PESTS

Q What is the cause of "cuckoo spit" and should it be controlled?

A *The frothy liquid seen on the young stems of many shrubs in late spring and early summer conceals the nymph stage of the spittlebug. Neither the adult nor the nymph causes significant damage but the "cuckoo spit" can be dislodged with a jet of water from a plant spray.*

Q How can mice and voles be prevented from digging up and eating crocus bulbs?

A *Make sure all bulbs are firmly planted, and remove dead leaves from the tops of bulbs after they die back to make it difficult for rodents to locate them. Bulbs can also be treated with rodent repellent before planting.*

Q The leaves of greenhouse ornamentals are becoming mottled, then turning yellow and brittle before falling. They show a fine webbing on the underside. What causes this?

A *This is caused by the spider mite, a serious pest of many indoor plants, particularly in dry conditions. Spray weekly with dimethoate or malathion on at least three occasions and increase the humidity.*

Q What is the cause of malformed new leaves on an established box hedge?

A *If the leaves develop in clusters that resemble tiny cabbages, the likely answer is box-sucker, which feeds on the new growths. The best solution to this is repeated sprays of malathion or dimethoate.*

Q Ragged holes have appeared overnight in the petals of our dahlias. What is the culprit?

A *Earwigs commonly produce this kind of damage on the flowers and leaves of dahlias and chrysanthemums. Remove dead leaves from the ground and spray on and around the infested plants with gamma-HCH. Alternatively, place inverted flowerpots filled with straw on short bamboo poles close to the plants to trap the earwigs, then shake them out daily and destroy the pests.*

Q Pansies growing in a pot have shriveled back, and seem to have been eaten through at ground level. Can this be prevented?

A *It is quite likely that this is caused by woodlice, which will eat stems and leaves of seedlings and young plants in contact with the soil. Good backyard and garden hygiene will help, washing containers before planting up and removing garden debris where they can hide. Next time, try dusting around the plants with gamma-HCH or use methiocarb-based slug pellets.*

Q Is there any way of dealing with aphids without using chemical sprays?

A *If you are patient, you can wait for ladybugs and hoverflies, the main predators of aphids, to come to the rescue and even encourage the latter by planting annuals such as* Limnanthes douglasii, *the poached-egg plant, near the affected plants. The trouble is that aphids transmit viruses, and exude sticky honeydew which encourages the growth of fungus, so it is wise to control them. A spray of pirimicarb affects virtually no other creatures as it is aphid-specific.*

Q What are the fat, white, C-shaped grubs with a brown head found in the soil during cultivation, and do they cause any damage to plants?

A *They sound like june beetle grubs, the larvae of the june beetle. The adults rarely cause serious damage but the grubs eat the roots and bulbs of many ornamental plants and can damage lawns. The simplest control is to turn over the soil and leave the birds to eat them, otherwise dust the soil with gamma-HCH.*

Q Phlox plants have suddenly developed distorted foliage and the flower display is reduced. There is no visible pest on the plant, so what can be done?

A *The pest is the microscopic nematode known as the stem eelworm, and it affects a number of other plants including aubrieta and helenium. There is no cure and affected plants should be removed and burned. Eelworms are easily transmitted, so take care when accepting plants from other gardeners. Examine them first before planting and dispose of any that look sickly.*

Q Hostas are frequently attacked by slugs. How can such damage be controlled?

A *Slugs are particularly fond of hosta leaves and can destroy a plant if not discouraged. They feed mainly at night, and during the day they hide under stones and in dead leaves so remove any garden debris from the locality. In addition, try metaldehyde or methiocarb pellets scattered in damp conditions. Alternatively, avoid planting the hostas out altogether and try growing them in pots.*

Q What are the tiny flies that rise up from the compost of glasshouse plants during watering? Are they harmful?

A *These are sciarid flies which lay their eggs in large numbers in potting compost. The tiny colorless larvae feed on organic matter in the compost and frequently damage young plants. The adults cause no significant damage, but are a nuisance. Hang sticky yellow traps around affected plants to catch adults and halt the life cycle.*

Q What pest causes the pale twisting tunnels in leaves of sweet Williams and how can it be controlled?

A *The damage is caused by leaf miners, which are the immature form of certain flies and moths. Although they affect numerous plants, including chrysanthemums, the damage is most serious to members of the dianthus family, such as carnations, pinks, and sweet Williams. Remove and burn badly affected leaves and inspect plants regularly for damage, squashing the larvae in the leaves as soon as they are seen.*

Q The edges of some leaves on a shrub rose have rolled tightly underneath on to themselves. What is the cause of this and how can it be remedied?

A *This is caused by leaf-rolling sawfly. There are a number of different species of sawfly that affect a variety of plants, but only one that produces this kind of damage. The insect lays eggs in the leaf and injects a chemical that makes it roll up in this way to protect the grub when it hatches. Hand-pick rolled leaves or spray with permethrin as a preventive.*

Q Is it possible to discourage moles from damaging a lawn without having to resort to trapping them?

A *Mole smokes are quite successful, although they occasionally kill moles. A recent method that seems to be effective involves the use of a metal stake that produces a high-frequency sound. This stake is pushed into the ground along the mole run and, periodically, emits a sound that drives the moles away.*

Q Should ants be controlled in the garden?

A *There are often so many ant nests around a garden that it would be pointless to try and control them completely, particularly as they do little* direct damage. On lawns, the soil they excavate may form heaps which are spread during mowing and provide a site for weeds to establish. Apply an ant-killing preparation, such as carbaryl or pirimiphos methyl, to the soil around the nests.

Q What are the waxy brown-red scales that have formed in clusters on the older branches of a fig tree?

A These are brown scale, a type of scale insect that affects a number of woody plants, including roses. The scale you see is not the insect but a covering beneath which the insect feeds on the sap. Deciduous plants can be sprayed with tar oil wash in early to mid-winter or with malathion or pirimiphos methyl during summer.

Q What control is possible for the gray-white caterpillars that completely strip Solomon's seal of its leaves?

A These caterpillars are the larvae of the Solomon's seal sawfly, which lays eggs in the stems of the plant, in batches of up to 20. The caterpillars go on to pupate in the soil under the plant and reemerge in late spring or early summer. To break the cycle, spray the plants with derris, permethrin or pirimiphos methyl as soon as the larvae are seen.

Q In the soil around wilting herbaceous plants are a small number of creamy-brown caterpillars, about 1½in in length. Are they the cause of the wilting and how can they themselves be controlled?

A These are cutworms, the larvae of various types of moth. They feed on roots and on the stems of plants at soil level and can kill the plants if they are allowed to continue. Remove and destroy the cutworms, then cultivate the area regularly to expose the grubs to their natural predators, birds. Treating the soil with gamma-HCH, pirimiphos methyl or a similar type of insecticide will also help.

Q Geranium leaves are showing small tattered holes but no pest is present. Earlier in the season, there were fast-moving green, winged insects around the plants. Are these the cause of the damage?

A This damage is characteristic of capsid bugs. They are sap-suckers and their feeding damages cells in young leaves and buds. When these expand, the damaged areas tear to produce tattered holes, but the bugs are long gone. Control them when noticed with regular spraying using a contact insecticide, such as derris or permethrin. Spray the ground under the plants and the undersides of the leaves.

Q Do crane flies cause damage in the garden?

A Not in the adult form, but the larvae are a serious pest of lawns and ornamental plants, particularly in areas that are being brought into cultivation. These leatherjackets are fat, legless, grayish grubs up to 1½in long, and feed on roots from summer to late spring. Regular cultivation exposes them to birds. On lawns, water thoroughly at night, then cover the area with black plastic. Remove in the morning when the pests will have come up to the surface, and leave for the birds.

Q What is the cause of brown scarring on the flower buds of Michaelmas daisies, which then go on to produce small leaves rather than petals?

A This is caused by tarsonemid mites, which also affect cyclamen and begonias among other plants. Lift and burn badly damaged plants of Aster novi-belgii as there is no spray available that controls these pests. Try plants Aster novae-angliae or Aster amellus, which will flower even if infected.

Q Circular holes are appearing in the margins of rose leaves, but no caterpillars are present. What is the cause of this?

A Leaf-cutter bees produce this kind of damage on roses, laburnums and lilacs.

They use the leaf material to build small nests in soil, rotting wood or sometimes even in pots of compost. Damage is not usually very serious and since the bees are such good pollinators, control is not recommended.

Q What causes the pale mottling on rose leaves? There are small yellow insects present which fly up when disturbed.

A The pest is called a leafhopper. They occur on many plants but roses and rhododendrons are the worst affected. They should be controlled generally, however, as they transmit viruses. Spray with malathion or pirimiphos methyl when damage is first noticed.

DISEASES

Q What is the reason for the shoots of clematis suddenly dying back in summer?

A Provided the plant is well fed and watered, the likely answer is clematis wilt, caused by a fungus disease. Cut out any wilted growth and spray the plant and surrounding soil with a fungicide such as carbendazim.

Q Cotoneaster shoots are dying back, but the dead leaves are still hanging on the plant. Is this a serious problem?

A Potentially, yes. This is a case of fireblight, which can affect a number of other plants in the rose family including apples, pyracanthas and chaenomeles. Cut out all diseased wood, which shows a red-brown staining under the bark and burn it. Disinfect your pruning tools afterward.

Q Why have all the softwood cuttings in a cold frame collapsed with visible fluffy fungal growth?

A The fungus Botrytis gray mold is common in humid conditions, particularly if there are any dead leaves present, through which the infection can enter. Water cuttings with a solution of benomyl and ventilate the cold frame during the day.

Q How can rose blackspot be controlled?

A This very common fungus disease appears in early summer as circular black or dark brown marks on the leaves, which fall early. In a severe case, the whole plant may lose its leaves. Rake up and burn fallen leaves on which the fungus overwinters and spray at regular intervals throughout the growing season, starting in early spring, with mancozeb or a specific rose formula, which will also help prevent powdery mildew. A foliar feed will help restore vigor.

Q If an ornamental cherry oozes amber-colored gum, is it a sign of disease?

A Not necessarily, but it could be bacterial canker, a serious disease of Prunus, both fruiting and ornamental. If the leaves are spotted in summer with small holes forming later, and with cankers forming in the angles of branches, it is likely to be this disease. Spray three times with Bordeaux mixture in late summer and the fall and prune in summer, when infection through cuts is less likely.

Q What can be done to prevent geranium cuttings turning black at the bottom and dying?

A The disease known as blackleg is probably caused by a fungus, which will spread rapidly to all cuttings in a tray or pot. Always use new potting compost and clean pots, take cuttings with a clean knife and select from healthy plants. Do not overwater and remove dying leaves promptly.

Q What is the cause of oval black spots on the leaves of weeping willow?

A Anthracnose is a fungus disease that causes serious problems to willows, particularly in wet summers. The leaves will turn yellow and fall early, and after a few years there is likely to be serious die-back. Spray small trees with Bordeaux mixture as the new leaves emerge, and repeat in summer. Large trees cannot be treated, but gather up and destroy fallen leaves.

Q The leaves of a flowering almond have become thickened and curled, then covered in blisters, which are initially red then turning pale. These fall early in the season and the tree is not thriving. What is the remedy?

A *Peach leaf curl affects flowering peaches as well as fruiting types. The spores overwinter on the plant and reinfect the developing buds. Spray twice with Bordeaux mixture in mid- to late winter, and then again just before the leaves fall. Remove all the affected leaves promptly if the infection is not serious.*

Q What are the pink patches that appear in lawns in late summer and fall?

A *This is a fungus disease known as red thread. Although unsightly, it rarely causes serious damage and may only last a few weeks. The likelihood of it recurring can be reduced by aerating the lawn and applying a general lawn feed during spring and summer. Severe attacks can be treated with a fungicide such as benomyl.*

Q What causes fairy rings on lawns and what is the way to treat them?

A *Fairy rings are caused by a fungus which spreads outward in ever larger circles. Although the outer rim is dark green, the grass inside turns brown, although it recovers in time. To speed recovery, feed the lawn and remove and burn the toadstools when they appear in summer and the fall. Mow the infected area separately, burn the clippings and disinfect the mower blades to prevent any spread.*

Q Are the pinky-red raised pustules that appear on dead wood a danger to live plants growing nearby?

A *This is coral spot, a fungus disease that is most obvious on dead wood in damp weather. It can, however, spread to live wood and is particularly damaging to magnolias and acers, which can be killed by a serious*

infection to the main trunk. Cut out all the affected wood to at least 4in below the pustules and burn the debris.

Q What is honey fungus and how can it be identified?

A *This serious disease of trees and shrubs can lead to the rapid death of affected plants. Leaves wither and discolor but do not fall and buds will fail to open in spring. There may be white fan-shaped fungus beneath the bark at ground level and tough dark brown "bootlaces" mong the roots. Remove and burn dead and dying plants, try to remove the bootlaces, which will spread the infection, and plant only annuals in the site for three to five years.*

Q Why have the blossoms and leaves on an ornamental crab apple failed to develop, yet have remained on the tree until winter?

A *Blossom wilt is the fungus disease that causes this problem. Remove and burn the affected spurs and give a tar oil wash in winter. In spring, spray with benomyl or carbendazim.*

Q If hyacinth bulbs have a light bluish fungus on the outside, is it safe to plant them?

A *If the infection is only slight, they may produce quite satisfactory flowers, but the risk is that the fungus may spread, killing the bulb and infecting others nearby, particularly if they are damaged in any way. Examine bulbs carefully before buying them and control slugs in the soil, which can damage the surface allowing infection to enter.*

Q What causes the brown marks at the tips of tulip leaves? The affected bulbs developed brown spots on the leaves and the flowers then rotted back.

A *This is tulip fire, a common but serious form of Botrytis fungus. Badly affected plants and bulbs should be lifted and burned, but spray every two weeks with mancozeb when the leaves are emerging until flowering.*

Q How can virus diseases be identified and how should they be dealt with?

A *There is a variety of symptoms, but one common indication is yellow blotching and mottling of leaves, which may also become distorted. Viruses are often spread by aphids and other sap-sucking insects, so controlling these pests will help prevent the spread of viruses. There is no cure for plant viruses and severely infected plants should be removed and burned.*

Q What are the orange-red pustules on the undersides of hawthorn leaves?

A *This is likely to be rust, which is a fungus disease that affects roses, box, sorbus and various other plants. It can be serious and will weaken the plant. Spray with mancozeb, thiram or a similar fungicide, rake up and burn fallen leaves, and try feeding, mulching and watering.*

Q Branches on an azalea are dying back and the cut surface of the branch has a purple staining. What is the cause?

A *This is probably silver leaf, despite the fact that the leaves naturally show the characteristic silvery color also seen in cotoneaster, poplars and species of Prunus. It can lead to the death of the plant. Cut affected branches back to a point where no staining is visible in the wood, then cut back another 6in. Feed and water the plants to improve vigor, but if the disease worsens, the only solution is to lift and burn the plant.*

Q What has caused the stems of all my sunflowers to rot with discolored patches? This has now occured for several years in succession.

A *This is sclerotina rot and it affects a large number of ornamental plants. It usually produces a fluffy white mass containing black resting bodies, but in sunflowers it is not so obvious. Remove and burn any stems that are discolored or rotting.*

COMMON PROBLEMS

Q If lichen and moss are growing on a tree, does it mean the tree is dying?

A *It could do. Such growths are seen on healthy plants in humid conditions, but they are more likely on trees suffering from die-back. Try to encourage healthy growth in the affected tree by feeding in spring and watering throughout the season.*

Q What causes the pale blisters turning to scabby patches on the undersides of leaves on camellias grown in the greenhouse?

A *This is probably oedema and is caused by the atmosphere and soil being too moist. The plant takes up too much water but is unable to get rid of it, and this causes the damage. Do not remove affected leaves, but improve ventilation and water moderately.*

Q Why do all the flower buds of a stephanotis fall before they open?

A *This is usually caused by dryness at the roots as the buds start to develop, but in a newly bought plant it is more likely to be the result of rapid changes of temperature as the plant is moved from one location to another.*

Q After years of flowering well, a clump of daffodils has failed to produce any flower buds at all. How can this be cured?

A *The name for this condition is blindness, and is usually due to the bulbs being too small. In an established clump, the bulbs have probably divided and are now congested and starved. Lift and divide the clump, taking care to feed and water in the growing season. In double varieties, blindness can simply be caused by lack of water.*

Q What could have caused the leaves of snapdragons to turn silver overnight?

A *Low night temperatures have this effect, and also make the leaves of* *morning glory and sweet peas turn white. If frost is likely, protect newly planted-out specimens.*

Q What is the reason for the stems of phlox splitting near the base?

A *This is usually caused by an irregular supply of water as the plant grows and also occurs in pelargoniums. Cut off badly damaged stems, apply a mulch after rain and water regularly.*

Q The new growth on a rose is distorted, with spirally twisting stalks bearing stunted, twisted, cupped leaves. There are no pests visible and the roses have been carefully mulched, watered and fed. What is the problem?

A *This is probably caused by damage from a hormone weedkiller, sprayed nearby on a windy day, from a sprayer that was not thoroughly cleaned out, or in the mulch, particularly if grass clippings have been used. Remove affected shoots and the mulch if it is the likely culprit, only spray garden chemicals in calm conditions and keep separate sprayers for weedkillers, foliar feeds and pesticides.*

Q Why should new roses not be planted on the same site as old roses?

A *The cause is not fully understood, but the problem is known as a specific replant disorder. The new bushes are likely to sicken and die back, perhaps because of a build-up of pests in the soil, which attack the new young plant where the old one was able to resist. You should either choose a different site or replace the soil to a depth of about 2ft over the area.*

Q What could have caused a lack of fruit on an otherwise healthy pyracantha after a good display of flowers?

A *If the weather conditions are poor while the plant is in flower, pollinating insects will be discouraged and fruit will not set. There is no remedy for this but it occurs infrequently.*

Q What are the blackened patches that have appeared on grass just a few days after the application of lawn sand?

A *This is scorch caused by applying nitrogenous fertilizer at too high a rate. It damaged the grasses and, in the long run, could cause too rapid growth in some areas. Follow the manufacturer's instructions to the letter when using any garden chemical and, in this case, check the setting on the spreader before use.*

Q How is it possible to eradicate slippery algae and lichens from a lawn?

A *These dark green growths will only appear on the lawn in areas that are always damp because of poor drainage. Try to improve drainage in the area by spiking the ground or, if necessary, laying land drains. The algae can be treated with dichlorophen.*

Q A variegated eleagnus is producing shoots with all green leaves. Should these shoots be removed?

A *Yes, and promptly. Most plants with variegated foliage are naturally occurring variants on a plain-colored type. They will often start to revert to the plain foliage of the original species, particularly if grown in deep shade and, since the all-green foliage contains more chlorophyll than the variegated type, it is usually more vigorous and will grow faster. If left unpruned, the plant may revert to the all-green type. Green shoots should be removed right to the base of the plant.*

Q What is the best way of clearing a garden pond of algae?

A *Algae is a common problem in newly established pools and will often clear up in time. These organisms thrive in sunny conditions, so one way is to grow waterlilies and other floating plants so that between 50 and 70 per cent of the water surface is covered. In addition, introduce some plants to oxygenate the water as algae need carbon dioxide.*

Q What could be the cause of acer leaves becoming brown at the edges?

A *Some acers, particularly the ones with finely cut foliage, are sensitive to cold winds and will show this kind of damage, particularly on young leaves, if they are planted in exposed positions. Remove damaged leaves as they may allow fungus diseases to enter the plant. Give the plant a foliar feed during the growing season to help it recover.*

Q What makes a garden compost pile turn slimy and smelly, and how can it be turned into a useful product?

A *If too much soft plant material, such as lawn clippings, is placed on the compost pile, oxygen is excluded and anaerobic rotting takes place. The result is the unappealing mess described above. Adding layers of coarser matter, such as bark or shredded paper will allow it to rot down properly. This also balances the chemical content of the compost, as grass is rich in nitrogen and the coarser matter is usually rich in carbon. Never place diseased plants on the pile, and avoid weeds, both perennial and annual.*

Q How can a blue hydrangea be encouraged to go on producing flowers of a good blue, instead of pinkish ones?

A *Blue hydrangeas need an acid soil to produce flowers of a true color, while pink hydrangeas need alkaline soil. When planted in an average garden soil, they start to fade in color and look rather dull. When the flower buds are forming, apply aluminum sulphate to blue-flowered types and ground limestone to pink-flowered types.*

Q What causes a shrub rose to produce a flower stem from the center of an open flower?

A *This is called proliferation and does, indeed, occur more frequently on old roses than on new varieties. It is usually caused by minor damage to the developing bud, perhaps as a result of late frost or an insect attack. If the problem keeps occurring, it may be due*

to a virus in which case the plant should be lifted and burned. Otherwise, no action is required.

Q Seedlings raised on a window sill have grown very long and pale. Can they be planted out and will they flower?

A *This etiolated growth is certainly caused by insufficient light. As soon as seeds have germinated, they need plenty of light and a window sill will rarely provide that. It is worth pricking the seedlings out and providing them with better conditions to harden off.*

Q Why should cuttings be covered over with a plastic bag when they are newly potted up?

A *Most cuttings will benefit from this treatment because they will continue to lose water from the tiny pores on their leaves as though they were still growing on the parent plant, but they do not have roots to take up water from the compost. The humid atmosphere created inside the plastic bag will discourage them from losing too much water too fast.*

Q What is the best way to improve clay soil?

A *The mineral particles in clay soils are tiny and, when compacted, will not allow the free movement of air and water through the soil. This makes for a heavy soil that is slow to warm up. The best way of improving clay soil is to add coarse grit, to open up the texture, and organic matter, such as well-rotted stable manure or garden compost to improve water retention and drainage. Lime can also be added but not on a soil that was already alkaline.*

Q Should soil pH tests be carried out in more than one location in the garden?

A *Yes, definitely. The use to which a garden has been put in the past may affect the pH of the soil in various areas, as can the underlying bedrock, which can vary from place to place. If using a chemical tester, remember to use sterilized or demineralized water so as not to influence the results.*

GLOSSARY

A

Acid (soil) With a pH of below 7 (see *alkaline* and *neutral*).

Aerate (soil) To loosen the soil in order to allow in air.

Air layering A method of propagation in which a portion of stem is encouraged to root by making a wound and enclosing it in a medium such as damp moss.

Alkaline (soil) With a pH of over 7 (see *acid* and *neutral*).

Alpine A plant that grows above the tree line in mountainous areas; loosely applied to rock-garden plants that enjoy similar growing conditions at a lower altitude.

Anaerobic A process carried out in the absence of air.

Annual A plant that completes its life cycle within the space of one growing season.

Aquatic Any plant that grows in water (see *bog plant*, *deep water aquatic*, *floating aquatic*, *marginal plant* and *submerged plant*).

Arbor A trellis supported on arches that carries climbing plants.

Arboretum A collection of trees.

Aspect A garden position that faces a certain direction.

B

Bare-rooted (plant) A plant lifted from the open ground (see *containerized plant*).

Bedding (plant) Annuals and biennials used for temporary garden display, usually flowering in spring and summer.

Biennial A plant that completes its life-cycle over the space of two growing seasons.

Biodegradable (material) A naturally derived material that can be broken down into its constituent parts by the action of micro-organisms.

Bog plant A plant that thrives in permanently damp conditions.

Bolster chisel A type of chisel with a broad blade splayed outward toward the cutting edge, used to cut masonry.

Bolting Premature production of flowers and seeds.

Branch A shoot from the main stem or trunk of a woody plant.

Broadcast To sow seed by sprinkling it evenly over an area rather than in rows.

Bulb Any plant with a modified stem acting as a storage system (see *corm*, *rhizome* and *tuber*).

Bulbil A small bulb-like organ, often borne in a leaf axil, occasionally found on a stem or in a flower head (see *bulblet*)

Bulblet A small developing *bulb* produced from the basal plate of a mature bulb.

C

Carpeting plant See *ground cover*.

Caterpillar See *larva*.

Chlorophyll Green pigment present in most plants.

Clay A fine-grained soil rich in nutrients but which has poor drainage capability.

Climber A plant that climbs by clinging to other plants or objects by means of twining stems or tendrils or adhesive tendrils. More generally, any long-stemmed plant that is trained upward.

Clinker Partially vitrified brick or mass of brick.

Cold frame An unheated structure made from wood, brick or glass, with a hinged glass or clear plastic lid, used to protect plants from the cold.

Compost activator Material that promotes the initiation of the composting process.

Compost (garden) Rotted organic matter.

Compost (seed or potting) A mixture of materials used as a medium for sowing seeds or potting plants.

Conifer trees and shrubs These are evergreen, with linear or needle-like leaves. Their seeds are normally borne in cones.

Containerized (plant) A plant grown in a pot or other container (see *bare-rooted plant*).

Coping Cast cement pieces, beveled wooden strips or masonry used to deflect rainwater from the face of a wall or fence.

Coping saw A handsaw with a U-shaped frame used for cutting curves in material that is too thick for a fretsaw.

Coping stone A stone used to form a *coping*.

Corm A *bulb*-like swollen stem or base, often surrounded by a papery tunic, that acts as an underground storage organ.

Corolla The part of the flower formed by the *petals*.

Cover A glass or polyethelene cover used for propagation, or for protecting early crops raised in open ground, or to warm the soil before planting. Also called a "cloche."

Crocks Broken pieces of clay pot used to cover the drainage holes of pots to provide drainage and aeration and to prevent the growing medium from escaping or blocking the holes.

Cultivar A cultivated plant or group of plants distinguished by one or more characteristics which are retained whether it is propagated sexually or asexually.

Cutting A leaf, shoot, root or bud that is cut off a plant to be used for *propagation*.

D

Datum peg A wooden peg set at a particular position, forming the point from which measurements are taken.

Deadhead To remove spent flowers or flower heads.

Deciduous (plant) A plant that loses all its leaves annually at the end of the growing season (see *semi-deciduous*).

Deep water aquatic A plant that grows right at the bottom of a pond or pool.

Division A method of increasing plants by dividing them into pieces, each with a root system and one or more shoots.

Double digging A cultivation technique in which the soil is worked over to a depth of two spade blades.

Double-leaf (of a wall) Having two layers of bricks.

Drainage The passage of excess water through the soil, or systems of drainage which are used to remove excess water.

E

Ericaceous A term describing plants of the family *Ericaceae* (heathers), usually lime-hating and requiring a pH of 6.5 or less, or compost with an appropriate acidity for the growing of plants which are termed ericaceous.

Erosion The process of soil being washed away or blown off the surface of the ground caused either naturally or by man's intervention.

Evergreen A plant that retains its leaves throughout the year (see *semi-evergreen*).

F

Fastigiate Erect, upright form of growth with branches close together.

Floating aquatic A plant that grows on the surface of a pond or of a pool.

Flower The part of a plant containing the reproductive organs, usually surrounded by *sepals* and *petals*.

Footing A narrow cement foundation for a wall, or the base of garden steps.

Framework plants The plants that form the basis or structure of the design of a garden.

Frost-hardy Describes a plant that is able to withstand frost without protection.

Frost-tender Describes a plant that will succumb to frost damage.

G

Gazebo A garden pavilion or summerhouse.

Genus A category of plant classification that identifies a group of related species.

Germination The development process of a seed into a seedling.

Green manure A plant grown to improve the soil.

Ground cover Usually low-growing plants that cover the soil surface and suppress weeds.

Growing medium Mixture in which plants are grown.

Growing season The period during which a plant is actively producing leaves and flowers.

H

Habitat The natural home of a plant or animal.

Half hardy A plant that is unable to survive the winter without protection but does not require protection all year round.

Hard landscaping An area of the garden covered with paving, cement, or another hard surface.

Hard pan A hard, compacted layer in the soil.

Harden off To acclimatize plants raised in warm conditions to cooler conditions.

Hardy (plant) A plant capable of surviving the winter in the open without protection.

Hawk A small square board with a handle beneath, which is used for carrying mortar.

Header A brick or stone laid across a wall so that its end is flush with the outer surface.

Herb A plant grown for its medicinal, flavoring, or decorative qualities.

Herbaceous perennial A non-woody plant in which the upper parts die down to a rootstock at the end of the growing season.

Herbicide A weedkiller.

Humus The organic residue of decayed vegetable matter in the soil.

L

Layering A method of propagation in which a portion of stem is induced to root while still attached to the parent plant.

Leaching The removal of soluble substances from soil or potting mixtures by water passing through.

Leafmold Decomposed fall leaves, used as a soil conditioner.

Level A tool with a bubble vial which is used for checking horizontal levels.

Loam This is normally soil of medium texture, easily worked, that contains more or less equal parts of sand, silt and clay and is usually rich in humus.

Lump hammer A heavy hammer with a block-shaped head.

M

Manure Bulky organic substances of animal origin (often mixed with straw) that are either dug into the soil or are applied as a mulch.

Marginal plant A plant that grows partially submerged in shallow water or in moist soil at the edge of a pond.

Medium A compost, growing mixture or any other material in which plants may be propagated or grown.

Mixed border A border

containing different types of plants: these can include a mixture of shrubs, herbaceous plants, bulbs and annuals.

Modules Molded plastic or polystyrene trays divided up into cells which are filled with compost for sowing seeds.

Mulch A layer of organic or other material applied to the soil surface.

Multi-sowing Sowing more than one seed in a pot or module cell and leaving them all to grow on.

Neutral See *acid* and *alkaline*.

Nosing The front edge of a step, often protruding from a riser.

Native (plant) Originating in the country where they are grown.

Naturalize To establish and grow as if in the wild.

Nitrogen An important plant food, especially used in the growth of leaves and shoots.

Non-degradable (material) One that is not *biodegradable*.

Nutrient A plant food.

Offset A young plant that arises by natural, *vegetative propagation*, usually found at the base of the parent plant.

Organic matter Material consisting of, or derived from, living organisms, such as compost, leafmold and farmyard manure.

P

Padsaw A small, narrow saw used for cutting curves.

Pan See *hard pan*.

Peat Partially decayed, humus-rich vegetation formed on the surface of waterlogged soils.

Perennial A plant that lives for at least three growing seasons.

Pesticide A chemical substance used for killing pests.

Petal A modified leaf, one part of the *corolla*, which is often brightly colored to attract attention.

Percolator A pit filled with rubble, into which water drains and percolates to earth.

pH The degree of acidity or alkalinity of the soil.

Phosphate A phosphorus compound (P2O5).

Phosphorus One of the major plant foods, important in the germination and development of seedlings and in root growth.

Pier A thick column of brickwork that buttresses a wall.

Pinching out The removal of the growing tip of a plant to encourage the production of side-shoots or flower buds.

Planter A decorative pot or stand for plants.

Pollination The transfer of pollen to the stigma of a flower which takes place in the process of fertilization.

Potash A potassium compound (K2O). The word potash is often used loosely to mean *potassium*.

Potassium One of the major plant foods affecting the size and quality of fruit and flowers. It can also increase resistance to frost, pests and diseases.

Potting compost See *Compost*.

Profile board Narrow wooden crosspieces nailed to uprights used to mark out foundations for walls.

Propagation The production of a new generation of plants by sowing seed, cutting or division.

R

Resistant variety A plant variety that shows particular resistance to a pest and/or disease.

Resting body A structure produced by a fungus that remains dormant for a period before germinating.

Rhizome A horizontal creeping underground stem which acts as a storage organ.

Riser The vertical part of a step.

Root ball The roots and accompanying soil or compost visible when a plant is lifted.

Rooting hormone A chemical compound in powder or liquid form, which is used to encourage root production.

Rootstock The crown and root system of herbaceous perennials and suckering shrubs, or the plant used to provide the root system for a grafted plant.

Rotovate To use a machine with rotating blades to break up the soil.

Runner A trailing stem that grows along the surface, takes root and forms new growth at nodes or the tip.

S

Scooping and scouring The techniques that are used in the propagation and growth of hyacinth bulbs.

Scree A slope comprising rock fragments, simulated in gardens as scree beds, in which drainage is particularly good.

Screed A thin layer of mortar applied to give a smooth surface on which to build brick or block walls, or as a finish for cement.

Seed A fertilized plant ovule consisting of an embryo and its food store surrounded by a protective coat.

Seed head A faded flower head that has been successfully fertilized and contains seed.

Seedling A very young plant raised from seed.

Semi-deciduous A plant that loses only some of its leaves at the end of the growing season.

Semi-evergreen A plant that retains only a small proportion of its leaves for more than one season.

Sepal One of the outermost modified leaves that compose a flower head.

Shrub A woody plant that branches from the base with no obvious trunk.

Silt A fine deposit of mud or clay.

Single-leaf (wall) A built wall that has only a single layer of bricks and mortar.

Soft landscaping A soft area of the garden, such as a lawn or gentle sloping bank.

Soil conditioner Material that improves the structure of the soil without necessarily adding to the plant foods.

Species A group of closely related plants within a *genus*.

Specimen plant A striking plant, usually a tree or shrub, grown where it can be clearly viewed.

Spur A slow-growing, short branch system that usually bears a cluster of flower buds.

Stretcher A brick or stone laid horizontally with its length parallel to the length of a wall.

Strimmer A hand-held electric-powered machine with a rotating blade or nylon cord, which is normally used for cutting long grass or other soft vegetation.

Submerged plant A plant that is grown in the deeper part of a pond or pool.

Subsoil The layer of soil below the topsoil which is lighter in color and lacking in organic matter, soil life and nutrients.

T

Tap root A strong-growing, vertical root.

Tender See *frost tender*.

Tilth A fine, crumbly surface layer of soil.

Topdress To apply a material such as organic matter or fertilizer to the surface.

Topiary The trimming or training of trees and bushes into decorative shapes, such as animals, birds and geometric forms lining an avenue in a formal garden.

Topsoil The upper layer of dark, fertile soil.

Trace elements Food materials that are required by plants in very small quantities.

Tread The horizontal section of a step.

Tree A woody plant with a single trunk bearing an elevated head of branches.

Trompe l'oeil A decoration that, while false, gives a convincing illusion of reality.

Tuber A swollen, usually underground organ for storing nutrients derived from a stem or root system.

V

Variegated Marked with various colors in an irregular pattern; particularly applies to leaves that have white, yellow, or cream markings on their edges.

Variety A naturally occurring variant of a wild *species*; also used to describe any variant of a plant.

Vegetative propagation The increase of plants by asexual methods, usually resulting in genetically identical plants.

W

Water table The level in the soil below which the soil is saturated by ground water.

Watering in To water around the stem of a newly transplanted plant to settle the soil around its roots.

Windbreak Any structure that shelters plants from strong winds.

Worm compost Plant material that has been converted to compost by worms.

INDEX

PHOTOGRAPHIC ACKNOWLEDGMENTS

GATEFOLDS:

On Top of the World: Garden Picture Library/ Linda Burgess (3 pictures),/Gary Rogers (2 pictures),/Ron Sutherland, Ron Sutherland/ Anthony Paul Design; John Glover; Andrew Lawson; Clive Nichols /Randle Siddeley

A Cut Above the Rest Eric Crichton (2 pictures); Jerry Harpur/Designer: Bobbi Hicks, New South Wales, Australia; Andrew Lawson; Clive Nichols/Hillbarn House, Wiltshire; Clive Nichols/17 Fulham Park Gardens - designer: Anthony Noel; Reed International Books Ltd/Guy Ryecart (4 pictures), /Steven Wooster (3 pictures)

All Change: Eric Crichton (2 pictures); Andrew Lawson; Clive Nichols/Brook Cottage, Oxfordshire; Reed International Books Ltd/ Michael Boys, /Jerry Harpur, /Clive Nichols,/ Steven Wooster, /George Wright (4 pictures)

Forest Fencing Limited 66.
Garden Picture Library 68,/John Baker 157 right, /Lynne Brotchie 91 bottom, 198 bottom, / Lynne Brotchie, Audrey Flower 19 bottom, / Linda Burgess 151 top left, 159 top right, 200 center, 206 bottom,/Brian Carter 165 top right, /Bob Challinor 164 bottom, /Karin Craddock 13 top, /Geoff Dann, Designer: Simon Fraser 54, /Vaughan Fleming 137 top, /Nigel Francis 96, /John Glover 12 bottom, 17 left, 27 bottom, 27 top, 30 bottom, 88 top, 94 /95bottom, 97 bottom, 136 bottom left, 137 bottom, 149 left, 160 right, 212 top, John Glover, John Duane Design 27 top, /Gill Hanly 20, / Neil Holmes 151 bottom left, /Michael Howes 199, /Noel Kavanagh 164 top, /Kate Zari Roberts 151 bottom right, /Ann Kelley 87 top right, / M Lamontagne 194 bottom, /Jane Legate 198 top, /Zara McCalmont 130 bottom, 193, / John Miller 11 bottom right, 91 top right, / John Neubauer 92 top, /Clive Nichols 150 bottom, /Jerry Pavia 88 bottom, 90 /91 top, 99, /Kevin Richardson 87 bottom, /Gary Rogers 206 top, /Alex Saunderson 23 right, /JS Sira 81 top right, 161 center, /JS Sira, Chelsea Flower Show 70 top, /Ron Sutherland 18 bottom, 51 bottom inset, 79 center left, 94 top, 210; Ron Sutherland,Chelsea Flower Show 1994, Cartier/Harpers & Queen Garden, Clifton Landscape & Design 156 bottom; Ron Sutherland, Duane Paul Design Team 18 top, 65; Ron Sutherland, Designer: Murray Collins 69 top; Brigitte Thomas 31 bottom right, 51 center inset, 78 bottom, 86 top, 89, 157 left, 165 bottom, 208 top right, 214 bottom, / Juliette Wade 92 bottom, 202, /Juliette Wade,

Congham Hall, Norfolk 29 right,/Steven Wooster 32 left; Steven Wooster/Chelsea Flower Show 1994, The Harpers & Queen Garden, Clifton Landscape & Design 49, Steven Wooster, Designer: Dr Ian Hamilton Finlay 95 bottom, Steven Wooster, Anthony Noel Design 138 bottom right; Steven Wooster/Saling Hall 236 bottom.

Jerry Harpur /Designer: Bonita Bulaitis, Ware, Herts 21 top left, /Mr and Mrs John Casson 12 top, 53 top, /Designer: Thomas Church, Pasadena, USA 126, /Designer: Jane Fearnley-Whittingstall, Wootton-under-Edge, Gloucs 26 bottom, /Designer: Simon Fraser, Hampton, Middx 20 bottom, 31 bottom left, /Designer: Christopher Grey-Wilson, Suffolk 196, /Designer: Ann Griot, Los Angeles, USA 52 bottom,/Designer: Christopher Masson 23 bottom left, /Designer: Hilary McMahon, RHS Chelsea 1991 50 /51 main pic, /Designer: Anthony Noel 26 top, /Designer: Stephanie Riley 8 /9 main pic, /Designer: Judith Sharpe 13 bottom.

Leisuredeck Limited 57, 67.
Marshalls Mono Ltd 20 top right, 22 bottom, 51 top inset, 55 center, 55 center bottom, 55 right, 62 top, 62 bottom right, 62 mid center left, 62 bottom center, 62 bottom left, 62 mid center right, 62 center, 63 right center, 63 bottom right, 63 top right, 72 top right, 72 left, 73 top right, 73 left, 74, 86 bottom right, 86 center bottom right, 86 center top right.
Clive Nichols/Ashtree Cottage, Wiltshire 93 top, /Mottisfont Abbey Gardens, Hampshire 93 bottom.
Reed International Books Ltd 200 left, 201 left, 201 right, /Michael Boys 52 above, 53 below, 69 left, 77, 84 left, 111 above, 111 below, 112 top, 114, 115 left, 119 orange, 119 green, 122, 128 top, 129 top left, 130 inset, 132 top, 133 top, 134 below right, 135 bottom, 135 top, 135 above left, 141 bottom, 146 below right, 146 below left, 149 top, 153 top left, 154 top, 156 top, 158 bottom, 158 top rght, 159 below left, 159 below right, 161 bottom, 207, 218 bottom, 220 bottom, 221, 236 top, / Mike Busselles 25 left, /Steve Campbell 202 bottom, 211, 213, /W.F. Davidson 136 bottom, 160 bottom left, /Jerry Harpur 4 title verso, 10 /1, 11 top, 25 right, 29 top left, 30 top right, 61, 71 right, 75, 81 left, 100 top, 103, 104 top, 105, 107 top inset, 107 bottom inset, 110 top, 116 left, 117 below, 118 bottom right, 119 yellow, 127 bottom, 127 top, 129 top right, 130 top, 134 top, 136 top, 139 center, 144 below, 145 bottom right, 145 bottom left, 146 top, 148 right, 148 left, 152 bottom, 152 top, 153 bottom, 155, 158 top left, 162, 163 above, 163 below, 164 inset left, 165

above left, 166 top left, 166 top right, 166 below right, 166 below left, 167 above, 167 below, 184 above, 189 above right, 194 top, 214 top, 222 right, 224 bottom, 238 right, /Neil Holmes 24 top, 71 left, 78 top, 97 top, 138 top, 160 above left, 161 top, /Andrew Lawson 147 top, /Kelvin Murray endpapers, title, half title, /Clive Nichols 112 bottom, 116 right, 118 center, 118 top, 120 top, 121, 123, 125, 152 center, 190 below, 224 top, /Peter Rauter 202 top, 216, /Guy Ryecart 170 above, 170 below, 171 top, 171 below, 171 center, 172 top left, 172 below right, 172 below left, 178 below, 179, 182 below, 183 above, 184 below, 185 above left, 185 below, 185 above right, 186 /7, 188 above, 222 left,226 bottom, 226 top right, 228, 229 left, 230 left, 237, /Ron Sutherland 59 top, 204, /Pamla Toler 55 top left, 60 top, /Michael Warren 110 bottom, /Steven Wooster 9 center inset, 9 top inset, 16 top, 22 top, 24 below, 28 below, 30 top left, 31 top, 56 above, 82 above, 82 below, 102 left, 104 bottom, 118 bottom left, 127 center, 138 below left, 139 top, 154 center, 168 below left, 168 below right, 168 top, 169, 172 top right, 173 below left, 173 above right, 173 below right, 173 above right, 174 /175, 175 bottom inset, 175 top inset, 175 center inset, 176 below right, 176 below left, 177, 178 top, 180 /1, 182 top right, 186 below left, 186 above left, 186 above right, 188 below, 189 below, 189 top left, 190 top, 191, 192, 223, 226 top left, 227, 229 right, 230 /1, 233, 234, 235, 239, 240, 241, /George Wright 10, 16 below, 28 top, 32 right, 63 left, 76 top, 83, 84 right, 85, 96 middle, 98, 100 bottom, 102 right, 106 /107 main pic, 107 center inset, 113, 115 center, 115 right, 117 top, 119 violet, 119 red, 119 blue, 119 indigo, 120 below, 124, 128 bottom, 129 below, 132 below, 133 below, 134 below left, 139 bottom, 140 bottom, 140 top, 141 top, 142 below, 142 above, 144 top, 145 top, 147 below, 149 below right, 150 top, 151 top right, 153 top right, 154 bottom, 176 top, 183 below, 205, 209, 217, 218 top, 220 top, 225, 238 left.
Tilcon Trupak 56 bottom left, 56 center bottom, 56 bottom right.
Town & Country Paving Ltd (West Sussex) 55 top center, 76 bottom.
Mark Williams 195 bottom, 195 above center, 195 top, 195 below center.

ILLUSTRATIONS ACKNOWLEDGMENTS
Main illustrations pp34-48 Pam Williams
Inset illustrations pp34-48 Vana Haggerty